The Chosen Island
Jews in Cuba

The Chosen Island
Jews in Cuba

Maritza Corrales

SALSEDO PRESS, INC.

Published in the United States of America in 2005
By Salsedo Press, Inc.
3139 West Chicago Avenue
Chicago, Illinois 60622

Design by Houwer Friman
Cover illustration: Stained-glass Jewish Community of Santa Clara

All photographs, unless otherwise noted,
are courtesy of the interviewee or his or her family.

ISBN 0-9771764-0-1
Printed in the United States of America

In memory of my mother
Dr. Olga Capestany Meulener

Acknowledgments

To Rosamari, because without her untiring logistical support my work would simply not exist.
To Rafael for his stoic tolerance of all my absences.
To Margalit, for her generosity and example as an historian.
To Adela, for her faithfulness to the *mameloshn*. Without her work of Champollion many documents would have continued to be mere hieroglyphs to me.
To Graciela and June, for their unconditional help, sensitivity and always present enthusiasm.
To Deisy, for so many hours dedicated to make up for my technological incapacity.
To the friends of Monte Barreto: Enrique, the two Sergios, Maritza, Ivette, for their unwavering support.
To Reynaldo, a great writer and editor, and an even greater friend.
To Tatiana for her beautiful photographs and her availability whenever needed.
To Houwer for his talent, professionalism and attention to detail.
To Debra, for the translation without which the dream of publishing this book would never have come true.
To the international Jewish organizations that never forgot to be the *brother's keeper* of the Cuban tribe.
And, above all, to the pioneers, who have the leading role in the interesting and multifaceted Jewish life in Cuba, and to those who, against wind and sea, stayed and made it possible to keep it alive today.

Contents

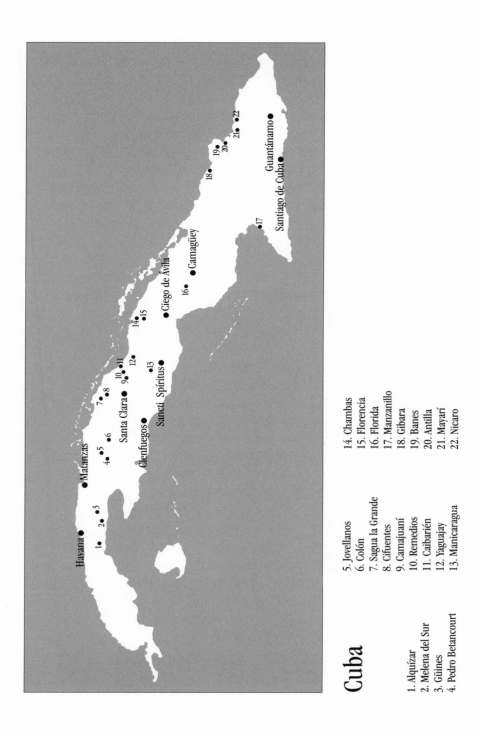

Cuba

1. Alquízar
2. Melena del Sur
3. Güines
4. Pedro Betancourt
5. Jovellanos
6. Colón
7. Sagua la Grande
8. Cifuentes
9. Camajuaní
10. Remedios
11. Caibarién
12. Yaguajay
13. Manicaragua
14. Chambas
15. Florencia
16. Florida
17. Manzanillo
18. Gibara
19. Banes
20. Antilla
21. Mayarí
22. Nicaro

Jews in Cuba

Various settlements: successive generations

The persistence of a cabalistic number

From time immemorial, the Jewish people have given significance to numbers. Thus, one possible interpretation of why there are thirty-six interviews in this book is that 36 is the exact multiple of 18, and 18 symbolizes the word *life*: it reflects the capacity the Jewish people have always had to multiply their lives, to arise from the ashes, to be reborn. Also, in the book of wisdom, the *Talmud*, thirty-six is the number of *tzaddikim nistarim*, of just men, simple and modest, necessary to produce a generation to save the world and Jewish life.

This book tells a story of regeneration. It recounts the lives of thirty-six men and women, who emigrated to or were born in Cuba and did not abandon the country, who adopted the project of the Revolution and kept the spirit of Judaism alive on the Island. They lived their Jewishness in very different ways, but all —in one way or another— lived it, shared its traditions and were nurtured by the deeply rooted ethic that is the essential legacy of the Jewish people to the civilization we know.

The three sets of interviews presented here frame the most significant temporal, geographic and ideological aspects that characterize this immigration.[1] The first emphasizes the ideological leanings of the *pioneer* immigrants and their descendants as Communists, Zionists and/or revolutionaries. The second, grouped under the subtitle "The Jews of the Central Highway," chronicles the settlement, primarily of Sephardic Jews, in geographic areas outside of the capital. The third portrays the immigrants and the first generation born in Cuba, who became part of the Jewish community and whose permanence has been decisive in the continuation of Jewish life on the Island after 1959.

Included are testimonies of militants who, having arrived during the Machado dictatorship (1925-1933), fought to liberate Cuba from it. They were arrested, jailed or murdered for having participated in the founding of the first Communist Party of Cuba (1925) and the organization of trade unions. They were persecuted, not for being Jews, but for the ideology they defended in their attempt to make the world better, faithful to one of the most profound ethical-philosophical Jewish precepts, *tikkun olam*.

During the same years, Zionist immigrants formed their organizations to work for the return to the Land that Abraham and Moses promised them. At the end of the 1940s and beginning of the 1950s, many went to Israel to fight for its independence and to participate in the most socialist and egalitarian model yet created by any society, the *kibbutz*. They departed Cuba with the sadness of having left behind the country which had so generously taken them in, and which, for many years, had been their "promised land."

Also among those interviewed are revolutionaries, intellectuals, scientists and artists, children of the first immigrants, who opposed injustice and —like their parents— sacrificed for the freedom of the land where they were born and rightfully considered their own. Although immersed in the euphoria and tumult of a revolution, these men and women remained faithful to their historic past and, conscious of the importance of their inheritance, defended their spiritual roots. Today, they are no longer part of the *otherness*, but ingrained in the very stock of our culture.

Waves of pioneers and their descendants

There had been two waves of immigrants in the history of the Hebrew people

---

[1] Some of the immigrants, whose stories are presented here, died before I embarked on this book. In some cases, I have been able to include interviews I conducted before their death. In others, I have relied on interviews conducted by others and on their own writings.

in Cuba prior to the period covered in this book: the *conversos* or Crypto-Jews, who landed with Christopher Columbus during the "Discovery" or came during the years of the Conquest and colonial domination in order to escape the Inquisition; and those who were called *Americanos* because they arrived with the United States Occupation (1898) after our War of Independence against Spain.

The reconstruction of certain facts based on oral histories of personal life experiences carries implicit temporal limitations, as well as inevitable subjectivity. For that reason, the time frame recreated here is only that lived by those *pioneers* of the Jewish community and their descendants, starting from the second decade of the Republic.

Their stories reveal the reasons for their displacement from their countries of origin and explain how Cuba appeared on the global map of Jewish migration. They illustrate the incorporation of these immigrants into the collective identity, their strategies of adaptation and the organizational structures created in their process of social, economic and cultural insertion. In addition, these testimonies explain their motives for remaining and supporting the revolutionary model since 1959. Above all, they reflect the pull of the two main ideological tendencies (Zionism and Communism), coexisting in permanent counterpoint, that shaped the distinct character of this community.

The popular perception of *turcos*, *sirios* and *polacos*

The traditional denominations of Sephardic and Ashkenazi Jews have no reference in the Cuban mind. As if by magic, in Havana, all Jews of Eastern Europe became *polacos* (Poles), and in the interior of the island, they became *sirios* (Syrians) or *turcos* (Turks), regardless of their nationality. Such linguistic characterizations did not strictly correspond to the actual geographic, ethnic or religious origins of these immigrants, but rather expressed the way in which a people free from xenophobia and religious prejudice popularly perceived them.

The Sephardic Jews arrived on the Island at a time when the Cuban economy was expanding. They came from the Ottoman Empire, compelled by the consequences for them —as a religious and ethnic minority— of the nationalist Revolution of the Young Turks (1908) that imposed mandatory military service, combined with the deterioration of the socio-economic conditions caused by natural calamities, the Balkan Wars (1912-13) and the

First World War (1914-1918).

The incorrectly named *poles*, who were actually Ashkenazi Jews from Russia, Lithuania, Romania, and, in their majority, from Poland, immigrated to the Island at the end of the Dance of the Millions,[2] after Cuba's economic growth had stopped. They left Europe as a result of the intensification of the pogroms following the peace accords of World War I, and came to Cuba because the coincidental, restrictive US immigration policy, as manifested in the Quota Laws of 1921-1922 and the Johnson Bill of 1924,[3] impeded their entry into that country.

Although for both groups the push forces were essentially similar (rejection of military service, misery and persecution as minorities), the pull forces and their pattern of settlement differed. Initially, both the *polacos* and the *turcos* were highly concentrated in the city of Havana —extending afterwards to the provincial capitals of Villa Clara, Camagüey and Oriente— and later on dispersing throughout the nation. Finally, they began a normal movement of internal migration from rural towns back toward the capital of the Island. In general, while the *polacos* remained congregated primarily in Havana, the *turcos* tended to move toward the east along the sugar route and the central highway.

The Jews of Inquisidor and Jesús María Streets

The Jewish enclave in Old Havana, in the areas around the port and the train station, brought together the smells and flavors of their varied places of origin, producing a complex social weave framed by streets that had the most inappropriate names for Jews: Santa Clara, San Ignacio, Jesús María and Inquisidor. The first *turcos* and *polacos* settled in this area, where they recreated their environment, their synagogues, grocery stores full of herring and *smetene*, their butcher shops, their seltzer stands and their bakeries brimming over with *pletzlaj, borekas* and *leicaj.*

During the first stages of their settlement, they inserted themselves as street venders in the so-called "informal economy." Later, as small merchants, they

---

[2] "The Dance of the Millions": The name given to the period of unbridled speculation in the sugar market in 1919 and 1920, which created an enormous economic bonanza for the island.

[3] Laws adopted in the United States between 1921 and 1924 limited the entry of immigrants to the country to 3% and later to 2% of the numbers of each nationality that resided in the United States —according to the census of 1910 and 1890, respectively. They principally affected Jews of Eastern Europe.

moved toward the center of the old city where they occupied a specific area of the capital that defined them as a community, and from which they began to spread out into the more exclusive neighborhoods in the 1950s.

To a certain degree, their commercial movement is reflected in their residential patterns. While the most religiously observant and least economically successful group remained relatively concentrated in Old Havana, the rest moved out to Santos Suárez, Vedado and Miramar, depending on their new socio-economic status.

The eternal and disperse peddlers

The *turcos* or *sirios* started out as itinerant venders, and some of them remained faithful to peddling until the end, perhaps because of the strength of this tradition in the Eastern Mediterranean and the greater freedom of action and movement it offered them.

Their organizational activity in the capital began with the founding of the Unión Israelita Chevet Ahim (1914), an orthodox synagogue and social center that, ironically, was situated on Inquisidor Street —a painful remembrance of their Spanish past. At about the same time, they formed two charitable societies: one that helped the sick and needy, *Bikur Holim*; and the other a women's organization, La Buena Voluntad, started in 1918. In addition, they opened a *Talmud Torah* (1924) in Havana for religious teaching that soon became the Theodore Herzl primary school. The creation of these institutions is indicative of two characteristics of this group: their greater religiosity and their profound Zionist beliefs that made them the initial force behind that movement in Cuba. However, within a short time, the *turcos* yielded leadership of these institutions to the *polacos*, and established their own Zionist organizations such as the *Macabi*. Nevertheless, despite this apparent evolving detachment from ideology, the *turcos* constituted the majority of Cuban Jews who went to Israel to fight in the war 1948.

In the decades of 1930 and 1940, they published in Spanish, not in *Ladino*, some sporadic and ephemeral magazines, such as *El Estudiante Hebreo*, *Bikur Holim*, *Belleza Israelita Cubana* and *Macabi*. These publications reported on different aspects of Sephardic life in Turkey, Spain, Israel and Cuba, as well as on national and international politics and news about the masons. One of these *turcos*, Roberto Esquenazi Mayo, became the first descendant of immigrants in Cuba to obtain the National Literature Prize (1951) with his work *Memoirs of a Student Soldier*, the story of his participation as a paratrooper in the Second World War. The recognition was repeated after the Revolution when another writer of Jewish origin received similar distinction: this time by the *polaco* Jaime Sarusky Miller who was awarded this prize for his life's work in 2005.

The First market study
and introduction of consumer credit in Cuba

The years that run from 1920 to 1925, the period of the greatest Jewish immigration, represent a true historical turning point for the Cuban nation. A profound structural and economic crisis, combined with other socio-political phenomena, created the conditions for radical solutions that lead to the Revolution of 1930. It was in this context that Jews, mainly the so-called *polacos*, began to enter the country on a massive scale and became a tangible presence on the Island. Cuba was for them, and would be a while longer —not a chosen destiny— but a convenient stop on the way to the *Land of Gold*, the United States.

Initially concentrated in Havana, the *polacos* also began as peddlers. The massive character of their arrival and their belief that they were refugees in transit, plus language difficulties, the intensity of the tropical weather and the Island's precarious economic situation, made the process of their insertion difficult. These impediments, however, did not prevent them from ultimately succeeding.

As a minority that had suffered constant persecution, Jews had created a unique international network of support and assistance. In connection with this organizational effort to help Jewish resettlement, Harry Viteles was sent to Cuba to analyze the real possibilities the Island offered for Jewish immigration. In his report, written in 1925,[4] he indicated that there was room for commerce and manufacturing in shoes, stockings, underwear, clothing for men and children and leather goods. This information enabled Jews to identify and enter niches in the market not yet exploited.

In addition, they were the first to introduce a system of consumer credit that made it possible for the poorer population to purchase their goods, thereby expanding their markets. Later, they moved into other commercial spaces, and, with greater productivity and more modern methods, replaced

---

[4] Harry Viteles. "*Report on the Status of the Jewish Immigrants in Cuba*," unpublished manuscript, 1925.

to a large extent other small established merchant groups. Furthermore, they developed new industries for items such as knitwear, zippers, ties and belts, which had previously been imported. As a result, the *turcos* and *polacos* advanced the industrialization of the country and became some of its most dynamic businessmen.

Organization and controversial activities in Yiddish

The *polacos*, because of their large numbers as well as their religious and political composition, were the most complex group and the one that gave a distinctive face to the Jewish community. Essentially, early Jewish life in Cuba was defined by the permanent counterpoint between the two dominant tendencies: the Communists, symbolized by Fabio Grobart, the *Kultur Farain* (1926), the Cooperativa (1933) and the *Folkcenter* (1941); and the Zionists, represented by David Blis, the Centro Israelita (1925) and the many organizations and clubs grouped under the Zionist Union (1924) —*Hashomer Hatzair, Hanoar Hatzioní, Betar, and Keren Kayemet Leisrael.* Lead by the so-called *polacos*, most of the Ashkenazi institutions were created between these two ideological currents. Out of these organizations emerge a variety of significant Jewish activists, including: four of the thirteen participants at the founding of the Cuban Communist Party in August 1925, the first martyrs of the Machado dictatorship, the only Jewish-Cuban combatant in the Spanish Civil War, the volunteers of the *kibbutz* movement at the end of the 1940s and beginning of the 1950s, some of those actively involved in the struggle against Batista and the first Jews to participate in the government after the Revolution. Of course, they also produced the prominent persons of wealth of this community after their deproletarization.[5]

The organizational structure of the *polacos* developed differently than that of the *turcos*. Whereas among the Sephardic Jews religious belief and mutual help took precedence, the Ashkenazi Jews placed central importance on cultural institutions that enabled them, in the early years, to overcome their nostalgia for their language, Yiddish, and for their traditions.[6]

However, once they decided to stay in Cuba, with the cooperation of international Jewish organizations like the *Joint* and *Hias*, they created a wide

---

[5] Margalit Bejarano. *"The Deproletarization of Cuban Jewry," Judaica latinoamericana: Estudios Históricos-sociales,* Magnes and Hebrew University, Jerusalem, 1988.
[6] Margalit Bejarano. *The Hebrew community in Cuba*, Hebrew University, Jerusalem, 1996, p. 57.

network of institutions to support immigrants, including schools to teach Spanish and skills, a Women's Association (1926) with a nursery for orphans and working mothers, a home for young unwed women to safeguard their morality (1928), and a Credit Union that contributed to their initial establishment as merchants. They formed cooperative and guild societies imbued with socialist ideas to protect their main economic activities: the *Shutzfarain far Peddler* (Union of Itinerant Venders, 1929), the Cámara de Comercio Israelita de Cuba (1936) (Hebrew Chamber of Commerce), and the Unión de Fabricantes de Calzado de La Habana (1942) (Union of Shoe Manufacturers of Havana).

Worried about the two diseases that most affected them, given the precarious conditions in which they lived and the traumatic shock of their displacement, they organized the Committee to Protect against Tuberculosis and Mental Illness (1927). Later, to deal with the serious situation of the refugees escaping Nazism, they created the Cuban Jewish Anti-Nazi Committee, lead by Communists, and the Cuban Hebrew Committee to Assist Victims of the European War.

In the sphere of religion, they added a purer variant of religious orthodoxy with the founding of the Adath Israel Synagogue (1925) on Jesús María Street, which, in addition to normal prayer services, oversaw specific aspects of Jewish law: food laws by application of the *shechita*; purification by way of the *mikvah*; attention to the dead through the *Chevra Kadisha*; and religious teaching provided by their *Torah Vadaat*.

Reflective of the importance Hebrews have always given to the transmission of tradition, culture and education, numerous schools emerged between 1924 and 1946 that were affiliated with the centers and preponderant tendencies of the community: the Autonomous School of the Centro Israelita, the religious Takjemoni, and the leftist Sholem Aleijim; and the schools of the Zionists, Yavne and Theodore Herzl. Culturally as well, the *polacos* were the most active group. They brought from Europe a strong Yiddish tradition, typical of the *bundist* movement that was socialist, not Zionist. From the 1920s, this tradition inspired them to write books in Yiddish, portraying their impression of the Island from a positive political perspective, and expressing their admiration for its historical leaders such as Hatuey, Antonio Maceo and José Martí, paradigms of freedom that they adopted as their own in their search for identity. They organized conferences on distinguished Cuban (the scientist Carlos J. Finlay) and Jewish figures (Albert Einstein), book and art exhibits, theater and literary groups. They founded newspapers, magazines and radio programs that also reflected their ideological tendencies and organizational affiliations: *Oyfgang* (1927-1930), organ of the Centro Israelita; *Havaner Lebn* (1932-1960), a Zionist daily and weekly; and the Communist periodical *Kubaner Idish Wort* (1942). The latter two also produced radio programs in Yiddish.

The Cuban Hebrews

The new generation, descendants of those first immigrants, has preserved —though not so faithfully— the Yiddish culture. Imbued with youthful eagerness, they served as vehicles of communication and bridged the two cultures. Their adoption of the language lead to a *boom* in publications, mostly written in Spanish, a sign that Jews were no longer a minority of strangers, but had become Cubans. Even the way they named their associations, such as the Agrupación Cultural Hebreo-Cubana (1953), using a hyphen to combine the two cultures, is an indication of this new interweaving of identities.

In 1950, having resettled in the neighborhoods of Vedado and Miramar after becoming part of the well to do and middle classes of Cuba, the *polacos* established the Patronato, which officially opened its doors in 1955. The Patronato's congregation was made up primarily of Polish Jews, former members of the Centro Israelita and a very few *Turcos*. Designed by the prominent architect Aquiles Capablanca, the building was an impressive architectural complex that included a synagogue, library, classrooms, a restaurant and halls for cultural and recreational activities —balls, banquets, etc. Although the initiative was questioned from the beginning as appearing elitist, the Patronato embodied an effort to bring together a very diverse community. In addition, to the world outside, it signified the new social and economic status achieved by its membership.

Like the Ashkenazi, in 1951 the *turcos* founded the Centro Hebreo Sefardí, also in Vedado, and undertook the construction of its Temple, which was inaugurated in 1959, shortly before they renewed their destined Diaspora.

This consolidation marks the completion of the first phase of the socio-economic insertion of the pioneers of this Jewish immigration to Cuba and the moment when the definitive profile of their *Kehillah* started to take shape. They were no longer a minority struggling against poverty and fearful of the consequences of intolerance, anti-Semitism and rejection, always present in their historical memory. Gradually, they had stopped being *polacos* and *turcos*, and

21

began to develop a new dual identity, defining themselves —with satisfaction and pride— as Hebrew-Cubans.

The Jews of the central highway

The Sephardic Jews that arrived in Cuba in the early years of the twentieth century came primarily from two cities of the Ottoman Empire: Silivria (Silivri), in the area of Istanbul, and Kirklisse (Kirklareli), which was close to Edirne. This defined geographic origin produced a chain of migration patterns based on kinship and community relations. The news that money flowed on the Island and "dollars grew on trees,"[7] as well as the similarity of language, race and ethnicity with their Spanish past, made Cuba their chosen destination.

In addition to their knowledge of Ladino, which facilitated communication, their traditional trade as peddlers made it less difficult for them to venture into the interior of the Island. They followed the path along the central highway to areas that were in full development because of the expansion of transportation and the sugar industry. As they made their way as peddlers and retail merchants, they ended up far away from their spiritual centers. The highly dispersed pattern of settlement, as well as the disproportionate number of single men among these immigrants, resulted in greater interaction and marriage with non-Jews, making the process of their integration into the social fabric of the host society easier and more fluid than that of the Ashkenazi.

These circumstances also shaped the institutional network they created. With Chevet Ahim in Havana as the mother organization, they formed societies in twelve towns and established four cemeteries across the Island. Thus, their presence was felt, not only in the capitals of provinces like Santiago de Cuba, where the natives of Kirklisse resided primarily, or in Camagüey, settled by natives of Silivri, but even smaller towns like Caibarién, Sancti-Spíritus, Artemisa, Campechuela, Colón and Manzanillo, among others.

The first associations were founded in 1921 in Camagüey and Holguín. The first cemetery was also established in Camagüey (1923), one of the most organized communities and the only one, in addition to Santiago de Cuba, that had a Rabbi as well as a Youth Union and a women's organization. In 1924, associations were created in Manzanillo, Ciego de Ávila, Camajuaní and Santiago de Cuba, the latter two having established cemeteries in 1925 and

---

[7] Margalit Bejarano. "Los sefardíes, pioneros de la inmigración judía a Cuba", in *Rumbos*, No.14, Jerusalem 1985, p.109.

1926, respectively. Still others were formed in Banes (1926), with a cemetery a year later (1927), in Matanzas (1928), in Guantánamo and Santa Clara (1929), which also inaugurated a cemetery in 1932.

Their coexistence with other ethnic groups established in Cuba was exemplary. As evidence of their rapid penetration and level of integration with the native population, they joined with Chinese immigrants in Camajuaní to form a kite team in the 1920s. In 1929, they participated in the traditional *parrandas*[8] with a float entitled "The Queen of Turkey." This mutual acceptance by the groups that composed the Cuban nationality happened not only on an individual social basis, but also in the commercial arena as well.

The first three decades of the twentieth century circumscribe the period of settlement, insertion and associational structuring for the Jews in the interior of the country. From then on, they began an internal migration from these towns back toward the capital for various reasons related to access to higher education, the desire that their children marry within the religion, and other aspects of social mobility, in general. Although many of the *turcos* living in the provinces moved to Havana, others stayed to become survivors and witnesses of that period of hard work, which was also a golden time of joy and harmony, as portrayed in these interviews.

1959: Decline and rebirth of a community

As noted, by 1959, the Jews in Cuba had entered a phase of complete consolidation. Few could imagine that a momentous Revolution was at the gates, and that this exuberant community life would vanish so quickly. The process of nationalization, initiated during the first years of the revolutionary government, affected them profoundly since they were concentrated in the commercial sector as wholesalers, owners of large department stores and shops and producers of consumer goods. As a result, and as part of the exodus of the middle and upper classes to which they belonged, more than 90% of the Jews on the Island emigrated, causing a true demographic catastrophe for their community.

Over time, they reacted to the economic measures imposed by the Revolution, shaping a migratory pattern that can be divided into four periods. In the years 1960-1962, when the large commercial interests were affected, they emigrated

---

[8] Parranda: a carnival in the towns of the interior, in which neighborhoods compete with floats and fireworks to show their best.

to the United States, Puerto Rico, Mexico, Venezuela and Israel. Later, when the "offensive"[9] of 1968 nationalized small businesses, they primarily went to the United States. In 1980, some went to the United States during the so-called "Mariel Boatlift," and in the 1990s, as a result of the difficult economic conditions of the "special period," they went fundamentally to Israel.

With that exodus, Jewish life languished in Cuba. More than 90% had intermarried, and they no longer had either a Rabbi, a *moreh*, a *hazzan*, or a *mohel*. Moreover, one part of the community was totally assimilated, and the other part subdued because of the government's religious policies that, without suppressing, disfavored religious practice. Yet, the community survived despite being reduced to its minimal expression and has become another example of the resilience and capacity of the Hebrews of the Diaspora to resist and adapt. Some of the men and women, whose stories appear here, assured this would be so.

Religious belief in Cuba: creole, utilitarian and pragmatic

A Cuban —as often said jokingly— believes in everything, and, at the same time, believes in nothing. It is true. With its peculiar insular religiosity that is mixed race, utilitarian and pragmatic, a product of the great syncretism that shapes it, Cuba is more flexible and open than any other Latin American country. The observation of the Jewish Agency that the "Hebrews in Cuba […] are seen as Cuban citizens, with equal rights,"[10] reflects the receptiveness that the Cuban people have always had toward immigrants and identity, an attitude that goes way beyond mere paternalistic tolerance.

In Cuba, Jewish origin has not been, by itself, a reason for exclusion. The peculiarity of being the only ethnic group in the country that also encompassed a religious community did not prevent its members who were not practicing Jews from being affiliates of the Communist Party or members of its Central Committee, something impossible in other socialist countries, or from achieving prominent positions in the central administration of the State (ministers), the diplomatic corps (ambassadors), or the military (high level officers). Cuban Jews have distinguished themselves in a broad range of intellectual and professional

---

[9] Offensive: the word given to the process that totally eliminated the last vestiges of private enterprise in the country.

[10] Nahum Sharon, Statements to the newspaper *Al Hamishar*, Israel, April 9, 1961, and the Archive of the Ministry of Foreign Relations of Cuba, Exp. 452.

activities that run the gamut from designing scientific projects in outer space to crafting nuances in socialist ideology.

Undoubtedly, some aspects of Cuban culture favored the understanding treatment that the Jewish community received all these years: the prominence given to the thought of José Martí, the guiding intellect of the revolutionary movement, with respect to the rights of all minorities; the profound influence of the antifascist legacy of the Spanish Civil War and the Second World War on the leaders of the Revolution; the recognition of the historic progressive role of Jews in Cuban struggles for independence as well as in international revolutionary movements. Prejudices harbored by the Spanish merchant class and some elements of the upper classes in the Republican years did not penetrate popular thought, making Cuba a country traditionally free of anti-Semitism. Moreover, there have been Jews whose access to the upper levels of the leadership of the country enabled them to instill greater comprehension of the aspirations and idiosyncrasies of this group.

Thus, when public religious institutions were nationalized (schools, cemeteries, hospitals) and all private industry taken over in 1961, the Albert Einstein School —sponsored by the Government— maintained its classes on Jewish history, Hebrew and Yiddish. In addition, the radio program in Yiddish continued broadcasting even when all the other programs in foreign languages had been cancelled, and the kosher butcher shop remained open as the only private business in the country. Moreover, the Jewish community conserved their social and religious buildings, although they no longer had a congregation large enough to justify their existence. Further, their members were the only Cubans who received special treatment when they decided to leave the country to emigrate to Israel, because they were considered to be returning to their motherland and not abandoning Cuba.

A generation lost or regained?

In the early 1990s, the crisis that battered the Cuban economy as a result of the fall of communism in Europe produced changes in Cuba that affected the life of the community. The disappearance of the socialist bloc created the necessity for new survival tactics suited to the new political-economic situation. Although economic hardships motivated some to leave, a series of reforms also gave rise to the revival of religious life on the Island.

Jewish life, as part of the larger society, had been dormant. The synagogues were in a state of deterioration, and a segment of Cuban Jews lived their Judaism in an internal exile. The words of the President of the Patronato, Dr. José Miller, express it best: "Community life was very poor. [...] Three synagogues with scarcely any activities, the services hardly obtained a *minyan*. Nothing was happening in the provinces. It was a depressing situation with a very uncertain future. [...] We knew we had young people [...], we knew that in the depths of their hearts something remained alive. The only thing we had to do was to reach them and rekindle that flame."[11] Thus, supported by the transformations that began in 1991 and were incorporated into the Constitution in 1992,[12] the temples abandoned their solitude, and Cubans initiated a search for new forms of religious identity.

Once more, the axiom that the third generation remembers what the second tried to forget was to be fulfilled. From a population of approximately six hundred members, at its nadir, composed of only a few original immigrants, where the last *Bar Mitzvah* took place in 1973 and the last wedding in 1976, the community has grown to 1,454 members of which 1,000 reside in Havana.

Progress in the Middle East peace process added to the environment of religious revitalization and allowed the flourishing of relations with the Jewish world abroad. The new reception found expression not only in the denominational sphere, but also in commercial and cultural arenas, and culminated with the visit of Fidel Castro to the Community in 1998. Shortly afterwards, and with the systematic help of numerous foreign organizations (Canadian Jewish Congress, American Jewish Joint Distribution Committee, B'nei B'rith, Weinberger Foundation, Miami Jewish Federation, Fundación Saltiel, Jabad), of individual synagogues (Kol Ami in Philadelphia, Netivot Shalom in Berkeley), of non institutional solidarity groups (Jewish Solidarity, Cuba-America Jewish Mission), or provided by *jubans*[13] in Atlanta, Chicago and Miami, among others, "the exhausted Cuban Hebrew community went from a culture of survival to a culture of community."[14]

The Joint —an organization that had been in contact with the Cuban Jewish life since the 1920s— centered the weight of its activities on religious teaching,

[11] Laura Paull and Evan Garell, interview with José Miller, in the documentary film *Havana Nagila*, 1995.
[12] Modifications to the Constitution in 1992 eliminated the definition of the Marxist Leninist State as atheist and strengthened provisions protecting freedom of religious belief.
[13] A name given to Jewish Cuban Americans.
[14] Jorge Diner, interview conducted in 1998.

education and assistance by sending *madrijim*, rabbis, and doctors, as well as on broad fund raising for the renovation of the synagogues, cemeteries and of the community, in general. From 1992 to 1995, the life of the communities in the provinces was also revived. Santiago de Cuba reopened its synagogue in 1995 and Camagüey in 1998. In addition, sections were organized to attend to different age groups: *Macabi Cuba*, between thirteen and thirty years of age; *Guesher*, from thirty to fifty-five; and *Simcha*, over fifty-five. The Women's Hebrew Association was reactivated and a Cuban chapter of Hadassah founded. A Sunday school was set up for children, as well as a program for adults, and ORT opened a center to teach different disciplines on the basis of pluralistic criteria.

The history of the Jews in Cuba, during these more that forty years, like that of their ancestors in the desert, is the story of this small percentage of men and women who stayed tied to the *promised land*, their chosen Island, that took them in or saw them born and who, unjustly, until the 1990s were considered a *lost generation*.

MARITZA CORRALES
Havana, Cuba 2005

27

PART ONE

The pioneers: Communists, Zionists
and revolutionaries

(Photo by Frédéric Brenner)

Avreml (Fabio) Grobart (1905-1994)
Fabio Grobart Sunshine

AVREML (FABIO) GROBART: One of the most important Communist leaders in Cuba and founder of the Party in 1925 of which he was a member of the Central Committee from 1926 until his death in 1994. Member of the Hebrew Section of the Agrupación Comunista de la Habana (1924) and founder of the Communist Youth League (1928). Organized, together with Martínez Villena, the first general strike against Machado (1930). Was imprisoned and deported. In Moscow, represented the Cuban Party in the Komintern. From 1931-32, worked organizing the Cuban sugar workers. Again imprisoned and deported in 1932. In 1933, he returned from Nazi Germany bringing the printing press of the Party and was elected Secretary of the Organization of the Central Committee of the PCC. Imprisoned again after the general strike of 1935. When the Party was declared illegal, he remained in hiding for a year and traveled clandestinely to Mexico. From 1952-60, was the representative of Cuban workers in the World Labor Organization in Vienna and Prague.

In 1960, returned to Cuba and was named Director of the Journal *Cuba Socialista*, a theoretical organ of the Party. Elected member of the Central Committee at the formation of the new Communist Party of Cuba (1965). Founded and presided over the Institute of the History of the Communist Party from 1973. A deputy of the Cuban Parliament. Published books contributing to the theory and practice of Marxism-Leninism in Cuba.

"A little nineteen year old polish Jew among the first in the struggle"

AVREML (FABIO) GROBART: I was born on August 30, 1905 in Trzciany, a *shtetl* on the border between Lithuania and Poland in the area of Bialystok that hardly even appears on the map. It was a small town of workers, the main industry of which was making products from hog hair. We were a very poor family. My father, Motel, worked in one of these factories making brushes. Mama, Raquel, washed clothes in the home of rich Jews. With the outbreak of the First World War, we moved to Bialystok because we were Jews, and we did not trust the local people.

My father went to synagogue every Saturday, but he wasn't fanatic. Rather, he was influenced by the *Bund*. I studied at the Zionist Hebrew school, but I didn't finish. When I was nine years old, my two brothers and I were orphaned, and we went to live with one of my mother's sisters in Gonyodz, near the fort of Ossovietz. Her husband was a tailor, and he taught me to be one as well.

To make a living, I tutored the children of wealthy families in arithmetic and religion. Like in Gorky's *My Universities*, I also read in the bathroom by candlelight. I became an apprentice to a shoemaker, but I left that because apprentices were the most exploited workers. I also had a job in the Post Office for a month wrapping and addressing packages.

FABIO GROBART SUNSHINE: It was the era of the pogroms, and that caused him to reject the type of cruel nationalism that existed among the Poles and Russians. The October Revolution triumphed and Lenin declared the independence of the regions that belonged to the Tsarist Empire, among them Poland.

In Poland, General Pilsudsky and his force took power, who, we could say, did not get along with Jews nor, of course, with the proletarian revolution. In 1920, they attacked the Russians who counterattacked, reached Warsaw and liberated it. My father remembers that those Russian soldiers were farmers who came in rags, but were happy and sang songs. When the Russians withdrew, the Polish troops reentered and took it out on the Jewish population. It was terrible. There he came to the understanding that the way to unite the poor was not by fomenting religious beliefs but by creating a socialist system.

Birth of *Avreml Simjovitch*

AVREML (FABIO) GROBART: At this time I get involved with youth organizations and become the provincial secretary. I fall in love with the Soviet soldiers whom I hear sing revolutionary songs, like the *Marsellaise* and *The International*, for the first time. They aren't like the tsarists or the Polish anti-Semites. I feel I am a Communist. We distribute the pamphlets of the Polish Communist Party at the Ossovietz military fort. Many young people are imprisoned. I escape, but have to go into hiding because the police are looking for me. It was the day before the first of May, 1924. My uncle, the tailor, helps me. He knows that if they arrest me, I will be tortured and sentenced to five or six years in jail for fomenting sedition within the army. I leave with a false passport: from Abraham Grobart, I become Avreml Simjovitch. I go to Bialystok where they advise me to go on to Grodno.

I stay in Grodno a number of months. I give classes and lectures until the police begin searching for me. The youth organization and the Communist party in Byelorussia were illegal. The non-Jews and the Zionist Jews alike did not consider Communists to be human. Something then happens that takes me to Cuba. An uncle in the Bund, who had participated in the Revolution of 1905 and who emigrated to Canada, found out that we had become orphans and sends a ticket to my older brother. My brother, who knew my situation, delivers it to me so I can get out of Poland. Afterwards, when I was in Cuba, I helped both of my siblings get out.

I cross a river on the Polish-German border clandestinely, helped by a group that worked to get out people like me, those who were politically persecuted or who didn't want to serve in the army. Germany was the transfer point to go to Holland from where a boat left monthly for Central America. I couldn't apply for a visa with the passport I had, and so in Edam, Holland, I got on a boat for Cuba. So, more like a sentimental than a conscientious Communist, I went first to Haiti and later to Cuba. I had a certain political consciousness, but it was not yet sufficiently developed to enable me to express my thoughts.

My first night in Havana, I stay in Tiscornia,[1] which was like a kind of prison for immigrants who didn't have relatives in Cuba. I left dressed in a Russian *rubashka*. It was summer of 1924. I was nineteen. There was a small Hebrew colony in the city that helped Jews who came from Europe. They learned that I had arrived and that I didn't have anyone to get me out, that I had no refuge. Among the Jews in Havana lived someone from Gonyondz, and he comes to find me. That's how I get out.

---

[1] Tiscornia: port of entry in Cuba. An encampment for immigrants similar to Ellis Island.

For the first time in my life I see black people. I hear the Spanish language for the first time, even though on the boat I learned a few words from a book that had certain expressions from Spanish to Yiddish. He takes me to his house in Marianao to spend the night and until I can find work. A good person. He asks me what my trade is. I respond a shoemaker, without knowing how to do it very well, and tailor, which I knew a little better. He finds me work in a tailor shop that belonged to a Jew on a street a little beyond Bernaza, where the Institute of History is. At least I had a place to work and earn something. I slept on a wooden table at the same workshop. I ate with the other operators at a cheap Chinese restaurant where the poorest people went. We ate for eight or nine cents. If you paid ten, you were a rich guy.

When the week ended, they gave me 1.50 pesos for the entire week of 12 hours of work a day. With this I couldn't even pay the rent for one room. At that time it was hard to walk a street in Havana and not see a sign that said FOR RENT, because a lot of people from Europe were coming. I found a house and took a room. I saw a young man I knew in Poland who had the same problem. He worked for a retailer and moved in with me to share the rent.

There are happenstances that sometimes change the direction of one's life. The owner of the house was a tailor, and his brother tells me that he is going to find me work. He calls the manager of a store to see if they need an apprentice, and sends me to the most famous store in Havana, J. VALLÉS, where the rich people go. The first week they pay me eight pesos. It was a very large shop with some eighty or ninety employees, both men and women. There I begin to notice Cuban women. I had never seen such pretty women. I worked there until 1930. I earned the sympathy of my co-workers at the tailor shop. Soon, they raised me to ten pesos and I got up to twelve pesos a week. With my personal needs met, I could send money to my brothers so they could buy tickets and leave Poland. It was my moral duty. That's how they finally got to Canada.

I am Lenin… meeting the Cuban communists

While working at the Jewish workshop, I had nothing to do at night. I didn't know Spanish, or Havana. At the end of the work day, I decided to walk around the neighborhood to see a little of the city. The first night I take care to remember the name of the street, so I can get back. The second night I go a little further to the neighborhood of the port of Old Havana, to San Isidro

Street, which was the street of the prostitutes, where the poorest lived. I had never seen this kind of life in Poland. For me it was something new.

But the biggest surprise I have during this walk is that I pass by a place where —I found out later— the workers of the Stevedores Union lived. The door of the house was open, and I see a portrait of Lenin hanging on the wall. I said to myself Lenin is here. I didn't know that Cuba had Communists. They were port workers, sympathizers of the Soviet Union. I decide to go in and I meet a black man at a table. Pointing to Lenin with a finger, I say: "I am Lenin." He got up and hugged me. He asks me where I am from. I respond that I am an immigrant, that I just arrived. I ask if there are Communists here. He answers yes and asks if I want to know them. We go to the Agrupación Comunista, which was on Zulueta Street, number 38, where they introduced me to Carlos Baliño about whom I knew nothing, an old Marxist of the last century who fought alongside Martí for Cuba's independence. At that time, he edited the newspaper of the Agrupación Comunista de la Habana. By making signs, I explain I am a Communist, and I begin to visit the place frequently.

I found out that there are Polish and Lithuanian Hebrews, clandestine members of the Youth and the Party, that belong to the Agrupación and who, like me, had emigrated for political reasons, and also others who had emigrated for economic problems. I get to know them, we speak in Yiddish. Two weeks later, I become a member of the Agrupación. There were two or three comrades who arrived in Cuba much earlier, and they explained things to me. I didn't enter blind. This is my first involvement with Cuban Communists. On the advice of the Jewish communist group, I look for a native teacher to teach me Spanish, and I quickly become a leader of the Hebrew Section of Havana.

The Communist Jews didn't have a place to meet. I rent one that was being leased on the first floor, on Zulueta, across the street from the Agrupación, which now belongs to the Center of the Valencianos, and I put out a call to all the Jews of the city, most of whom were supporters of the Soviet Union. It is 1925: we were not yet persecuted. We rent a place that was not Zionist. We Polish communists had been taught that Zionism was anti-communist. The Jews knew we sympathized with the Soviet Union and that we weren't Zionists. Today we could not say Zionists or not Zionists because there are also Zionists of the left.

Monument to the first Martyrs
of the Machado dictatorship,
Jewish Cemetery of Guanabacoa.
(Photo by Frédéric Brenner)

Workers and merchants:
La Unión Cultural Hebrea / Centro Israelita

Many Jews went on the street, to sell ties, they began as merchants. We were not.
We were workers, tailors, shoemakers, painters. The community was divided.
Those that opened a little shop would not go to a place where there were people
of the left. They went to Egido Street, to the Centro Israelita, founded in 1925.
The Unión Cultural Hebrea was ours. The Agrupación was born when we
didn't yet have the dictatorship of Gerardo Machado, an enemy of the Soviet
Union. Although the prior president was prejudiced against communists, he
didn't hold the same intense hatred for them as did Machado. The Communist
Party of Cuba, on the other hand, was illegal from the day of its formation.

The founding Congress was held in a house near Paseo Street, where a relative
of Julio Antonio Mella[2] lived. It was later converted into a theater. The Hebrew
Section elected as delegates to the founding of the Party: Magidson, Gurwitz,
Grinberg, and Wasserman as translator. They were communists who arrived before

---

[2] Julio Antonio Mella, student leader, founder of the Communist Party of Cuba, assassinated in Mexico on
orders of the Cuban dictator Gerardo Machado.

me, at the end of 1923 and beginning of 1924. All this happened in August, 1925. The First Congress brought together delegates from the Agrupación Comunista of Havana, Guabanacoa, Manzanillo and other places, some five or six. With them, the Communist Party of Cuba was officially established. I met Mella there. The true founders of the Hebrew Section, some twenty members in Havana, were: Grinberg, apparently the most knowledgeable of the group and who left for the United States a little afterwards; Gurwitz, a communist from Lithuania who had asthma; Magidson, who later emigrated to Mexico; and Wasserman, the interpreter, who was a teacher and an honest man. Only Wasserman knew Spanish, and Grinberg knew a little.

When the Party was set up in 1925, the Jews maintained a cell in Yiddish because many had not yet learned the language, except me who had a teacher. That enabled me to understand the Cuban workers. Once, the Polish Embassy invited me for my birthday and asked me to speak to the Hebrews who were there and explain what I did to organize the Communist Party in Cuba. I told them that it was because I knew Spanish and because others went to the United States to try their luck. Many workers remained here, and I was chosen to be one of their leaders, not as a Jew but as a Communist. I became one more Cuban who didn't speak Spanish well. I knew the rules of working underground, something that Cubans didn't know. For them the underground was the clandestine movement during the fight for independence against Spain. That was why I was named to the Central Committee.

At that time, the persecution of Cuban Communists had not yet started. The first secretary of the Party was from the Canary Islands. They expel him from Cuba. Others go because they have family; they sacrifice the Party in order to save the family. I don't have anything to lose. I don't have family. I came alone and was not married, but the Spanish married Cubans and had something to worry about. I feel the need to take the place of those who left. Already in 1926, I am called to the Central Committee, to which I have belonged ever since. I suffer through many calamities. I am wanted by the police, they detain me, they deport me and I go into exile.

Yunger Simjovitch:
the little Pole at the constitution of the Party

The first time I am imprisoned is in 1930, in solitary, but they don't deport me. There was a Jew, David Utiansky, who had progressive ideas and got along well with me, although he was not a member of the Party. He contacted someone in the Government. The second was in 1932, and this time they deported me. Through the German embassy, they were able to get me out to the Soviet Union. There, I participated in the meetings of the Communist International until I came back after the fall of Machado.

FABIO GROBART SUNSHINE: Papa was in prison many times. They deported him, but he always managed to return to his new homeland, to give himself fully to the struggle for a free and socialist Cuba. Many of his comrades were murdered by the different dictatorships that took turns in our country. He carried out organizational and ideological activities and trained revolutionary cadres in the Communist Party of Cuba and in the Young Communists, of which he was also a founder. He also organized solidarity assistance to other peoples like sending volunteers to defend the Republic during the Spanish Civil War, support for the people of Ethiopia against the fascist aggression of Mussolini, solidarity with the struggle of the people of Nicaragua for their independence, the campaign for the freedom of the Bulgarian revolutionary Jorge Dimitrov, and with the Soviet people during World War II against Nazi-fascism.

At that time, my father had a different name: Yunger Simjovitch. Every time they caught him, he gave another name. It was the only thing he could do to avoid being linked to earlier arrests. The identity card didn't exist then. Each time he was deported or had to travel, he would get a new passport with a different nationality and a different name. Abraham was his real name. Fabio is the one that a Party comrade gave him and that he made official after the triumph of the Revolution in 1959.

The "mastermind" of Cuban Communism

During the Cold War following the Second World War, the murders of the working class activists multiplied, including sugar workers (Jesús Menéndez), port workers (Aracelio Iglesias) and transport workers in the capital (José María Pérez). My father was also on the black list. The FBI, the American embassy and the Cuban police launched a campaign against the shadowy Jewish agent of the Kremlin, the man of sixteen languages, the mastermind of Communism. The Party ordered him to emigrate in 1951. He left illegally as a sailor on a boat and almost drowned in the Gulf of Mexico. During the Batista dictatorship, he worked within the ranks of the World Federation of Unions in charge of solidarity work supporting the struggles of the Cuban people and other peoples of Latin America and the world.

Our return to Cuba, at the end of 1960, was cause for great joy because my parents always felt themselves to be Cuban. Cuba held a great attraction. As a boy, I sometimes went to the countryside. There are special things —the typical smells of the houses of the peasants, the Cuban flowers, the butterfly jasmine…the way of Cubans, their hospitality, cheerfulness, the beauty of our landscape, of our women— they are different than those of any other country.

I remember that, in 1948, my mother asked my father when Communism, the revolution, was going to succeed in Cuba, and he said: "within twenty years." The Revolution triumphed in 1959, almost ten years early. And then, she, as a good Jew, laughed at him: "You said twenty years, but Fidel did it in less than ten."

In 1959, the goal of their life's work was fulfilled. The Communist Party of Cuba was reconstituted in 1965 from all the revolutionary organizations that had fought. In that act, Fidel spoke words of respect for that "little Pole who came to our country when he was only nineteen years old and was among the first in the struggle of generations of Cubans." As he had been before the Revolution, he was elected a member of the Central Committee of the new Communist Party, in which he remained active until his death on October 21, 1994.

He directed the journal *Cuba Socialista*, the theoretical organ of the Cuban Revolution, which is an historic source of how the Revolution was made, work that he shared with Fidel, Raúl, Ché Guevara, Carlos Rafael Rodríguez and other leaders. Later, Fidel gave him the task of creating the Institute of the History of the Socialist Revolution of the Cuban Communist Movement. He had the honor of representing the Cuban Communist Party at the Congresses of the Communist and Workers Parties of other countries and to receive important decorations of Cuba and other friendly countries, including Poland and the Soviet Union. He was the second Cuban to be awarded the Order of José Martí and the National Labor Hero Gold Star. He was elected deputy to the Parliament, and, because he was the oldest, he presided together with the youngest woman, over the "Table of Ages," a beautiful symbol of respect and historic continuity among revolutionary generations. In addition, he was assigned —at different congresses of the new Party— to introduce Fidel as its General Secretary.

Fabio Grobart Sunshine.
Havana, 2005.
(Photo by Tatiana Santos)

FABIO GROBART SUNSHINE (b. 1942): Master's Degree in Chemical Engineering (Prague, 1965); Doctorate in Economic Sciences (Soviet Union, 1981); senior researcher (Cuba, 1982); professor at the Center for International Economic Research, of the Faculty of Economics and the Department of Science, Technology and Society of the University of Havana; secretary of the department of scientific policy of the National Council of Science and Technology (1976-1980) and permanent representative of Cuba in the working group of CAME on prospective science and technology (1981-1988); co-founder and Cuban representative in international networks: Latin American Network of Prospective Studies, the Latin American Node of the "Millennium Project" of the University of the United Nations. Has published more than 100 articles in journals and books in Cuba, in fifty foreign countries and international bodies, including CAME and ONUDI.

Fabio Grobart, the son: a Cuban Jew

Mama was born in Alenitze, close to Warsaw. They were nine siblings. She had a twin who died and, as in the story of Mark Twain, they never knew which one had survived. The family maintained Jewish traditions, but they weren't orthodox. They mixed well with the Polish. My grandmother had a rooming house, and my grandfather was a specialist in Singer sewing machines. Grandpa died in the First World War of appendicitis. At that time, they didn't know how to treat it. They put him in a bathtub, gave him castor oil, and it burst. They lived in a petit-bourgeois environment and didn't feel discrimination.

Not so with my father's family. He was from a *shtetl* on the border between Poland and Byelorussia, on the Polish side, close to Bialystok, that then belonged to the Russian Empire.

Mama came to Cuba in 1924, the same year as my father but for different reasons. She had gone to Warsaw to work in a workshop where they made hats for the opera, in the area near the Great Theater. The singers gave her tickets to the upper gallery. She loved the opera and when I was a child, she always sang me those songs. There she met a young man, a good person. He had some means. He traveled to Cuba and set up a business, an important store, and they got married by correspondence. He brought my mother to the Island, and afterwards she brought her whole family.

They were happy until she met my father. Her husband was a man with excellent economic status, and my father was a poor man who was always being persecuted. But she fell in love with this young romantic who fought for the happiness of the world. She divorced, and they married and spent their whole lives as nomadic fighters for the revolution.

She also dedicated herself to the struggle as a leader of the Socorro Rojo Internacional, a Communist organization that helped political prisoners. She was put into prison, together with Justina Álvarez, the secretary to Blas Roca[3] and his wife for many years, with Conchita Valdivieso, a girlfriend of Antonio Guiteras.[4] Somewhere there is a photo of four women in the jail of Guanabacoa.

In my mother's family, there were both workers and members of the middle class. The uncle from New York, who was a marine in the Second World War, had a business in the International Diamond Center. He appears in the movie *Marathon Man*, starring Dustin Hoffman.

The sons of immigrants wanted to be *mambises*[5]

I was born in Havana in 1942 and wanted to be just another Cuban. As sons of immigrants we wanted to be Cubans, we played the same games, we wanted to be *mambises*. My friends were Cubans. Our parents, Jewish Communists, had their own friends like Epstein, the editor of the Communists' newspaper, Jaime

---

[3] Blas Roca Calderío: for many years the General Secretary of the Cuban Communist Party.
[4] Antonio Guiteras: a popular leader in the struggle against the Machado dictatorship. He was assassinated in 1935 by Batista.
[5] Mambises: Cuban guerrilla fighters of the nineteenth century in the struggle for independence against the Spanish colonial rulers.

Novomodi and Berta Burstein, the sister of one of the martyrs of the Machado dictatorship. As children, we saw each other, but only sporadically. Here the Jews were not isolated as in other countries. It was one of the advantages that Cuba offered. There wasn't discrimination, although one day a boy spit on me because his mother told him we had killed Christ.

I didn't study in a Jewish school. They wanted me to go to the Sholem Aleijim to learn Yiddish, but, although it was a progressive school, I wanted to be in Vedado and not in Old Havana. So, because of the neighborhood in which we lived, I went to primary school in Vedado, to the Columbus School, a lay school on 19th Street, and to kindergarten at the Edison School in La Víbora.

My parents spoke Yiddish between themselves, but I insisted that they speak Spanish. The confusion bothered me. I wanted to understand what they were saying. My father always liked to speak and read in Yiddish. I used to buy him books and magazines and other works in Yiddish published in the Soviet Union so he could read them. Mama cooked Jewish food, *gefilte fish*, herring, *kneidlach*, but I always asked for Cuban dishes, like rice, beans, chicken and rice. I liked Cuban food.

I wouldn't say there was a traditional atmosphere in our house. They always told me they had stopped being religious because God was a very strict God that instilled constant fear, which they considered to be an idea that held you back. They thought that it wasn't worth believing when they always killed Jews, in spite of their belief, and that it was better to fight for freedom. But we commemorated the Holidays: at Passover we ate matzoh and gefilte fish. Papa knew all the Jewish holidays. On Purim, he would say that the moon was here or there, that on that date his mother had died. But since we weren't believers, they didn't take it to its religious consequences, but rather as something they had lived fully when young and that they still shared. Saturdays were holidays, and they went to *Kultur Farain*.

My father never stopped helping his Jewish compatriots. The progressive Jews of the left used to get together at the Kultur Farain. They kept their customs and traditions, sang, put on plays. They also discussed politics, offering their solidarity to the struggles of the Cuban people, taking food to the political prisoners. The Jewish communists edited their own newspaper, the *Kubaner Idish Wort*, and for many years they broadcasted hours in Yiddish on the radio station of the Communist Party of Cuba. Their children went to the Sholem Aleijem school. They organized a cheap restaurant (La Cooperativa) where the revolutionaries, generally people of scarce means, could eat free. Many Cubans began to like Jewish cuisine.

It was a mixture of cultures, of communist life, of Jewish life. "For my father, to be Jewish was to be historically, culturally, traditionally, and genetically from that nation; it was a nationality. However, at the same time, he excluded religion as the only way to feel Jewish. He believed it was a way of thinking, venerating the ancestors and identifying with their history, origins, and suffering. It was a form of human solidarity, but it didn't mean that you had to live in a state called Israel, nor that you couldn't integrate into the life of a nation."[6]

The environment of a life

Look, my father transmitted to me many positive and negative experiences of Judaism. He knew the Bible very well; he had command of it, taught it to other children in Poland and taught me some things too. But he developed a rejection of the religious focus. By himself, not because someone told him "this is not so, this should be some other way." Everyday life was so rich and could be seen from different perspectives, and it was his life experience that convinced him that religious belief wasn't the way. Anyway, he transmitted the traditions to us. I didn't live it, but I received it through stories my father told me. And my son also received it from my father's stories, not from me. I left it up to my son. If he wanted to go to the community, it was his personal decision. Whatever he felt, I would welcome it. He had to think with his own head; he had to decide what was good, what was bad, what suited him, which ideals were important for all humanity, and which were insignificant. He had to find his own answers.

My parents were married in a civil ceremony, and they did not have me circumcised. By chance, because I really didn't know, I married a woman who was half Jewish, half Czech. My grandmother, my mother and my half brother are buried in the Jewish cemetery in Guanabacoa. Papa said he wanted to be buried with his comrades. He was more Cuban.

The Jewish Cubans were very active in the social struggles and contributed to the formation of the Cuban nation. There wasn't a progressive movement in the world that the Cuban Jews didn't support. When they brought back Mella's ashes, several Jews were wounded in the protest rallies. One of them, Boris

---

[6] Miriam Greenberg, unpublished interview, 1998 (Author's files).

Waxman, was treated so badly that he died a few days later of gangrene. It was at this protest that they killed the first Cuban pioneer who had been together with Archik,[7] a young Jew, who had recently arrived in Cuba. Afterwards, they created the Young Communist League, with my father present.

There was always a common language for noble causes

There were Jews of all tendencies, capitalists and proletarians, but a common language was always found to help the noblest causes. Those who were not militants, but sympathizers, the wives and friends, contributed to the struggle of the *Auxilio Español* (Spanish Auxiliary) at the initiative of the women of the Hebrew community who brought food for the political prisoners. These were ways of organizing solidarity.

When the Jewish Communists needed some material support for their work, the Jewish capitalists helped. They never denied it, even though they had other ideas, other life styles. Those rich Hebrews, who did not sympathize ideologically with the leftists, donated financially to the cause because they had personal ties to those other Jews. They passed the collection box on Muralla Street, and the store owners always gave.[8] I think they were sincere.

The Jewish community was divided by social, religious and ideological class origins. One part reflected the interests of the Hebrews who had done well and who adopted the position —closer to the religious and to Zionism as an ideological current— of creating a country in the *promised land*. The other part was composed of those who had not made religion the center of their devotion and whose political leanings were more universal in character. They didn't consider going to Israel, preferring to become part of the Cuban people.

Many Jews married Cubans. It wasn't that they didn't remember the ancestry of their fathers, rather that a Jew born here felt Cuban. There wasn't any difference of nationalities, they had totally integrated into the national life and carried on a full life within the new Cuban nation that is also as new as Israel. Revolutionary Cuba is a new country that must confront many difficulties, both external and internal adversities. And the Jews that live here also have contributed to the improvement of our life. Some decided to go where things are already done. Others decided to do them here, where there is still a lot to do.

---

[7] Arón (Archik) Radlow, head of the League of Pioneers and member of the Central Committee of the Communist Youth. His interview and that of his daughter Myriam are included in this part of the book.

[8] They called it "passing the collection box," just like that collected at mass in the churches.

Poster of the Yidishe Geselschaft Far Kunst un Kultur (Jewish Association for Art and Culture), announcing a lecture by Comrade Avreml Simjovitch on "The development of Cuban democracy and its relationship to the Jewish Community," October 8, 1938.
(Courtesy of Margalit Bejarano)

Fabio Grobart with Jone Jazan on their arrival in Cuba. Havana, 1924.

45

Fabio with his grandaughter.
Havana, 1966.

Mother, grandmother and aunts of
Fabio Grobart Sunshine in Alenitze.
Poland, 1921.

Celebration of Grobart's 75th birthday with his family and General Raul Castro.
Havana, 1980.

Richard Wolf (Ricardo Subirana Lobo)[1]
(1889-1982)

Hannover, September 22, 1887

The midwife Laise Lippelt, born Wilke, a resident of Hannover, presented herself before the employee signing this Civil Register and reported that Marianne Wolf, born Neumann and wife of the merchant of goods Moritz Wolf —both of the mosaic religion— residing with her husband in Hannover, Engelbostelerdamm # 7, on September 16, in the presence of the informant, gave birth to a male child who was given the names Richard Riegel.

That which is expressed above is hereby confirmed on the principle register for births of the Civil Register of Hannover I.

Hannover, February 2, 1938

---

[1] The testimony on Richard Wolf (Ricardo Subirana Lobo) summarizes original documents obtained from his family, an interview with Eumelio Caballero in 1990, and an article by Inge Deutschkron, Weekly Supplement of MA´ARIV, Israel, May 26, 1978. I am grateful to Graciela Dysenchauz, Margalit Bejarano and the Wolf Foundation for providing these materials.

Subirana and wife Francisca in front of the Capitol. Havana, 1925.

A wandering Jew with an island in his heart

Richard (Ricardo) Riegel Wolf was one of 14 children of Moritz Wolf, a merchant of metals and a pillar of the Jewish community of Hannover. He was the brother of Leopold Wolf, teacher and first cantor of the synagogue of Halle/Saale. It was in his home that Ricardo learned to respect education, work, and the ethical and moral values that were to be decisive in his life. Following the teaching of this deeply rooted humanism, Ricardo became a socialist during the government of the Kaiser and a member of the illegal Social-Democratic Party. Convinced that the rigid atmosphere blanketing Germany had a reactionary smell inconsistent with his ideas, he gave in to the heavenly descriptions of his classmates and, fortunately, he immigrated to Cuba in 1913.

He was not the typical Jewish immigrant who came from the shtetl to the Island in the 1920s. He was a student of chemistry, who one day, after much effort, made an important discovery: the recovery of residual iron during the founding process, which was applied successfully in steel mills around the world and made him a millionaire.

As stated in the family album started by his brother Leopold in 1907 at the time of his father's death: "Undoubtedly, hidden in Richard was an artist, an actor or opera singer, who in his early youth put on plays in the hallway of No. 3 Lilienstrasse for the neighborhood children, and who as a single man was a scrap dealer and lived in Düsseldorf with a tenor singer who transmitted his enthusiasm for Wagner." His love for music never diminished and forged his great friendship with Pablo Casals.

He might be seen as a typical wandering Jew, because he lived in Cuba, Barcelona, Italy and even settled for a while in Istanbul where he established a leather factory. He was married in the German city of Laatzen to a Cuban, Francisca Subirana, who was a tennis champion in the 1920s. Contrary to tradition, he adopted her surname. But despite all this, he continued to miss Cuba, maintaining an umbilical chord to the Island to which he always returned. Perhaps it was his advanced social spirit, combined with his artistic sensitivity or passion for gambling, that created a permanent bond to this land, to the Revolution and its leader, Fidel Castro.

I am Jewish...

"A mutual friend introduced us," he told Deutschkron. "The first thing I noticed about him was a small pendant with the image of Jesus and, for that reason, I said: I am Jewish." To his astonishment, Castro embraced him and confessed that Jewish blood from his ancestors in Spain also ran in his veins.

That day marked the beginning of his active involvement with the Cuban Revolution. He gave advice and promoted support for Land Reform. Although he was offered the position of Minister of Finance, he didn't accept it. He was already 73, too many years for what he thought, logically, would be his last job. He wanted to do something definitive: to bring together, to unite in understanding those two countries that were his personal choices —although he wasn't born in either of them, to plant the basis for a fertile relationship between Cuba, his adopted country, and Israel, his spiritual country. Consequently, he requested to be, and was named by the Revolutionary Government in 1961, Plenipotentiary Minister of Cuba in Israel.

"Subirana had located in Cuba and from here, or from Italy or Israel, he attended to the business and administered the family fortune," reports Eumelio Caballero. "He never used the Island as a place to develop his entrepreneurial life. There is no record of any properties of his having been nationalized or delivered to the Revolutionary Government. He lived off interest and money invested in shares and companies. In Cuba, he never had any political affiliation, but he told me of his past involvement with German Zionist movements of the left. He was an active Zionist militant until he began to represent Cuba. He told me that, because of his relations with the Zionist left, he had worked closely with leaders of the European Social-Democratic movement."

The Ten Commandments of Agriculture and the VIP sheep

Without doubt, the many similarities must have attracted the attention and admiration of the Cuban revolutionaries: the spirit of sacrifice of the Israeli pioneers that allowed them to flourish in the desert, the idyllic socialist experiment of the kibbutz, the struggle of that people against British imperialism, and the small David who fearlessly confronted Goliath. Fidel called Israel "that heroic country."[2] He had read *The Revolt*, by Menahem Beguin, and he showed special interest in the agricultural development it achieved and its sheep herding projects.

Despite the difficulties imposed by the political alliance between Israel and the United States, Subirana successfully promoted the collaboration of Israeli agricultural technicians, and he created a Friendship Association that substituted the official channels. This is how Peretz Rosenzweig came to Cuba with only a letter signed by Subirana, which served as a visa. Rosenzweig named citrus groves "Lenin" and "Marx" and wrote *The Ten Commandments of Agriculture*. Thousands of copies circulated in all of the agricultural centers of the country.

Fidel wanted a special sheep, adaptable to Cuba, and instructed his ambassador to buy one hundred sheep to be *cubanized* to create a new race, capable of thriving in the conditions on the Island. Charter flights were authorized to transport them. Cuban Jews, who wanted to immigrate to Israel because a socialist society no longer offered them possibilities to continue their private businesses, would travel to Israel on these same planes on their return flight to Israel. Dr. Prato observed: "The sheep traveled in first class and my wife in tourist class."

Cuba, at that time, was the only communist country that permitted a Zionist Union on its territory. When all private schools had been nationalized, the Cuban Government maintained Jewish children's access to teaching of their traditions. Further, they facilitated the emigration of citizens of Hebrew origin to Israel without limitation because they considered them to be returning to

---

[2] Jonathan Prato, first Israeli diplomat in Cuba; cited by Deutschkron.

their native country. They also left the kosher butcher shop in the hands of the Jewish community, which for many years was the only private business to survive in Cuba.

Perhaps, one could also find a little of Subirana's work behind these attitudes that reflected a high degree of empathy and understanding of Jewish reality. As expressed by a representative to the World Jewish Congress in 1975: "The Jews of Havana have told me that Subirana had been very useful in a whole series of matters that required the cooperation of the Government." [3]

The only Cuban Embassy that cost nothing

Exactly as he had promised Fidel, the Cuban Embassy in Israel was entirely paid for by him, including the salaries and costs of representation. Subirana purchased land in the neighborhood of Herzliya-Pituah, perhaps because it most reminded him of Havana, and contracted an Israeli architect named Rechter to build the Cuban residence facing the sea, surrounded by papaya trees and tropical plants native to the Island.

"I greatly admired him," states Eumelio Caballero. "He was a Cuban revolutionary. A very human man, very cultured, with a sharp nose to penetrate things, to see the future in the world of business, a man sympathetic to all the just causes of the world. I respected him a lot and he helped my development, my attitude towards life, and my discipline in work.

I will tell you an anecdote. I lived pretty far from the Embassy, and I had to take the bus, but on two occasions I missed it and arrived late. The second time it happened, I found an alarm clock on my desk. Subirana called me and spoke to me like a father. 'You are very young and I want you to understand the message I want to convey with this clock, and it is to avoid this possible conversation: You have arrived late for the third time and that is not permissible.' He was very admired by the rest of the Diplomatic Corps in Israel. Everyone knew his origins, of his success as a businessman, and was surprised that he was the representative of revolutionary Cuba. This supposed contradiction fascinated them."

Up until his advanced age prevented him, from his base in Israel, he attended Cuba's diplomatic relations with Italy, where he was decorated as Gentleman of the Great Cross of the Order of Merit of the Republic of Italy. He also carried out other functions such as being traveling ambassador to China. On

---

[3] Lavy Becker, *Report on the Jewish Community of Cuba*, June 1975.

Subirana and Francisca's tombstone in kibbutz Gash.
Tel Aviv, 2004.
(Courtesy of Graciela Dysenchauz)

September 9, 1973, Cuba broke off diplomatic relations with Israel. Since he was already 86 years old, and his wife "Panchita" was very sick, Subirana decided to stay in Israel.

Although it now houses the Wolf Foundation, the embassy has remained as it had always been, frozen in time: the Cuban flag, the portrait of Fidel with the dedication "To my great friends, Ricardo and Panchita, with sincere friendship," and the diplomatic license plate on the car. Established by Ricardo and Francisca in 1975, the Wolf Foundation is a kind of Israeli Nobel, which gives an annual award to scientists and artists of any nationality, race, color, religion, gender or political affiliation for their contribution to humanity and brotherly relations among peoples.

Richard Wolf and Francisca Subirana died in Israel in 1982, and although far from the Island —in order that their link with their other homeland not be severed— they were buried outside of Tel Aviv in the Kibbutz Gash, founded in 1948 by Cubans of the Hashomer Hatzair. They are a symbol of love and understanding between our two peoples.

---

* All the photographs, except the ones of the graves and the Embassy, are courtesy of the Wolf Foundation.

Subirana and Fidel Castro;
dedication written by Castro.
Havana, 1960.

Presentation of Subirana's diplomatic credentials to Itzhak Ben-Zvi, President of the State of Israel, and Golda Meier, Secretary of State.
September 1, 1960.

Reception honoring Cuba's National Day with a group of Cuban residents in Israel.
Hotel Accadia, Israel, 1961.

Subirana and Francisca with Itzhak Rabin and wife at the head table at an event in Israel.

(date unknown)

Former Cuban Embassy building. At present Wolf Foundation.
Tel Aviv, 2004.

(Courtesy of Graciela Dysenchauz)

Arón Radlow, at the right,
reading the Cuban Jewish Communist
newspaper, *Kubaner Idish Wort*.
Havana, 1942.

Arón Radlow Givner (1917-1995)[1]
Myriam Radlow Zaitman
Luis Lapidus Mandel (1937-1995)

LUIS LAPIDUS MANDEL: Distinguished architect. Principal planner of the Botanical Gardens of Havana, urbanizations, plazas, movie theatres and hotels. Graphic designer of the Cuban pavilions in the World Fairs of Osaka (1970), Seville (1992) and of Cuban Architecture in Berlin. Titled Professor of the Faculty of Architecture of the University of Havana, head of its Department of Architectonic Design and principal professor of the History of Architecture. Member of the Central Methodological Commission, of the Curriculum Commission and of the Scientific Council of the Faculty. Visiting Professor at the universities of Hamburg, Delft, Polytechnic University of Mexico, Rome, Tuscany, Rio Grande de Sur, Florida, Tulane and Venezuela, among others.

Member of the Executive committee of the International Commission of Monuments and Sites and vice president of the Cuban Committee of the same. Member of the Cuban chapter of the International Association of Art Critics. Director of the magazines *Arquitectura-Cuba* and *Arquitectura y Urbanismo*. From 1985 until his death, Vice Director of the CENCREM, National Center of Conservation, Restoration and Museology. Recipient of the award of Distinction of Cuban Education from the Ministry of Higher Education.

Author of numerous books and publications in Cuba and abroad.

---

[1] The testimony of Arón Radlow consists of extracts from two interviews conducted by Margalit Bejarano (1984 and 1987), Collection of Oral History, Hebrew University of Jerusalem.

Poster for an Antifacist meeting of the Unión Juvenil Hebrea de Cuba (Hebrew Youth Union of Cuba), 1941. Arón Radlow is listed as one of the speakers.

Leaders and speakers of the meeting, including García Agüero, Radlow, and Matterin. Havana, 1941.

The first leader of the League of Cuban Pioneers

MYRIAM RADLOW ZAITMAN: Born on April 5, 1943, in Havana. I am the oldest daughter of Arón Radlow Givner and Eva Zaitman Baigelman. My parents came to Cuba as children. My father was born on March 2, 1917, in Lomza, a small town in Poland, and arrived on the Island in 1927. My grandfather, who was a carpenter, died when my father was seven years old and his mother remarried on the condition that she would immigrate to Cuba because she already had a brother here.

ARÓN RADLOW GIVNER: I began Hebrew school at the Centro Israelita. I was there about six months when I told my mother: "I don't want to go to the Hebrew school because they speak a lot of Yiddish and very little Spanish, and I am never going to learn the language. I want to be in a Cuban public school that doesn't cost anything, and there I am going to learn Spanish much faster." I studied only up to the sixth grade in public school.

We lived in Old Havana, in a very small apartment that was divided by a curtain. In order to pay the rent, which was thirty-two pesos, we had to rent out beds at five pesos a head to young Jews who had recently arrived in Cuba. Imagine such poverty; we had to have four strangers sleeping there in the house with a simple curtain dividing the room.

I began to work at thirteen in a shoe factory, the owners of which were religious Hebrews. We worked on Sunday instead of Saturday, but with the doors shut because the government didn't allow it. They paid me one and a half pesos a week. I was a lining cutter. Later I learned to be a shoemaker, that is the one who makes the complete cut and sews it, and then they paid me between fifteen and eighteen pesos, which was a big salary. But every once in a while I got arrested and put in jail, and I lost my job.

I had artistic talents, of a singer, of a reader. One of the workers in the factory came to me and asked me why I didn't go to the Unión Cultural Hebrea, the Kultur Farain, because they had a theater group there. I already knew about this and went to the plays there, sneaking in without paying. It was a very advanced society for that time. They put on revolutionary plays in Yiddish. Once, I played the part of Gabroche in *Les miserables*, by Victor Hugo. I began to develop politically in this environment. Jazán[2] was the one who taught me

---

[2] Jone Jazán, Jewish Communist leader, who was deported from Cuba in 1931 and died in the Soviet Union.

and the whole group. He talked to us about the Soviet Union, of the workers movement, of the help given to the political prisoners that was called *Mota* in Europe, and in Cuba it was called the International Workers Defense.

There, with Jazán, I organized the first group of Cuban pioneers and, later, the Communist Youth League. I was elected head of the League of Pioneers when I was sixteen, and a member of the Central Committee of the Communist Youth in 1931. We were about forty members. In 1935, when the general strike began, they sent me to Oriente, to Santiago de Cuba, to lead the strike of the children and to help the teachers. We put out a national call asking children not to go to class.

The Jewish participation in the Cuban revolutionary movement wasn't very numerous, but it was high quality. Fabio Grobart and others, who weren't as important, were deported by Machado to the Soviet Union. Later some returned and continued fighting, like Jaime Novomodi, Dora and Mordechai Epstein.

The *polacos* who won the lottery

MYRIAM RADLOW ZAITMAN: Mama came with her parents when she was six years old. When they arrived in Cuba, they were lucky and won the Lottery, and they built a little hotel. My mother's family, the Zaitman-Baigelman, lived in Warsaw and had a bakery. One of my uncles was a little hunch backed and said it was from carrying baskets of bread when he was very small. The oldest of them, Mat, went to the United States later and set up a bakery-sweet shop called Famous Pies.

Grandmother, Chaya Sure, was a seamstress in Poland and with this skill she put together enough money to bring over her family. She came in 1927, well before the War, because she had a premonition that something was going to happen. She always said *ij job guevust* that means "I knew it. I knew that it was going to happen." First she sewed at home, and later worked for one of my paternal uncles who converted the house into a tailor shop and called it TALLER GIVNER.

My parents met each other at the Society, at the Kultur Farain, and they got married in 1941. At first, we lived on Jesús María Street, later on Compostela, above Boris Kalmanovitch's cafeteria. That family was crazy about me. They lived in the building next door and through a little hole in the railing that separated the two houses they passed me back and forth, from one balcony to the other. From there, we moved to Vedado. Each of the three uncles and their families slept in one room and Grandmother in the living room, behind a curtain to have a little privacy. The uncles all went to the United States, but my parents, my brothers, Grandmother and I stayed. We lived there until I was married in 1961, and then we moved to Santos Suárez.

I did first to third grade at the Modern Hebrew School that Ida Glezer had on 15th and E streets. I finished primary school at the one at the Centro Israelita directed by Elías Eliovich. Papa insisted that I continue studying, but I wanted to be economically independent. So, I enrolled in the Pérez Academy on Inquisidor and Sol to become a Commercial Secretary, and I graduated in 1958.

At fifteen I began to work at the Compañía Quincallera Remis S.A, known as the ALMACENES DAVID, in Old Havana, a wholesaler of variety goods, of which my father was a client. The owners, David and María Schizik, had to hide me each time the inspector came because I wasn't yet of working age. I earned thirty pesos a month working only half-days.

Later José Kopel proposed to my uncle Abraham that I work in the afternoons in his leather warehouse, LA CASA KOPEL, on Teniente Rey Street, for thirty pesos more. Kopel and my father had a small business together, a coffee-soda stand. Mama used to say to me that there "for one cent you had a cup of coffee, they gave you a toothpick, a glass of water and a napkin." My little office, which was made of cardboard, was so small that each time I stood up, my head hit the ceiling. When the Kopels left the country, they put me in charge of their business. When it was nationalized, I was given a job at the EMPRESA DE PIELES Y SUS DERIVADOS (LEATHER AND ITS BYPRODUCTS), until 1966, when I began to work at La Casa de las Américas. I have been in this very same office for thirty-nine years. The only thing that has changed is my title: from secretary to the Chief of the Office of the Presidency.

Papa worked as a shoemaker until 1941, when he set up the coffee-soda stand I spoke about. Later he sold wholesale to the stores, riding around on his Cushman motorcycle with the side car, until the triumph of the Revolution. Then they needed leaders with political training, experience, and trustworthiness, and they sent him to administer the old CASINO hosiery factory and the LILY doll factory.

With our sacrifice we are contributing to the future

ARÓN RADLOW GIVNER: In 1961, all of us Hebrews of the old guard became militia. We were about 20 or 25 activists. We walked the 62 kilometers.[3] You will ask why I sacrificed myself, and the others left. Because there are very few idealists in the world. Because you had to be an idealist, like the Jews in Israel are idealists who make sacrifices. I was never in Israel, but I looked at those pioneers and combatants who have a gun in their hand, just as the Cubans have a gun in their hand to defend the Revolution. They are more idealistic than I am.

When the Revolution came, I knew that I was going to lose out personally, and I said that to the comrades, but we were content because we believed that, by sacrificing, we were contributing to the future. I don't regret the things I did at all. If the Revolution failed in one thing, in another thing it succeeded, understand? Socialism is the future, of that I am sure, but you have to make a lot of sacrifices and not all generations can sacrifice.

Ideas are free; each person should do and think what he wants

MYRIAM RADLOW ZAITMAN: My father did not believe in God and Mama even less. Papa was the black sheep of the family, the Communist as they said. However, I have heard comments that my maternal grandfather, Arón Zaitman, was very religious and went to synagogue everyday. He died when my mother was pregnant with me. It was my paternal grandmother who taught us the traditions. We had to speak Yiddish with her because she never learned Spanish. She was a great cook. At home we only cooked with vegetable oil, and we never bought pork, but, contradictorily, we bought ham at the EL ESPLENDID, the Jewish grocery store on 4th Street in Vedado. There we bought sour cream and pickles that the owners made.

Grandmother always fasted on Kippur. I also did it for a long time when I was studying at the Hebrew school. We never observed the Sabbath; Pesach and Rosh Hashanah, yes. Papa said our ideas were free, that he didn't want his children to be like him, that each one should do and think what he wanted.

The *polacos* learn to play dominoes

When we went to the beach, we would go to the Casino Deportivo (Sports Casino), where the Jewish colony concentrated. We also participated in the youth activities that took place every Tuesday at the Patronato. That is where I met Luis, although we had seen each other at the Club. Mama admired him because he would jump from the stairs of the pool, and that got everyone's attention. Also, he was the nephew of one of my mother's good friends. They

---

[3] "Sixty-two kilometers:" the graduation exercise of the National Revolutionary Militia.

always played dominoes together. The Jews learned to play dominoes in Cuba and became fanatics. Upstairs at the Casino there was a room for dominoes and cards. In the summers we went there early in the morning, taking lunch with us, and in the afternoon we all went upstairs to play.

Actually, our world was pretty closed. I married a Jew and had a Jewish wedding. The circle of Communists who came to the house there were also Jews. All the Communist Jews are present in my wedding photo. The wedding took place in the house of some relatives, the last ones that Grandmother was able to rescue from Poland before the Holocaust. Grandma made the entire meal, all the dishes of Jewish cooking you can imagine. They brought the *huppa*, as well as the rabbi, from the Patronato. It's common. In Israel, people are not religious but maintain the tradition; they are Jewish.

In Cuba they don't even know what anti-Semitism is

I never felt discrimination. Maybe we could talk about our discrimination against the others. No one told me I had to marry a Jew, but we constantly heard: "Look what so and so did, he married so and so who isn't Jewish." It was something that was in the air. Luis's stepfather always exclaimed: "The worst of us before the best of them."

Luis's schoolmates called him *El Polaco*. Me, blond, not *polaquita*. Even so, everyday they asked me my surname. My daughter used to say: "Mama why did you name me Batia. You could have named me Ana, Marta, any other name. With this name and those surnames…"

Papa worked actively with Sara Tilchin in the Yiddish radio program, before and after the Revolution. They reported the news of the country and the world and something about the Jewish societies.

ARÓN RADLOW GIVNER: There was never anti-Semitism in Cuba. The kind that we know… never. It's that in Cuba they don't even know what anti-Semitism means. A Cuban doesn't know. You say to him you are an anti-Semite, and he asks you "what's that?" We had our places, our radio hour. For ten years we kept our radio hour in Yiddish. Because of our influence, we were able to have acts of remembrance of the Warsaw ghetto celebrated nationally in Havana, and broadcast on television. Delegations were sent to Poland every year from 1962 to 1968, and the Government paid for two or three Hebrew delegates. I went twice, in 1963 and 1967, as head of the delegation.

65

Luis Lapidus.
Havana,1994.

A Lithuanian, Jewish and Bolshevik family in Manicaragua

Luis was born on January 18, 1937, in a small town in the mountains in the former province of Las Villas, in the central region of the Island. His real name is Zelik Leib Lapidus Mandel, "a name that was too strange for that country clerk in Manicaragua,"[4] who registered him as Zoilo Luis. His life is almost a soap opera. He only found out who his parents were when he entered the Institute. A little before he died, he made a visit to Israel during which he learned, for the first time, things about his mother who had died when he was only eleven months old. No one had ever spoken to him about her. His uncle Moishe told him the story. His mother, Berta Mandel, was a Bolshevik and had to flee Lithuania because she was being hunted. She got to Cuba in 1937. I remember that in the family they said: "Imagine, you know what she did. An old man came along who was cold, and she took off her jacket and gave it to him."

---

[4] Isabel Rigol: Biographical sketch of Luis Lapidus in *La Encrucijada en el Tiempo*, unpublished book.

66

They had a store called EL CICLÓN (THE CYCLONE) in the town. When his mother passed away, his father left Luis with his sister-in-law, Pola, and her husband. Pola was very possessive and never let the father get near Luis. One day, when he was already 40 years old, the phone rang and a voice said: "This is your father speaking. I am at the Riviera Hotel, dressed like so and so. Can you come to see me?" He was a tall and corpulent man with blue eyes. He had remarried. Luis had a half brother, Jack, who was an engineer. When they met each other, Jack wanted to set up an engineering and architectural firm together and call it LAPIDUS AND LAPIDUS.

Luis grew up with Pola and Isaac Rachman, first on Jesús María and Acosta Streets in Old Havana, across from one of the synagogues to which he went every Saturday for Sabbath. "What he liked most was the sweet wine and the pancakes that they gave out after the ceremony…because the children understood very little of the prayers that they said in Hebrew… (…) and those people with beards and peculiar clothing seemed strange to them."[5]

None of my generation achieved a true identification with the Jewish religion. These things created a kind of distance with us. My uncle was not very religious, he ate *treif*, ham and all the rest, and he didn't fast. My aunt fasted, but she didn't impose it on us. She did it in a very subtle way, indirectly, without obligations.[6] "Close to where they lived were the Convent and the arch of Bethlehem, the Plazuela and the Church of the Holy Spirit, among many other places whose functions and names had nothing to do with those other inhabitants who, like the Rachman's, brought traditions and customs from a world very distant from that of the Spaniards, the blacks, mulattos, Chinese, or the common Cuban, an extremely mixed population that shared that little piece of Old Havana with the Jews."[7]

I feel a little strange, odd, and different from the average

Luis recalled years later that in that compact neighborhood and section he "felt a little strange, odd, different from the average; that he was embarrassed when at Passover they sang psalms and he thought the neighbors couldn't understand what was going on inside; when he wasn't allowed to go to the neighborhood movie house with his friends during Holy Week, because they

---

[5] Isabel Rigol: Biographical sketch of Luis Lapidus in *La Encrucijada en el Tiempo*, unpublished book.
[6] Laura Paull and Evan Garell, documentary film Havana Naguila, Havana, 1994
[7] Isabel Rigol, op.cit.

Luis' Bar Mitzvah.
Havana, 1950.

were showing together with "Tarzan" another Mexican film, very bad, on the life of Christ….'All this is tinged with a certain heartbreak, nostalgia, a little sad, my Jewish childhood in Old Havana."[8]

> *Some wait for the Jewish house*
> *To celebrate the Jewish Passover,*
> *The bitter festival of the Diaspora.*
> *Pale, the mother sets the table,*
> *The father pours the ritual wine*
> *And exalted, intones his searing psalms.*
> *Grandfather bites his unleavened bread, and cries.*
> *The sister anxiously watches the door*
> *And only the little boy quiets, disconcerted and alone.*[9]

---

[8] Paull and Garell, op.cit.
[9] Luis Lapidus. Fragment of the unpublished poem "Good Friday," cited by Rigol.

He studied at the Yavne School and later at the Institute. At the University he matriculated in Architecture. When the University closed in 1955, he went to work in one of the family import businesses and sold pieces for radios, televisions and hi-fi equipment. Afterwards, he worked at various architectural firms, where he participated in the construction of the Riomar building. He dipped into philosophy, Rosicrucianism, and literature. He became a fervent aficionado of good films and avant-garde art. Decidedly, Luis was not going to carry on the family business, but he would be the young man who would return to the revolutionary path initiated by his mother many years before, in far away Lithuania. It was the most logical path for a Jew, "because the Jews who have suffered so much, who have been harassed, have to be on the side of change."[10]

A rooted and not-wandering Jew

In 1959, he was placed in the Department of Rural Housing of the Institute of Land Reform. The reality he touched in the Cuban countryside, together with his memories of the poverty and social injustice that he knew from his infancy in Old Havana, led him to decide to stay and not follow the path of his loved ones, the new wanderers, who left Cuba.

He finished his degree in architecture and got involved in joint projects of housing, schools, social programs for agricultural and fishing cooperatives in the furthermost reaches of the country. The purpose was to eliminate the dramatic inequality between the capital, beautiful and grandiose, and the rural areas, miserable and destitute, but not less beautiful. With the architect Isabel Rigol and her team "of the big leagues," he planned and took the first steps for the restoration of the Convent of Santa Clara and the rehabilitation of the Plaza Vieja, as part of the recuperation of Cuba's artistic and architectural patrimony.

Luis was one of those "young people who had his eyes wide open and his heart ready to live intensely the experience of working in the rural zones of the country after 1959."[11] That experience "sealed the cause that governed his life and gave him the support he needed for the material and emotional losses he would have to confront."[12] He devoted himself as a revolutionary,

---

[10] Paull and Garell, op.cit.
[11] Isabel Rigol. Biographical Sketch of Luis Lapidus, in *Cien Años de la Escuela de Arquitectura de La Habana*, ISPJAE, Havana, 2000.
[12] Idem.

and that essentially defined his identity. In 1994, a year before his death, he visited Israel where he renewed contact with his other roots. "I had belonged to various Zionist organizations when I was a boy. It was my dream to visit Israel, which had signified so much in my formation and which had such symbolic force for us." [13]

This symbiosis of idiosyncrasies and cultures led him to state: "I am a Cuban Hebrew. Basically, I am Cuban; that is my nationality. I am a Jewish Cuban. The personality is enriched. That is one of the things that have made me hang on to being Jewish. People do not give up what they have. The more components one has in his development, his vision of the world tends to be superior...sometimes even suffering is enriching. We Jews are educated to think with international consciousness, as citizens of the world, but if one evolves fluidly, without contradictions with his environment, he feels part of that context and it becomes his homeland. I have always thought this; I have a great attachment to this country."[14]

And, it is in this country that he died, on April 12, 1995, and he was buried in the Jewish cemetery in Guanabacoa. His friends of the world planted a tree with his name in the sacred place of Anuradhapura, as testimony that "the projection of his shadow reaches further than our frontiers and our time."[15]

Due to circumstances of life, Arón died in Miami. But, as Fabio Grobart said to one of his friends when someone criticized him, "Archik, wherever he lives will always be a Communist."

---

[13] Paull and Garell, op.cit.
[14] Idem.
[15] Isabel Rigol, Biographical sketch in *La Encrucijada en el Tiempo*.

Myriam as a debutant at the Patronato at age sixteen.
Havana, 1959.

Luis at Rachman's store on O'Reilly Street.
Havana, 1955.

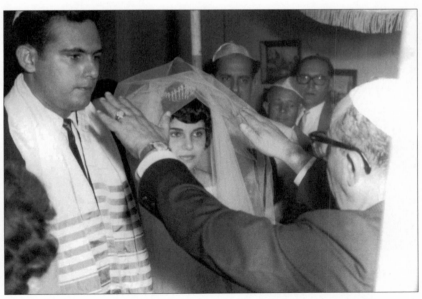

Under the huppah: Luis and Myriam's wedding.
Havana, 1961.

Luis at Yad Vashem Museum.
Israel, 1994.

Myriam with Wilka, a Peruvian peasant.
Casa de las Américas.
Havana, 1970s.

José Blumenkrantz (1905-1999)
Israel Blumenkrantz

JOSÉ BLUMENKRANTZ: Treasurer of the Pro Histradut League, 1948-1949; president of the Keren Kayemet Leisrael (KKL), 1952-1954; president of the Pro Histradut League, 1949-1953; president of the Zionist Union 1955-1956; member of the executive committee of the Centro Israelita and the Hebrew Chamber of Commerce; First Vice President, treasurer, administrator and executive director of the Patronato and the House of the Hebrew Community, from 1966 until his death in 1999.

Blumenkrantz, a man to remember

JOSÉ BLUMENKRANTZ: I was born on August 19, 1905 in Ostrolenka, a town in Poland on the border with Germany. I came to Cuba in 1926 because my sister-in-law spoke to me about the Island, a place of transit to the United States, the *goldene medina* of the Jews of Europe for more than a century.

I knew carpentry because my grandfather was a construction supervisor. A week after landing on the Island and without knowing the language, I began to work at a sugar mill in the town of Pedro Betancourt in Matanzas. A year later, I brought my girlfriend, Golda Kauffman, from Poland, and

75

we were married, but only in a ceremony at the synagogue. Our relatives always joked and said we weren't really married because we didn't have a civil ceremony.

I left carpentry and became a peddler, traveling all over the Island. Later on, I set up a general store in Manguito, another small town in the same province where we were one of only two Jewish families. All went well. In 1934, I moved to Havana and opened a pants factory in Old Havana with another countryman, but I kept the store in the town until the depression forced me to close. I rescued what I could of the debts and set up another store in Trillo Park in Central Havana. There the business prospered, and within two years grew considerably.

I brought all of my mother's family, except her older sister who was living in Belgium. Life wasn't as bad there as it was in Poland. She stayed in Belgium and died there. My father's family didn't want to come, and they all perished in the Holocaust.

My name is Israel for that dream he had and could not fulfill

ISRAEL BLUMENKRANTZ: I went to primary school at a school in the neighborhood and Sara, my sister, at the Encinosa Academy. During the Holidays we attended the synagogue in La Víbora. In those days the Hebrew school of Figueroa was converted into a synagogue. Grandfather went daily to the one on Jesús María and Cuba Streets. There were two, one next to the other. He went to the one that was closest to Cuba Street.

Actually, the ones who observed the rituals at our home were my maternal grandparents. When they got old and came to live with us, the tradition grew. We were not kosher until they moved in. To tell the truth, grandmother was very *frim*, but grandfather hid so he could eat what he wanted. Papa wasn't such a strong believer as he was a Jew. He observed the tradition, but without falling into orthodoxy. My parents spoke Yiddish between themselves, and they hired a teacher so we would learn.

The pro-Franco Spanish and the José Martí Forest in Israel

From the time he opened his business in Havana, Papa got involved in the Zionist Union in which he held many offices. In Poland he belonged to an organization of young people that formed to go work in Israel. He admitted to me that he gave me the name Israel because of that dream that he couldn't

Israel Blumenkrantz at the Synagogue.
Havana, 2005
(Photo by Tatiana Santos)

fulfill. He was shaped by that movement, and its teachings were a guide for him in life.

When the State of Israel was established in 1948, a project to create artificial forests was organized. Papa presided over the Keren Kayemet in Cuba. With a lot of effort, he succeeded in creating the José Martí Forest in Israel. A good number of pro-Franco Spaniards gave money for that Cuban forest in Israel, only because Papa asked them for it. His human relations were excellent. Of the entire colony he was the Jew who had the most friends among the Spaniards. He was the representative of the Labor Party in Cuba, with both Ben Gurion and Golda Meier. In 1964, he attended the Zionist Congress, and he worked in the Zionist Union until the end when it closed.

Papa was an important personality in the Jewish community both before and after the Revolution. From 1959 on, he worked even harder to preserve the life of the community. There was a large emigration in the 1960s and 1970s, and it became a very personal thing for him, one that made him very happy, to give his religious services when they no longer had rabbis, to teach the children and youth all about Jewish culture and tradition.

If my two children are happy here, I am staying.

It was a decisive moment. The whole family decided to leave, including the Kauffman's, who introduced the factory for plastics in Cuba that Kalusin later perfected. The fellow who was going to be my brother-in-law had an important position, and he explained to us that the process that had begun with the big warehouses and department stores would continue down to the smallest strata. So, I spoke to Papa. I told him it was the time to sell and that I could get the money out if he wanted to leave. He responded: "I only have two children. If they are happy here, then I am staying."

When he went to the United States to visit family in 1984, they asked him why he hadn't left, like everyone else. He answered: "My children are happy there, because no one has bothered me and I feel very respected."

Judaism is a philosophy that fits and will always fit at any time

Independently of how much he was respected by the community for his work and leadership, people also admired how he handled the whole process of the nationalization of his business. We knew what was coming, and we prepared, we made an inventory. When the person arrived who was going to take over, we showed him what we had done. The difference, in merchandise worth more than 100,000 pesos, didn't amount to more than 250 pesos. Then, the woman said to Papa: "José, you can't go, we need you to stay working here." For ten years, religiously, they paid him the value of the business.

Since we lived in Santos Suárez, they offered him a job as an employee at a shop that was on Jesús del Monte. There he found a comrade who belonged to the Empresa and who had been one of our suppliers. He asked Papa to assist him and be the director of the stores of the Municipality. Papa didn't want to do that, but he agreed to be the chief of the warehouse that supplied the stores in the area. Once there, he started to organize, to introduce initiatives, to shift personnel around to jobs that matched their abilities, to say "This doesn't sell, now take out this other product." He applied all his experience as a merchant to improve his center and to teach others.

I think he expressed himself about Cuba the way he did because of the manner people always treated him, for the recognition he got for all the good he was doing. He had a very humanistic vision of life. "He harmonized his ideas and his Jewish customs with revolutionary ideas from the point of view of what was human and just… There are canons and laws that are learned in

Judaism. Call it religion, customs or ethics. Judaism is a philosophy that fits all times. It is a philosophy that fits and will always fit in whatever time."[1]

The Star of David on the facade

Before the University had closed, I had studied up to the fourth year of Civil Engineering. Sarita entered the same year, 1956, in Architecture and got caught in the closing. So, she did all her studies for her career after the Revolution. Precisely because she was an architect, they called on her when the directors of the Patronato received a significant donation to restore the synagogue. The building was important architectural patrimony of the 1950s, well conceived by the architect Aquiles Capablanca, with first class materials.

Architect Isabel Rigol, from CENCREM, had already outlined the guiding principles to be followed. The fundamental task was to maintain the original image and concept of the synagogue. She had to work in new ways, with new materials, and also to take into account the different functions (computer rooms, video rooms, etc.) to be placed in a space that, up until then, had been totally unused, that had been the *mechitzah*.

Sarita noted that there was nothing explicit on the exterior to indicate that it was a Jewish building, only subtle symbols on the door —placed at street level— and the arcade. The star is the element most commonly recognized as belonging to the Jewish people and, at the same time, it is also the center of the flag and shield of Israel. In our country, where there exists a certain perception of the Israeli-Palestinian conflict, the star provides another image, another understanding.

Indisputably, all the city signs that indicate where synagogues are located, and in particular the one for the Patronato, are manifestations of respect and of the freedom of expression of the Hebrew religion and culture that has always existed in Cuba.

---

[1] Miriam Greenberg. Interview of Sara Blumenkrantz, Havana, 1998. Unpublished document. Files of the author.

Participants in the radio program of the Zionist Union.
Havana, 1950s.

Dinner at the Centro Israelita;
Blumenkrantz and wife, Golda, are in the front.
Havana, 1940.

Event at the State of Israel School
on the seventeenth Anniversary of Israel's Independence.
Havana, 1955.

Entrance of the Beth Shalom Synagogue
of the Patronato after its restoration.
Havana, mid-1990s.
(Photo by Damaris Betancourt)

(Photo by Tatiana Santos)

Elena Nudelfunden Perelmuter

He didn't have a single saint in the house

I was born in Warsaw in 1921, and came to Cuba with my mother when I was four, in 1925. My father had immigrated in 1922. In Poland, my mother's family was very poor. My father's was not so poor, but he was the black sheep. His brother was a Rabbi, and he turned out to be a Communist. He was a shoe pattern cutter. When he got to Havana, a countryman took him to Camagüey where he worked for a time, until he had saved up enough money to bring us over. Later, he set up a small shoe factory, a hole in the wall on San Isidro Street, between Habana and Damas, or Compostela. But business was very bad, and we went through a lot of hard times.

When I was thirteen, my mother died of cancer very young. Papa got remarried to another Jewish woman, who was a beautiful person and very religious. My father wasn't religious and Mama very little. But look what happened: now, as an old woman, I have become religious. I married a Cuban, not Jewish, who was a chauffer for hire. Of course, Papa didn't like it. He accepted it because I was his only daughter, and he wasn't going to throw me out. My husband wasn't a racist, he didn't care that I was Jewish and he didn't put a single saint in the house. He respected me and knew that I wasn't going to let him have one either.

We went to the *Folkcenter*, which was a Communist club, because my father was a Communist. I remember the theatre, which was very good. There was a man who worked with the plays who later set up a clothing workshop on Monte Street. At the end, they told me that he left.

The ones who were badly off, really had a hard time

I studied only up to sixth grade at the public school. To help my father, who was very poor and also sick, I had to start working when I was very young as a seamstress for a Hebrew on Acosta Street. The *Froien Farain* society helped us with twelve pesos a week. With that we bought milk and stale bread, left over from the day before because it was cheaper. Life was very hard. We complain about things now, but please; before, the ones who were badly off, really had a hard time.

I also worked selling in a store on Muralla Street that belonged to Guinsburg and Berman until after the Revolution. One day, we arrived, like we did every morning, and the owner wasn't there. They had gone without telling us anything. They left only nine pesos in the cash box. So, we opened the store, and I and another boy were named managers after it was nationalized. Later, they sent me to LA FERIA (THE FAIR) on Egido Street, and to the one that sold plastic shoes where I also became the manager. I think they always named me because I am very tidy; I like order and everything in its place.

Guinsberg and Berman's store on Muralla Street.
Havana, 1950.

Elena with Sophia Chanivecky at Adath Israel Synagogue.
Havana, 2004.

(Photo by Tatiana Santos)

(Photo by Tatiana Santos)

Salomón Mitrani Barlía

A Cuban communist in the War of 1948

My parents were Turks. Mama was from Kirkareli and Papa from Stambulía.[1] Very poor, so poor that Papa went around without shoes in the snow to look for milk. His older brothers got excited about going to America and were the first to emigrate. When they got to the United States, they worked in a match factory, one of those assembly line types, like Charles Chaplin in *Modern Times*. They couldn't stand it and decided to come to Cuba.

On my maternal side, Grandfather Jacov was an engraver. I must have inherited my artistic streak from him. But he was a man who never had any luck. The Turks believed he was falsifying passports for Jews so they could emigrate, and they gave him such a beating they almost killed him.

Papa came alone from Turkey when he was only thirteen, in 1913, before the war. My grandfather Salomón starved to death in Istanbul, and his younger brothers stayed there with Grandmother Esther. When my father got to Cuba, it

---

[1] We have maintained the pronunciation of the person providing the information with respect to the names of the cities.

wasn't easy to find his brothers. They had moved to Colón, a small town in the province of Matanzas, where they worked as peddlers, selling clothing and fabric. They were among the first immigrants before the avalanche during the war.

Maybe she is lame or missing a leg

The family prospered in Colón and decided it was time to get married, but in Cuba there weren't Jewish girls to choose from, and that was an important requisite. Some of the older Jewish women told them that there were young girls in their families who had stayed in Turkey and in France, because many had already emigrated fleeing from the outbreak in the Balkans.

The normal procedure was to send photos. My three uncles accepted their brides from photos, but Papa —although Mama was very beautiful— said that the photo wasn't good enough, and he wanted a photo of her whole body because "maybe she is lame, a dwarf or missing a leg." When they sent it to him, he fell in love with her. My mother came with my grandmother and a sister. They were married in Colón, in 1921, and they moved to Havana to the corner of San Nicolás and Rayo, where I was born on August 4, 1922.

His brothers also came. They opened a fabric store on Monte Street. They were looking for a name and Mama, recently arrived from France, said they should call it LA TORRE DE PARÍS (THE TOWER OF PARIS) because she thought it was very beautiful.

A Jewish *turco* in an Arab neighborhood

There were never problems between Arabs and Jews in Cuba. We lived in harmony; we got along in a normal way. Although he never denied his origins, we never lived in Old Havana because Papa —I don't know why— didn't want to live among Jews. Papa was a free thinker and also a Mason. He only went to synagogue on Kippur.

My grandmothers were the ones who preserved tradition, the ones who set the rules. More my paternal grandmother, Esther. Grandmother Ventura, like Mama, was more modern. During Passover, they cleaned the house, changed all the plates and flatware; they bought everything new. We didn't have a refrigerator, only a round freezer, but they kept the things separate. Oddly, they got the Passover products in the house of Boris and his brothers, Russians who weren't Jewish. Even though it is an offensive word among Turks, we called them the *lonzos*, because they were as big as bears.

On Sabbath we didn't turn on the lights, and Grandmother, who was a heavy smoker, stopped smoking at six o'clock in the afternoon. You couldn't say a word to her; she would say: "I don't want anyone to talk to me, I am going to the *Kal,* and after I will come to eat." She put on a veil and walked to Chevet Ahim. I remember that Mama wanted to cook, but Grandmother never let her because she was afraid it wouldn't be kosher. Grandmother was a tremendous cook. I can still taste the flavor of her *borekas,* of the *agristada* (brain soup with lemon), and the *yurlikas,* of the *tapadas.*

Better to buy from the *polacos*, they sell cheaper

I was also a peddler. It was the only thing Papa could teach me. I went to school only up to the fifth grade because, in 1933, Papa couldn't pay anyone to carry the bundles of fabric, and I had to begin to help him. The economic situation was very bad. We had closed the store and were buried in debts. So we made sacks with the things we had and sold them. We left at six in the morning and came back at four or five in the afternoon. I sat on the curb to wait for Papa to put out the merchandise. At first we sold for cash. He would say that it was a store that had gone bankrupt, and we were liquidating what was left. He told this story for years. There were some who asked us, with great irony, how many times the store had gone bankrupt.

I was always self-employed. I was a peddler all my life until 1962, when I went to work at the zoo as a painter with a big paintbrush. There, I fine-tuned the brush a little: I painted a mural for the Peasant Worker Alliance. Once, some Jewish peasants sent for me from Topes de Collantes.[2] I don't know how they got up there, or how they opened a big store in the mountains. They invited me to visit them because they had two interests: to marry me to their sister and to go into business with me. They wanted to come to Havana. You know, among Jews the issue of dowry was common. Also some people from Sancti Spíritus made me a proposal. In the end, I didn't accept the marriage proposal, but we did begin a business together.

Then I suggested to Papa that it would be better to start to sell on credit. He got along well with people, and he developed a good clientele in Luyanó.[3] Before he had to go to the provinces, to Matanzas, Pinar Del Río. It was a lot

---

[2] A town high up in the Escambray Mountains.
[3] A neighborhood, some distance from Old Havana.

of effort. Now he could sell in the neighborhoods of Martín Pérez, Lawton, Arroyo Naranjo, Mantilla, and Sevillano. I was already selling on credit, because it was easier. I had some cards with the name THE TWO FRIENDS (for Leoniko, the guy from Topes) on which I noted down what they were paying me: a peso a week. The profit margin was 100%. We bought from my brother-in-law who was working in the ALMACENES CENTRO, of Tianno, behind the Church on Teniente Rey and Bernaza. It was better to buy in cash from the *polacos* because they sold cheaper.

A Jewish Communist who fought in Israel and was a militant in the Zionist Union

In the period of the Constitution of 1940, the Party had to choose its delegates.[4] Papa called me and commented that people were joining the Popular Socialist Party. He asked me if I wanted to join because it was the best Party there was. He didn't join because he wasn't a Cuban citizen, but I did and began to work with Agapito Figueroa.[5] Those Communists were to be admired: they had nothing, they were dying of hunger, and they still gave their all to the Party.

I was named president of the Party Youth in Luyanó —in the section that had a pretty big Jewish colony, but they didn't belong to the Party. The Communist Jews primarily lived in Old Havana. We organized meetings to mobilize the workers and young people, we handed out leaflets, we sold the *Mella* magazine and the newspaper *Hoy*, we collected dues, and we raised funds for the Party. As a joke, they said that the Popular Socialist Party (PSP) stood for "pidiendo siempre pidiendo" (asking always asking). I led the Youth for more or less eight years up to 1948, when I went to the war. By this time, I was already distancing myself. I didn't like the attitude of the group of Hebrew Communists when we asked them for support to fight in Israel. I couldn't bear Jews being criticized.

My work with the Zionist Union and the Keren Kayemet (KKL) came after my return from Israel. At nineteen years of age, I entered San Alejandro School to study sculpture; I also liked to paint. When the KKL began its activities to raise money, each club set up its stand, and I got fully involved. With its two *menoras*, ours won all the prizes at the Purim Fair on March 24, 1951,

---

[4] In the late 1930s, a constituent assembly was elected by the various political parties in the country to draft a new national constitution.
[5] Agapito Figueroa, leader of the metal workers union.

Mitrani and the twelve aboard the Yagiello,
1948.

commemorating the fiftieth anniversary of the organization. Later, I painted a mural on the KKL premises on Prado. I was secretary of the KKL some two or three years, while they gave their parties. I was politically active in the youth of the Zionist Union and spoke on the radio program they broadcasted on Radio García Sierra.

We have a *minyan*

The thing of Israel happened this way. I had friends within the Jewish Youth, in the KKL with Regina Algaze, and in the Sephardic Society. I was also friends with Salvador Bennun, who was a cousin of my brother-in-law. One night, Salvador says to me: "Listen, Mitrani, do you know there are a bunch of Cubans that are going to Israel?" Really, we were very surprised. They had been so quiet about it. Well, in truth, at that time there wasn't much freedom of expression. We agreed to go look for information so we could also form our own group.

The next day, we went to Betar, to the Unión Juvenil Hebrea, the youth organization of the Communist Jews, to Chevet Ahim, to Macabi and to the Zionist Union that was on Prado, next to the Arab Society. We asked everyone, and they all answered that they didn't know anything about it. Word got out, and young Hebrews went to find out. Israel Bichachi and David Bakalchuk wanted

91

to join. So, we were four. Then, Jaime Goldberg appeared and made the fifth.

They told me that if we didn't belong to the Irgún, we couldn't go, and that Communists couldn't join. It didn't matter to me how, just that I was going to achieve the goal I set for myself. They had their ideas, and I had mine. I didn't pay attention to what they were saying and said to myself: "Above all, I am a Jew, and I am going with them where I have to go." That helped bring together many people.

Later, in the 1950s, I was among Menahem Beguin's body guards when he visited us, because he asked that those who fought in Israel be the ones to look after him. We set up guard shifts for eight to ten hours at the National Hotel. I defended Beguin because he was Jewish, not because I was in favor of him. I was a Communist, and he of the Irgún. His party was very conservative; his methods and ideology were different from mine.

We went again to the Zionist Union. The organization had a spokesperson, Primitivo Ramírez, who defended our cause on Radio García Serra. He was a Hebrew revolutionary at heart —and, oddly, he was black. A nice love story. He also signed up, as did Elías Tacher, Isaac Barrocas, Israel and Rubén Behar. Until we were ten, and then we had a *minyan*.

We aren't doing anything, we are playing

Finally, a man called Solowiejczyk showed up who told us what we had to do in order to be able to get there. They also brought an Israeli to give us military training. Since we couldn't do it in the open, we went to the area of the Laguito, which at that time was pretty far outside Havana. But the guy made it seem like we were in Israel: halt, arm and disarm, commands, etc. A man passed by, asking questions, who turned out to be a journalist, and the trainer treated him badly and threw him out of there. Shortly after, police cars showed up with *bichos de buey*[6] and machine guns. They asked what we were doing, and we said nothing, that we were playing. You can imagine that they didn't believe us. They told us: "You are under arrest; you're inciting rebellion against the State."

They took us to the police station in Marianao, which was on a bridge. There they took our finger prints and our past histories. I was trembling. Like a good *turco*, I had carried my peddler's sack so I could go to work after we finished the training. But it was also the time of the elections, and it was full of leaflets

---

[6] Bichos de buey: whips that the police used.

of my party. I was a Communist, and if they discovered the package, who was going to convince them that we didn't want to overthrow the government and that we weren't preparing for it at the Laguito? To make things worse, the Israeli had a revolver hidden in his sock. By luck, Isaquito was a minor, and they kicked him out of the jail. He took my package and the revolver, and we breathed with relief. From there they sent us to Príncipe prison where we spent two or three days among delinquents.

The morning after my return, some neighbors came to see me because they had read that one Salomón Mitrani had been arrested, who had been part of a group that wanted to overthrow the government. I stood firm: that it was some other Salomón Mitrani, not me.

Solowiejczky told us that we had to pay the passage; that we would go in a boat that was coming from New York. We went to Muralla Street to see the Hebrew merchants, store by store, to ask them for money. They told us that they were always giving money for the clubs, and now we were also asking them to give money to us. Finally, they did it, and we were able to pay for three or four tickets. Then we asked our fathers and, despite the logical contradictions it caused, we got it.

Old Havana emptied of Hebrews

The day of our departure arrived, and Old Havana emptied of Hebrews. Everyone found out that some Cuban Jews were going to fight for Israel's independence. They came out to the docks to see us off, but Mama didn't want to say goodbye to me. It was very emotional. We sang the Hatikva. They followed us to the edge of the bay in small boats that were overflowing.

In all that tumult, a couple of guys had hidden on the boat without our knowing it. The ship, under English flag, was called the Yagiello. It had served to transport soldiers during the Second World War. The crew was Polish, the officers were Italian. We had paid for ten passages in third class. And then, suddenly, we find out that there were two boys —the French boy and Benjamín Fridman— who were stowaways, hiding in the life boat. We asked them not to move from there; that we would bring them food. But one day at lunch, the Italian officer, who always counted the table said: "*Uno, due, tre... duodeci.* It can't be! You were ten, and now you are twelve." They arrested them. The captain threatened to hand them over to the English in Gibraltar. Meanwhile, they made them mop the boat. Poor guys; they didn't let them rest.

The Jews seeing the combatants off on their day of departure to Israel. Havana harbor, 1948.

In Havana you were asking and here also?

Fortunately, we made friends with the crew, and the officers liked us a lot. They let us walk around in first class, swim in the pool and look for food that was a little better because they only gave us soup and spaghetti. We played cards with the crew to earn money. What were we going to do? We had to pay the passage of the stowaways. But what we got from them wasn't enough, and we had to go back again to some of the Cuban Hebrew merchants who were on the ship. They were going to Europe. We explained our situation to them. They said: "You don't rest. In Havana you were asking and now here too?"

We approached "Papa" —that's how we called Hemingway— in the same way. He invited us to eat at his table because he liked Cubans. We told him our problem, and he gave us money. We have a photo of him from the day the boat stopped in the middle of the Atlantic. He took out his fishing rod. I never saw him try to catch anything, but it served well for our portrait with him.

We docked in Funchal, Lisbon, and Genoa. We disembarked in Rome, and we went to Ventimiglia and Marseille. Europe was still in ruins from the war. You could feel it. Marseille was the point of departure for Israel. They put us in an encampment of immigrants that had been a former Nazi concentration camp. They gave us food out of buckets, and we slept in bunks on duck cloth. The people were full of lice. It was a real League of Nations: Algerians and Moroccans who were fleeing the Arabs that mistreated them in their countries; Germans, Austrians; lot of little French girls with numbers tattooed on their arms, who had lost their entire families; and Canadians who were going to fight, like us.

We left in the *Habima*, a ship built to transport one thousand people, but was carrying like five thousand —mothers nursing their children, many elderly and very few young people. Many times we crossed with the lights out because the English were very hostile to the ships. Since we were going to fight, they sent us to the hold, because they didn't want the British to see us. When we were in the port of Pireo, in Greece, I recalled my father. It was the route he took when he left Turkey for Cuba. Now I was following it in reverse.

The Sephardic Jew spoke in Yiddish and convinced them

Finally, we arrive in Haifa. They asked us what we came for, and we answered that we were Cuban combatants. They gave us some little cards with no photo, like an identity card with date of birth and name. When they saw Primitivo, they insisted he was Arab and couldn't enter. We told them he was Sephardic. Everything was so absurd. So, the Sephardic Jew began to speak in Yiddish and convinced them. Nevertheless, they decided to test our statements and sent us to bathe ourselves. In the bathroom, there were five doctors to examine us to see if we were really Jews. How embarrassing! They were women! After the examination, they took our portraits, enlisted us and sent us to Galilee. There we met people from all over the world: Panamanians, Colombians, Argentineans, Venezuelans, Germans, and Canadians.

I have two loves

Why did I go? Because I saw so much suffering, so much devastation of our people, for the love that I had for a nation that I didn't even know. I have two loves: This land Cuba that I love so much, as well as Israel. It was very emotional the first time we walked in our country. We were there so that no one would harm it; we knew that it wouldn't be like it was before because now there were those who would defend it. When the first group returned, we also decided to leave, but we promised that if there was another war, we would come back, because our struggle was worth it.

Postcard Mitrani sent from Israel to his family: " This is a group of our regiment. There are Colombians, Cubans, Argentineans, Greeks, Turks, a pole from the "Altalena." We might even have Chinese in this beloved army. Kisses, Salomon."

Cuban combatants upon their arrival in Tel Aviv. Mitrani with cigarette in foreground. 1948.

Wedding photo of Mitranis' parents, Havana, 1921.

Cuban Jews in front of the Vatican in transit to Israel, 1948.

Prize winner for the best stand at the Keren Kayemet Leisrael, Purim.
Havana,1951.

Mitrani working on sculpture.
Havana, 1942.

קומט אלע צום גרואנדיעזן בשרץ באנקעט לכבוד
דעם גרויסן יידישן נאציאנאלן העלד און באפרייער

מנחם בעגין

דינסטיק דעם 16-טן מאי 9 אזונט
אין האטעל „נאציאנאל"

NINGUN HEBREO DEBE FALTAR

AL GRANDIOSO BANQUETE EN HONOR DE

Menajem BEGUIN

EL LIBERTADOR DE ISRAEL

MARTES 16 DE MAYO DE 1950, A LAS 9 p. m.

EN EL HOTEL NACIONAL

LAS ENTRADAS PUEDEN SER ADQUIRIDAS EN BERNAZA 216, ALTOS, TEL. W-7240

LOS INGRESOS SERAN DESTINADOS A LA REANILITACION Y COLONIZACION DE LOS VETERANOS DE LA GUERRA.

Poster of the banquet in
honor of Menajem Beguin.
Havana, 1950.

Banquet in honor of Menajem Beguin at the National Hotel.
Havana, 1950.

(Photo by June Safran)

José Altshuler Gutwert

Suma Cum Laude in Electrical Engineering (University of Havana, 1953). Doctor in Technical Sciences (Science Academy of Czechoslovakia, 1974). Professor of Electrical Engineering (1960-1966). Senior Researcher. Director of the Engineering Section of the Ministry of Communications of Cuba (1959-1961). Vice Rector of the University of Havana (1962-1963). Director of the Institute of Basic Technical Research (1967-1982). Vice president of the Cuban Academy of Sciences (1976-1982). President of the National Space Commission (1974-1985). Director of the Technical Science Section of the National Commission of Scientific Degrees (1977-1995). President of the Cuban Society of History of Science and Technology (1993-2004). He has published articles and books on electro-technical theory, history of science and technology, spatial activities, and higher education in Cuba. He received various medals: the Rafael María de Mendive, Combatant of the Underground Struggle, and Ñico López; and diplomas as Founding Member of the Cuban Movement for Peace and the National Commission of the Cuban Academy of Sciences.

First to escape from the holocaust

My mother was born in 1900 in Radzilow, a village in Poland. She had heard about Cuba from a friend of hers, who had immigrated to the Island. She wanted to go someplace where she could study. The narrowness of the town suffocated her. But, above all, she wanted to go because she could feel the anti-Semitism and was convinced that, in the long run, they would kill everyone. It was my mother's firm belief. Unfortunately, she was right: in 1941, the pro Nazi Poles put all the Jews in a barn and burned them alive.

In 1924, my grandfather accompanied Mama to Rotterdam, to take the boat. She came alone and, unlike many others, didn't intend to keep traveling to the United States. She came because she wanted to start a new life here. Although she tried to bring and save her family, she was only able to get her younger sister out. In 1935, another sister escaped the Holocaust because she made *aliya* to Israel. The others perished, and she never overcame that pain.

My father came from Ivye, a small town in what is Belarus today. He emigrated in 1923 in search of a more promising future. He didn't think like my mother. He was always an optimist. Although he wanted to improve his life, he was a bad businessman. He wasn't cut out for business. Like many, he began selling *esquimo* pie, clearing rust off sewing machines, and he had a seltzer water stand —"the water of the polish"— and, oddly, he even became an assistant to a Japanese cook.

Of course, he was also a peddler, an occupation he would turn to more than once. He bought goods from Dworin, the father of Adela, the current vice president of the Patronato, and from other Hebrews on Bernaza Street who gave him credit. I still have his wooden suitcase. Inside, it had a compartment where the things were held by an elastic and some thumbtacks. He carried it in one hand and a bundle of clothes in the other. He sold at the bus and train stations, and at some work centers, especially on the days they got paid. From this, many good friendships were born. He was very well liked. He also was so lightning fast at calculations that he astonished everyone.

My mother and my aunt worked in a clothing store. Mama told me that, at the beginning, she would go days without eating, chewing gum to fool her stomach. One of the first things she did upon arrival was to enroll in a private academy to learn stenography and typing. But this didn't last long because she met my father, and they were married on January 1, 1929, in the Adath Israel synagogue.

They went to live in Melena del Sur, a town about sixty kilometers from Havana, and I was born there at the end of that same year. Papa bought a general store with money that a brother in the United States sent him. Before that, with two partners, he had set up a store in Piedrecitas —a small town that I can't even find on the map— and another in San José de las Lajas. The economic crisis of 1933 totally ruined him, and we moved back to Havana. Despite having lost everything, Mama was happy because she couldn't stand the colored earth of Melena del Sur.

How am I going to send a letter to my family with that address?

From the colored earth we went to live on Inquisidor Street, in the oldest part of the capital, but when my mother discovered what the name of the street meant, she made us move. She said, how can I send a letter to my family with that address? So, we rented other places, always in Old Havana. The last one was an interior room of a house on Lamparilla Street, between Aguacate and Compostela. I was about five or six. There, at the beginning of 1935, Papa set up a refreshment stand on the first floor of an adjoining building. It didn't matter that he worked more than 12 hours a day, because the business went bankrupt at the end of the 1940s, and he was forced to go back to peddling.

The street we lived on was very mixed, with few Jews. I remember that it had a refreshment stand across from the movie theater, in competition with my father. A Chinese grocery store and another one owned by Spaniards were on the corner as well as a butcher shop that still functions today. On the same block were the studio of a Catalonian woodcarver, of anarchistic-socialist tendencies, and a hardware store, property of a Spanish Falangist whose children and I went to the same school. In a certain way, I miss that hardware store because you could find just about everything there. He may have been a Falangist, but he knew how to buy.

Next to our room, in the living room of the house, two brothers manufactured purses for women. Their mother was Argentinean. They had a row boat, which they invited me to take out into the bay once or twice. A taxidermist worked in a small room he had rented on the roof, and there was a business on the first floor that installed loud speakers for public activities. Turning the corner, onto Aguacate, there were two or three contiguous houses that had become brothels, with their corresponding *souteneur*. This was the life that surrounded me. The neighborhood wasn't one of the worst. In fact, the location of the house was convenient for me because the Havana High School was right there.

Even without being religious, it was a treif *marriage*

When I got married, Mama accepted the fact unwillingly, because Mercedes wasn't Hebrew. The Jewish community had always been strongly in favor of marriage within the religion. At heart, underlying it was the idea of betrayal, but more than religious sentiment, I think for my mother it signified her identification with the people to which she belonged. It was a feeling of belonging that she was convinced should continue. Despite everything, she was passionate about her grandson. I think her satisfaction would have been even greater if she could see the scientist and university professor that he is today, respected for his work and loved for his human quality.

My father wasn't religious; he was always a liberal thinker. He said that the Bible stories weren't anything more than *maisalach*, little tales. My mother, however, went to Adath Israel. She conserved habits that had a religious origin, although she wasn't a practicing Jew. She didn't observe the Sabbath, but ate matzah on Passover and kept up with the big Jewish holidays. They spoke Yiddish, although very contaminated with Cubanisms. They addressed me in Yiddish, but I responded in Spanish. Sometimes they took me to the Centro Israelita, to theater productions or to some concert. They both thought I should make my Bar Mitzvah, but in the end I decided for myself. Already at thirteen, my principles were well defined.

Mama didn't eat pork. She rejected it. But my father did; I would say he even enjoyed it. We ate some typical foods: kneidlach, which my wife incorporated into her recipes; and *borscht*, which I discovered in Poland, was not a genuinely Russian dish as we had thought. The fact is, if you worked like my father from eight in the morning until twelve at night, or went out like my mother very early and returned at mid-day to prepare something to eat, to go running again before two in the afternoon and finish at the shop at six, it was very difficult to maintain traditions.

We ate in a cheap Chinese restaurant, located across from the Church of Christ that, paradoxically, served Cuban food. Once or twice a month my parents shopped in the grocery store on Acosta and in the bakery. Our life was very modest and our clothes threadbare, which didn't matter to us, but eating did. Occasionally, we went to the Hebrew Cooperativa on Compostela, a restaurant run by people of the left, where one could eat cheaply and well. We maintained the custom of drinking tea, which was a European thing. In Cuba, tea was sold at the pharmacy. If you drank it, it meant you had an upset stomach. I still keep some of those tinplated boxes in which the brand *Swee Touch Nee* came that Mama used to bring.

When my father died, we buried him with all the ritual in the Hebrew cemetery in Guanabacoa; the same for my mother and aunt. It was the first time that I participated in a religious ceremony. Later, I did it on a few occasions so as not to get out of practice, but I only felt linked to the community by my origins. When my mother died, I continued to pay her dues in Adath Israel. For some years I have been a member of the Patronato, and I generally attend when there is a cultural or social event to which I am invited. I even gave a lecture there. I have good friends in the community, where I also buy products for the Jewish Holidays. On principle, I am neither an opportunist, nor a renegade.

He has a runner in his blood

My parents were leftists and principally fraternized with Spanish and Cuban friends of all colors, all of the left. In my father, this came from a very strong family history. His older brother, Moisés, was a well known militant socialist who was persecuted for his political activity and was sent to prison in Brest Litovsk. Maybe for that reason, the family changed its name. When the Bolsheviks entered Ivye, they named him mayor of the town or something like that.

In Cuba, my father joined the Popular Socialist Party, but he wasn't an activist. My mother worshipped José Martí, our national hero. When, in a discussion, a neighbor called him "Misguided Joe," she considered that to be true blasphemy. Martí was a sacred symbol.

The Catalonian carver I mentioned lived on Lamparilla, half a block from home. I remember he made a sickle and hammer to put in his lapel and also the star shaped protection that encased the diamond of the Capitol after it was returned.[1] My father and various Cubans and Spaniards of the left would meet in his studio at night to talk about the latest news of the Spanish Civil War. I went with him. The group also participated in the rallies in support of the Spanish Republic and to raise funds for the Party newspaper that took place on the grounds of La Polar beer factory. There, I listened for the first time to speeches of such notable political leaders as Juan Marinello, Blas Roca and Salvador García Agüero. That would be 1938.

---

[1] A diamond that marked the kilometer zero on the central highway. It was stolen and later appeared in the desk drawer of the then president of the Republic, Ramón Grau San Martín.

On Sundays, without fail, one or two friends would come over to talk, seated in the doorway of our room. Years later, one admitted to me that one of the reasons he came over so frequently was because my mother served bread and butter and tea, and this way he could complement his not so very abundant diet that day.

When I entered high school in 1941, my ideological inclinations were already formed. There, I studied with another comrade who thought the same. We read *La pupila insomne*, by Martínez Villena,[2] and *Los fundamentos del socialismo en Cuba*, by Blas Roca.[3] At fifteen or sixteen, I joined the Socialist Youth. I wrote a column entitled "Science Update" for the magazine *Mella*. On one occasion —I think it was at the end of the 1940s— I even was taken to court with the rest of the editorial council, accused of carrying out subversive propaganda, but we were acquitted. I don't have any copies to show you, because I had to get rid of the ones I had, and a good part of my library, when the repression intensified. The Party was very strong in our neighborhood. My parents felt it was their world. So, this was the environment in which I grew up.

Teresa, my Asturian teacher

My parents always insisted that I study. I was the only child they had. I went to kindergarten at a public school on Habana Street. Since it was very far from home, my parents transferred me to a little school that an Asturian teacher, Teresa García, had on a roof on Lamparilla Street. I went through primary school with her, and I prepared for the entrance exam for high school. I was her favorite student. Sometimes, she called me José de Arimatea, like the disciple of Jesus Christ. Papa paid $1.50 a month for the classes. I remember that they were able to buy me the entrance text for high school in a used book store because Teresa was kind enough not to charge that month. Five years later, after finishing high school, we decided that she should accompany me to the graduation ceremony. Although Teresa was a practicing Catholic and belonged to a religious brotherhood, our relations were always superb. We had a very important thing in common: we were both poor and didn't have aspirations to become millionaires.

I was always interested in science, especially physics, inspired perhaps from

---

[2] Rubén Martínez Villena: Cuban intellectual and revolutionary, leader of the Communist Party.
[3] Blas Roca Calderío: for many years the General Secretary of the Cuban Communist Party.

High School Graduation day with Teresa his teacher, parents and aunt.
Havana, 1947.

reading some excellent books: *Mathematics and Imagination*, by Kasner and Newman, *Biology and Marxism*, by Prenant, *Where has Science gone?*, by Planck, and two on Einstein's theory of relativity, one by Papp and the other by Born.

My secondary school study was free of charge. I acquired the books with the prizes I won for being the best student: three pesos for each subject in high school and ten at the university. But I needed some additional money, for which we went to one of the workshops of the diamond industry, which the Belgian Jews had established in Havana during the Second World War. It was a very attractive offer, but, after much analysis, my parents decided that "it was better that I dedicate all my time to my studies even though we would continue to live on a tight budget."

He has only one defect: he is a Communist

Then, another opportunity presented itself. Someone had asked one of my professors for a tutor in physics, chemistry and mathematics. She gave him my name, making clear that I had only one defect: that I was a Communist! I learned of that afterwards. What is certain is that, after talking with my teacher

Teresa, it turned out that she knew the mother of the boy and spoke to him. A Jesuit priest of Italian origin, who functioned as the spiritual father of various wealthy families of Havana, was the one who opened the door for me. Naturally, I said good morning to him, which I suppose he wasn't expecting. Apparently, I was approved, perhaps because I didn't carry a bomb under my arm like all the Communists in the caricatures of the time.

That's how I began to give private classes to the son of a wealthy family in Marianao. From time to time we talked politics, of a the future, of socialism. "Well, when socialism comes, neither you nor I will have problems earning a living because we will be professionals," he said to me. With my first pay for the classes, I bought our first radio, which had electronic tubes and a loud speaker: a PHILCO. Some years ago I gave it to a friend, and it is still working. I replaced the crystal receiver with headphones that I built myself and that were so poor I could only hear some comedy programs that I liked late at night. During the day, the nearby stations crowded out the others. In order to follow the episodes of the Chinese detective, Chan Li Po, that were the rage at the end of the 1930s, I went to the house of the watch maker across the street. His son studied at the School of Arts and Trades and had introduced me, in a very elementary way, to the world of radio. Of course, a little while after acquiring the radio, my parents discovered it and began tuning in regularly to a program of the left in Yiddish that was broadcast by a small station in Old Havana for years.

"Since he is poor, the only thing he can do is study"

I finished high school in 1947. Our graduation took place in the America Theatre with a lot of pomp. If I remember well, the newspaper *Havaner Lebn* published a photo of the Jewish graduates, emphasizing that I, the son of workers, was first in the class. Someone told me that the father of a classmate asked his son how it was possible that he earned grades inferior to mine if he lived in much better conditions. His answer was: "Very simple: since he is poor, the only thing he can do is devote himself to study."

Before coming here, we rented two rooms in the building across the street. It was the only time, in all those years, that we had two bedrooms. It was because my aunt lived with us. Our room was very small. I slept on a stretcher with legs that we put under my parent's bed during the day. When I was at the university, someone gave us an old rocking chair, but you couldn't rock in it because there wasn't enough space.

In order to study, I mounted a small blackboard on the wall in the hall, which was really two broomsticks and a piece of black oilcloth. At night, because of the heat, I opened one of the two doors of the room and put up a sheet as a curtain so that the light didn't bother the neighbor. When I heard him awaken, I turned off the light until he was asleep again because, if not, he would begin to grumble vulgarities. Later, I invented a way of studying on the roof. I got light from a bulb connected to an extension cord several meters long that was plugged into my bedroom.

I would have liked to have been a physicist, but in Cuba practically the only career opportunity for that was to be a secondary school teacher, a difficult job to get.

Cuba, a tropical paradise for Jews

If there had been some incident that one could qualify as genuine anti-Semitism, I don't remember it, and if I don't remember it, it wasn't important because it didn't leave any real mark. In my personal experience, the core of my problem was not that I was Jewish but that I was identified with socialist principles. When I finished my university studies, everyone knew my political ideas. But this detail escaped the Cuban Electric Company —which wasn't Cuban, but an American monopoly— and they hired me when I graduated in 1953. A month later they fired me without any niceties after an agent of the secret police had visited my house. Imagine, one of its employees was a Communist and, on top of that, a Jew.

Something similar happened in secondary school. I remember one professor, who was very Catholic and very far right, saw me discussing physics with some friends in the classroom and remarked: "How about that? A Jew and a Communist." That time the order was reversed. But I must admit that, despite the commentary, she always gave me the maximum points on exams. Also, another teacher pointed out that it didn't seem right that someone of my origin should win the Cuban History Prize. He gave me second prize. Those were the only two occasions that I recall being criticized for being Jewish.

Well, trying to remember, also that Falangist hardware owner, when the neighbors commented that the Nazis were killing Jews, he answered: "It must be for some reason." But none of that, in my opinion, was sufficient to consider it an integral part of the way the Cuban people thought. They were solely the attitudes of a minority of reactionaries with small minds. Of course, there was racial discrimination in Cuba, but that was basically against black people. I think that other manifestations of the phenomenon were very marginal.

By the way, I want to tell you something that happened to me in the United States. I was invited by the Smithsonian, and I participated in the annual meeting of the History of Technology Society in 1995. It was the first time that someone from Cuba attended, and they made a point of mentioning it. Everyone was very nice. At the final banquet, I was seated at a table with a distinguished American researcher and his wife, and a Japanese couple. During the conversation, the Japanese gentleman commented that my surname didn't seem Latin, but German. I answered that I was Jewish. Hearing that, the wife of the American professor whispered to me: "You were very courageous to say that." I was very surprised that someone would say that to me.

University Reform, Radio Havana Cuba and the Cosmos

I worked in a refrigerator enterprise, the profits of which were used to support the underground of the Communist Party during the struggle against Batista. At the beginning of 1959, Enrique Oltuski had just been named Minister of Communications and had asked his comrades of the July 26th Movement to recommend engineers who knew about telecommunications. Someone mentioned my name, with the usual tag line: "He is capable, but a Communist." Oltuski didn't care. That's how I began at the Ministry and became a founder and director of the Telecommunications Advisory Council.

There, with a small team that we formed —mostly students— and with the unreserved support of the leadership of the Ministry, we promoted a truly technical revolution. The antiquated telegraph system was automated, telex was introduced, and the creation of a coastal network for maritime radio-communications was planned. In addition, we established two large international short wave communication centers, the transmission center in Bauta and the receiving center of La Chorrera. And something no less important: the modernization of the curriculum at the university in Electrical Engineering, which gave a decisive boost to the teaching of this specialty in Cuba.

Almost immediately, we realized the urgent necessity of having a high potency short wave plant. Practically all of our communication channels passed through the United States, and, naturally, there was a danger that in time of crisis they could not only be interfered with, but cut off completely. Our idea for the radio transmission center had a two-fold objective: to make possible the

110

establishment of flexible point to point communications for commercial and diplomatic matters with the outside world, and to broadcast to the entire world, particularly Latin America, the truth about our revolutionary process. This was the beginning of Radio Havana Cuba, built in record time. Its broadcasts premiered with excellent results during the Bay of Pigs invasion.

The reform of the study plan for Electrical Engineering was related to the urgency of graduating engineers who knew about electronics and high potency broadcasts. In the academic sphere, it served to guide other plans that were implemented after 1960. Since my time as a student, I was critical of the teaching method and the performance of professors who acted like feudal lords, as well as the lack of an up to date scientific and technological focus. I suppose that is why, when they created the National University Council, they included me in it. Principal responsibility fell on Carlos Rafael Rodríguez and Armando Hart. When we began the discussions, everyone thought of a popular and progressive university, which wouldn't actually be socialist, but events overtook us and very soon imposed on us a different reality.

From 1966 on, I was involved with the Intercosmic Program of the socialist countries, as vice president and president of the National Space Commission. The most important results of our participation in the program were the inclusion of Cuba in international satellite communications, the application of remote sensory techniques for agricultural and environmental purposes in the national territory, and the first Cuban scientific experiments in outer space undertaken in 1980 by our cosmonaut.

Klezmer music and religious chants: the soul of the people

I work here. Yes, I know I have already sparked interest in my collection of *klezmer* music, of Al Jolson, Perlman, Jan Peerce, Gershwin, Bloch, the chants of the synagogue, as well as my collection of Jewish family trees. I simply felt that it was part of my family tradition and, to a certain point of my past, with all its virtues and faults. I still remember the music and some of the words of the theme song of the Yiddish radio program. When I visited some of my mother's relatives in Liverpool in 1955, I was able to acquire some of those records. Later, some friends who knew about my interest in this music sent me others. The melodies that they sing in the synagogue, on the holidays, express the soul of a people, and I always find that moving.

Father with mandolin.
Poland, 1920.

As a child with his parents.
Havana, 1939.

As President of the National Space Commission with the two Cuban astronauts.
Havana, 1978.

Greeting the Pope at the Vatican.
1984.

(Photo by Peggy Myers)

Jaime Sarusky Miller

In 1931, while Joseíto Fernández was writing Guantanamera and Kid Chocolate assaulted Philadelphia with his punches, Jaime Sarusky Miller was born in the Cuban Florence (Ciego de Avila Province). A real *criollo*, whom everyone called, however, "the Polaco." In his library of innumerable volumes, are photographs of him having a beer with Wifredo Lam, talking non-existentially with Sartre and Beauvoir, leaning over Bergman in a pose that would make even Bogart envious. Novelist and journalist, his novels *La Búsqueda and Rebelión en la Octava Casa* obtained mention in the Casa de Las Américas Prize (1961 y 1967); *Un hombre providencial* won the Alejo Carpentier Prize in 2001. Other books he has published are: *El tiempo de los desconocidos* (1976), *Los Fantasmas de Omaja* (1986), *El unicornio y otras invenciones* (1996), *Aventuras de los suecos en Cuba* (1999). He received the José A. Fernández de Castro Prize for Cultural Journalism, the Distinction for National Culture, the Order Alejo Carpentier and the Cuban National Literature Award in 2005.

A difficult childhood

My father, Moisés Sarusky, arrived in Cuba when he was twenty two in 1924. He came from a village in Poland called Stawski, in the province of Lomza. He was a shoemaker, the eldest of nine brothers and sisters. He first worked repairing railroad tracks, in the northern zone of Cuba between Santa Clara

115

and Nuevitas. He saved as much as he could and, later, moved to Florencia where he had various businesses: a general store, a shoe factory and another store in a nearby town.

He continued saving money to bring over the next younger brother and, one by one, the other five. He also helped them establish themselves. In 1940, when Germany had invaded Poland —with the help of a friend who owned a wholesale business on Muralla Street and a Spanish Falangist— he attempted to get his parents and his two youngest brothers to Cuba. But he died at thirty eight, and, with his death, the fate of my grandparents and two aunts was sealed in the *Shoah*.

My mother, Hashke (or Juana) Miller, was from Pinsk, today Belarus. She met my father here, and they married in 1928. I was born in 1931. It was a difficult birth, the consequences of which she suffered for two years until she died at twenty six in 1933.

I had a difficult childhood and adolescence. My relationship with my tutor was very problematic because he managed the money that my father left me. It made me uninterested in business or money. I was very rebellious. When my parents died, it was hard for me to accept the authority of some of my uncles. They never took me into account. My life was unstable; they switched my schools and homes as if I were a gypsy. This may explain my urgent need, consciously or unconsciously, to belong, and to have roots. All of this influenced my way of viewing life.

We were the only Jews in Florencia. For Rosh Hashanah and Yom Kippur we went to Chambas where they improvised a synagogue in a room of a house, which families of nearby towns also attended. When mama died, one of my aunts came to live with us, and she lit the Sabbath candles. Papa always spoke in Yiddish to her. My family, like the Jews of the shtetl, kept the special days. My parents and one of my aunts are buried in the Jewish cemetery in Guanabacoa. I also have relatives who are buried in Jewish cemeteries in the provinces, like in Santa Clara.

The Torah, the Bible and the Cuban *orishas*

In Havana, they enrolled me as a student at the Candler College, a very good Protestant school, but I was a prisoner. Since I didn't have family in the city, I wasn't allowed to leave the school on weekends, like other students. This exacerbated my rebelliousness, and everything came down to "I leave or I

Sarusky with his mother in Florencia. 1931.

escape." So, my uncles arranged for some friends, who lived above Moshe Pipik restaurant, to pick me up on weekends. Later on, they let me go out alone. I took the 22 bus, and I felt like the freest boy in the world. After that family immigrated to the United States, I lived in the rooming house that belonged to the owner of Moshe Pipik, where I ate breakfast, lunch and dinner.

On the anniversary of my father's death, I went to the Adath Israel Synagogue, then on Jesús María, and to the Centro Israelita on Yom Kippur and the New Year. I wore a blue winter suit even though the heat was like August, because that was what the occasion called for.

Everything was linked with solemnity and fear, about which I developed very personal feelings from the time I was very young. That fear of the divine bothered me a lot; it angered me. These are things that are not always talked about. When I went to say *kadish* for my father and read the words in Hebrew, I didn't understand anything. I was simply acting out of fear that I must be faithful to the memory of my father. There are more intimate details: the lengthy arguments, the religious confusion where Judaism was mixed with Protestantism and the Cuban belief in the Island's Patron Saint, the Virgin of

La Caridad del Cobre, linked to the orisha, Ochún, in Santería.

I had practically no Jewish upbringing, only some contact with the community. I did attend the *B'nei B'rith* because Marcus Matterin[1] invited me to collaborate. I wrote a story, and I gave it to him. I think he was my accomplice; one needed courage to publish something that attacked an institution so established as the dowry.

From a bad businessman to writer in bohemian Paris

I began working in the store of my two uncles on Muralla Street. When they split up, I went to work in the office of the jewelry store CASABLANCK, on Monserrate Street. I was there about two years until, in 1949, because of a crazy romance, I became a merchant. The truth is that the girl's father thought that the best way to trap the wild boy was to buy him a store in Marianao and put them to work together. The store was called LA FERIA. It lasted four years, only because I didn't find a buyer sooner.

It's a lamentable story that has to do with an act of liberation like the previous ones. I didn't accept the dowry, and my whole family was mad at me. It was one of the most significant decisions of my life. If I had consented, I would have fallen into a moral dependence. He presented me in Yiddish to other merchants as "my future son-in-law, for whom I set up a store in Marianao." My family said it was a way to help the couple prosper. Maybe it was like that, but I had a different moral view, and, despite being very much in love, I opposed it. I explained to my girlfriend that we would do it with my money. I went to my uncle, but I was only nineteen and couldn't get my inheritance until I was twenty one. The Cuban came out in me. I wasn't going to become a nobody, but it wasn't simply machismo, it was a matter that transcended gender. It was her father's interest opposed to mine, to my way of thinking. It was a much more profound attitude. So, I said to her: "The best thing is for you to go home, and we will continue seeing each other without the store." The only thing that remains of that adventure is the story that Matterin published, "It seems they were very much in love," an ironic look at the subject of dowry.

I had already started to write, to publish in *El Sol* newspaper of Marianao. I submitted articles about the Cuban and international situation. That was in

---

[1] Abraham Marcus Matterin, distinguished community leader from the 1940s until his death in 1982 who also encouraged Jewish and gentile authors to write on Jewish subjects and published them. His interview appears in the third part of this book.

As President of the "Cuba House" in Paris with Nicolás Guillén, the Cuban National poet. 1955.

the years 1951, 1952, 1953… Although it meant living in tighter quarters, I built a barbacoa[2] in the same store. Young writers and journalists got together in the store, and it became a kind of literary circle. In addition, when it was the anniversary of Martí or some other patriotic date, instead of using the two display windows to show pants or shirts, I used to fill them with materials related to these historic occasions.

When I decided to break with everything, I just about gave the store away because I couldn't find someone to sell it to. I was never a good merchant. Someone gave me a little more than 2,000 pesos for the place. It had a lot more merchandise, but I took it and left without saying anything to my family. I was twenty one. I burned my bridges and went to Paris for about five years. I said to myself: "I am going to try to learn and know as much as I can." But I knew from my first days there that I wasn't going to stay. I needed my roots.

Rebellious Cubans in France

For a year, I was president of the "Cuba House" at the University City of Paris. Saúl Yelín[3] was also there. We had problems with the director because

---

[2] Barbacoa: an improvised structure made of discarded materials, frequently constructed by poor people to increase the available living space by taking advantage of the high colonial ceilings to put in an additional floor.
[3] Saúl Yelín: a Jewish Cuban, one of the founders of the motion picture industry of the Revolution.

she severely restricted the daily life of the students, the use of hot water, heat, and female visitors. We had fierce arguments, so fierce that we began to light firecrackers, and they reported us to the police, which added to other problems. I had to leave the "Cuba House." After I left, they came to arrest me at six in the morning, accusing me of being an international agent. But they quickly released me.

We are speaking of the 1950s, which were very difficult times on the Island. The majority of the students belonged to and worked with the three established groups: the Popular Socialist Party, the July 26th Movement and the Revolutionary Directorate. We protested in front of the Embassy of the Dominican Republic, because the dictator Trujillo was selling arms and planes to Batista. From there we went to the United States Embassy. The police caught the Cubans. Some comrades said to me: "Don't let them get you so you can report to the press what is going on." And that's what happened. Stories came out in the most important newspapers, in *Le Monde*, for example, that objectively reflected our situation.

A social agenda always surfaces in my work

In Paris, in summer of 1955, I coincided with Saúl Yelín, with José Altshuler, who had been in England on a scholarship, with Roberto Fernández Retamar and Adelaida de Juan.[4] There, I also became a good friend of the "Moro" Fayad Jamis,[5] a step toward Arab-Jewish co-existence.

When I got to Havana in 1959, Moro was waiting for me on the dock and took me to the newspaper *Revolución*. Saúl, who was then working on the foundation of Cuban cinema, also asked me to get involved. So, I worked on many things. I was a journalist until 1964, writing for the pages of *Revolución*. I was a teacher of American History at the Marianao High School, and of Cuban and Spanish Literature at the Cepero Bonilla Junior High. I was Editor in Chief of the cultural page of *La Gaceta de Cuba*, with Nicolás Guillén as director, and of the Saturday Supplement of the newspaper *Granma*. Later, I was on the staff of the magazine Bohemia, for seven years, in the Ministry of Culture (1977 to 1984), and since then, I have been a member of the Editorial

---

[4] Roberto Fernández Retamar, current president of the Casa de las Américas, is an essayist, poet and university professor. His wife, Adelaida de Juan, is a professor, essayist and art critic.
[5] Fayad Jamis, poet, editor, painter and journalist, was born in Mexico, of Arab descent, which is why he is known in Cuban intellectual circles as the "Moro."

Board of the magazine *Revolución y Cultura*.

When I began to write, I was interested in minorities that were not well known, those that were forgotten, and social issues. One can't be a writer in the modern world and ignore those subjects. I am not a priest of the Middle Ages, enclosed in a monastery. Without intending to, a social agenda always surfaces in my writing.

I think that the subject I am working on currently is the most difficult. I don't know if it will be a novel or a testimony. I am summing up aspects of my life, mixed with fictional persons. I don't know to what extent it might be interesting, in the context of the country, among so many other subjects. It is the story of a Cuban who is also Jewish and trying to rediscover his Cuban roots, a process of conflicting identity.

Board of the magazine *Revolución y Cultura.*

When I began to write, I was interested in minorities that were not well known, those that were forgotten, and social issues. One can't be a writer in the modern world and ignore those subjects. I am not a priest of the Middle Ages, enclosed in a monastery. Without intending to, a social agenda always surfaces in my writing.

I think that the subject I am working on currently is the most difficult. I don't know if it will be a novel or a testimony. I am summing up aspects of my life, mixed with fictional persons. I don't know to what extent it might be interesting, in the context of the country, among so many other subjects. It is the story of a Cuban who is also Jewish and trying to rediscover his Cuban roots, a process of conflicting identity.

Sarusky with Ingrid Bergman.
Paris, 1956.

Sarusky with the famous Cuban artist
Wifredo Lam.
Havana, 1968.

(Photo by Tatiana Santos)

Rafael Hernández Rousseau

Rabbis, Cardinals and *Mambises*:
a non aggression pact

I was born in New York in 1935. My father had emigrated from Cuba during Machado's dictatorship because his best friend, Ramiro Valdés Daussá, had been jailed, and they warned Dad that the police were also looking for him.

He arrived in New York in February of 1931, in the middle of winter and amid the Great Depression. There were soup lines and unemployed people selling apples. It was a tremendous shock. He was lucky, however, thanks to his level of education. Since he was a lawyer and spoke English perfectly, he was able to get work collecting bills from clients of an underwear factory. It turned out that the owner, Gad Rousso, had a younger sister, Victoria. When my father met her in May of that year, it was love at first sight, and they married three months later in August. He was a Cuban from a very Catholic family from Camagüey, and she was a Sephardic Jew from Monastir, who had arrived in the United States in 1922.

In Cuba, Dad had gone to the Belén primary school, a famous Jesuit school in Havana. As was common among well-to-do families in Cuba, his father sent him to high school in the United States. Thus, Dad and his brothers went to high school at a military academy in Virginia. At that time, he had already abandoned his religious beliefs. He only believed in God and nothing else. However, although Mom was also not observant of her religion, she made him promise two things before they were married. First, that the wedding would take place in a synagogue with a Rabbi. Thus, my father, whose name was Francisco, became Abraham, and they married in the synagogue of Riverside, New York. I still have the *Ketuba* (Jewish marriage contract). Second, that if a male was born he would be circumcised. So on the eighth day, without warning me, they sealed the pact.

My father always said that he was so in love that it didn't matter to him if Mom was Jewish, Muslim or Buddhist. For him, like for most Cubans, that was not a problem. But there is an exception to every rule. Generally, in mixed marriages, it is the Jewish side that is opposed. In his case, it was not that way. My mother's family accepted my father, but, contrary to the open attitude of Cubans, it was not easy for my paternal grandmother to approve of the marriage. For my grandmother, who was both very Catholic and a strong nationalist, it must have been traumatic when Dad suddenly appeared with a Jewish American wife and a son.

In part, I come from a *mambí* family. Grandfather Antonino ran off when he was 16 years old to join the Independence War in 1895, and my great-grandmother, Inés Betancourt, spent the whole first war against Spain from 1868 to 1878 living in the bush. She was also a cousin of Salvador Cisneros Betancourt, the Marquis of Santa Lucía, and my Grandmother Herminia, her daughter, was a cousin of Cardinal Manuel Arteaga Betancourt, Cuba's first Cardinal. On the other extreme, my maternal great-grandfather was a Rabbi in Salonica. Thus, on my Sephardic side —my grandparents Samuel Rousso (of Istanbul) and Rachel Covos (of Salonica), and the Cubans Herminia Llopis Betancourt (of Camagüey) and Antonino Hernández (of Camajuaní)— there are Rabbis, Cardinals and *mambises*. That was something that should have carried weight in the implicit non aggression pact which I imagine was agreed to between my parents. In any event, they didn't raise me in either of the two religions.

From New York to Jovellanos:
among Bar Mitzvahs and *bembés*[1]

Papa ended up being a partner in my uncle's factory. Although he was doing well, he didn't like the business. Also, he missed his country and his profession, which he loved. So, in 1937, he decided to return to Cuba. The first memory I have of my life is arriving in Havana, by boat.

We first went to live to Cifuentes, a very poor town with a single paved street in Las Villas province, where my father had been appointed a municipal judge. Later, we moved to Jovellanos, a town in Matanzas province, with a large afro-Cuban population and its *santeros*.[2] It was very peculiar. In those towns there were so many illiterates who didn't even know Spanish, but people asked me to speak in English, as if I were some kind of circus attraction. Of course, when I spoke, no one could answer me, and I began to reject English at an early age. Mom spoke to me in English, but I responded in Spanish.

There were a handful of Jewish families in Jovellanos: the Zimmerman's who had a Pharmacy; the Shapiro's and the Gurian's, who both had clothing stores; and Garmizo who was the owner of the rope factory and another store. All these stores were on Real Street, which was the main business street. Mom got along well with them, as well as with the Cubans. Everybody in town called her the *Americana*, the judge's wife; they never called her a Jew.

I had two groups of friends. During the day, the white kids were my school mates and, in the afternoon after school, the *negritos*[3] were my buddies in mischief. My best friend was Nolio, whose father was an important *santero* and very respected in the town. Once, we asked him how to remove evil from a dead black hen by witchcraft so we could take the pennies people had left on it and buy candy. I lived a very happy childhood, although I saw, at first hand, the misery and extreme poverty in which our people lived. I believe that experience had an influence on me and on my attitude towards life.

From the time I was four until I was thirteen, we visited family in New York every year, except from 1941-1944, due to the War. I have beautiful memories of those vacations with my uncles, aunts, my grandmother and my cousins. I never saw such a united and affectionate family as my Jewish family. I always

---

[1] Santería rituals commemorating a saint's day.
[2] *Santero*: A priest in the Santería religion.
[3] *Negritos*: In Cuba, this term is of affection commonly used between friends. It can also be used pejoratively, but in the context used here it is a term of affection.

remember those days with love and nostalgia.

As you see my life developed in two places, in two very different atmospheres. In Cuba, I fell asleep every night to the rhythm of the drums of the bembés; I grabbed sugar cane off passing trains and pennies off dead hens with my friends, the *negritos*. In New York City, I went to the Roxy to see Paul Robeson in "Show Boat" and to Yankee Stadium; I played stick ball in the street with my multi-national friends in Washington Heights, the neighborhood where I was born; and I participated in my cousins' Bar Mitzvahs.

A "Big Five" Jew becomes a socialist manager

When I was thirteen, we moved to Havana. I came under protest. I didn't want to leave my town. I locked myself in my room for three days, but later on, as I made new friends, I slowly forgot the town. I went to the high school in Vedado, and not to Belen as my father did. But, at the University, I studied law because Dad was a Judge, although what I really liked was economics, business, sports and music. So if I appraise my life, I can say that the only time I was a lawyer was the day I graduated from the university; I was a good athlete, but not a very hot pianist; and, modesty aside, I was a pretty good businessman.

I love sports. In my teens I stood out as an oarsman and guard on the football team (American style) of the Vedado Tennis Club (VTC), called The Marquises as all teams of the VTC were called. The VTC was one of the "Big Five" Clubs. Generally, Jews were members of the Casino Deportivo and not of these more aristocratic clubs, but Victor Frankel and I were members of the VTC and never felt any discrimination as Jews, although many of our teammates went to Catholic schools.

Starting in the early years of the Revolution, I worked in Foreign Trade, international banking and real estate. I was Director of Economics and of Foreign Business Administration at the Ministry of Foreign Trade, a General Manager of various importing state agencies, Director of Exports at the National Bank, Vice-president of the Cubalse Corporation, etc. My work has always been related to trade and business, which is what I like. Maybe my genes had something to do with it. It's funny. My father who was such a learned person could never make a business succeed. However, Mom, who didn't go beyond sixth grade, used to advise him: "Frank, that business is no good; don't do it, you will lose money," and, unfortunately, she was always right. I believe that there is something, like an instinct, without doubt due to historical reasons,

128

which explains why we have perhaps developed a little more in business than others have through the ages.

I had a completely lay education. I studied in public schools, never in a religious school. Mom didn't eat pork and she cooked with oil, but she told me that it was because she didn't like fat, that it was bad. She saturated me with eggplant, she made delicious cookies, with different forms that, I learned later are typical dishes of Sephardic cuisine. I knew that I belonged to a Jewish family and that my aunt Flora, her husband and two of their children died in the Holocaust. I was surprised, and I admired my grandmother Nona when she spoke Ladino, remaining true to the tradition it signified. I knew of my Judaism. In New York, I participated in Jewish traditions with my family, but they didn't instill in me any religious concepts. My parents never wanted to influence me, and they let me decide when I was an adult.

In Cuba, nobody ever called me a Jew or said anything deprecating to me. Cubans don't care very much what religion you profess or to what ethnic group you belong. For thirty five years living in the country no one was interested to know if I was Jewish or not, until one day in 1973 when Maritza, a girl very steeped in historical studies, looked me in the eye and, without hesitation, shot the question: "Are you Jewish?" I was so taken by surprise. Three months later we married. All these years, with that persistence of hers, she has continued researching and writing about Jews in Cuba. This book is a reflection of that.

His parents in New York City.
1934.

With his mother and all his Jewish relatives from New York
the day of his departure to Cuba.
1939.

The rowing team of the VTC.
Havana, 1955.

As a football player.
Havana, 1955.

In a business meeting with the President of Hino Motors.
Japan, 1970.

Maritza and Rafael's wedding.
Havana, 1974.

(Photo by Frédéric Brenner)

Enrique Oltuski Osacki

Distinguished revolutionary and leader of the July 26th Movement in the plains. One of the signers, in the Sierra Maestra, of the Land Reform Law. Has served in important posts in the central administration of the State: Minister of Communications in the first cabinet of the Revolution, in 1959; Vice Minister of Industries with Ché and of the Central Planning Board; Director of the North Coast cattle development plan and of the Sugar Enterprise of Matanzas. Since 1977, he serves as Vice Minister of the Fishing Industry.

Recipient of various decorations, including: Founding member of the PCC, Medal of the 20th Anniversary of the Attack on the Moncada Barracks, Medal of the 20th Anniversary of the Landing of the Granma, of the Insurrection, the 30th and 40th Anniversary of the FAR, and Félix Elmuza.

Graduated in Engineering from the University of Miami in 1955. Has published various articles and two books, which recount the struggle against the Batista dictatorship and his experiences as a revolutionary.

I baptized myself Enrique.

My father's name is Berol, which in Cuba was translated as "Bernardo." He was born in Brest-Litovsk, a city in the current Belarus, which belonged to Poland at that time. Mama, Jashe, was born in Kobrin. Papa went by bicycle all

133

the way from Brest to Kobrin to court my mother. Although it was like twenty kilometers, it was worth it to go on foot to see a woman as beautiful as Mama. They were both nineteen when they married, and they took the boat practically on their honeymoon. It was 1929. I was born in 1930. They must have made me somewhere in the Atlantic Ocean; maybe that's why I have been working in the fishing industry for twenty-four years.

Papa left Poland fleeing from military service. He came here dazzled by the riches described in the letters written by one of his relatives who had immigrated to the Island but ended up leaving for the United States, like the majority of those who considered Cuba a springboard to get to America. My parents wanted to stay; they planted themselves here. Since Papa had been a shoemaker in Poland, he first established himself in that trade in Old Havana, which is where I was born. When I was six months old, he went to Santa Clara where he set up a small shoe factory on the narrow street of Santa Bárbara, a street of poor people. We lived in two rooms of the house; the rest was the factory.

There are two curious things about me. First, that my name is Erol and not Enrique. I baptized myself Enrique in high school because I told my father I couldn't go on with so many strange names. He did all of the paperwork to change it for me. Up to that time, ever since primary school, everyone had called me Eri, because my name didn't stick. Second, I was born on November 18, 1930 and not the 25th as appears on my identity card. My parents say that they hardly spoke any Spanish when they went to register my birth, and there was no way that the clerk could understand them.

In 1931, while pregnant with my sister, my mother became ill. The doctors advised her that a change of climate would be beneficial and that she should give birth in Poland, because Cuba was too hot and humid. We stayed in Poland until 1935, because the economic crisis prevented my father from putting together enough money for us to return before that. In Poland, I learned to speak Yiddish, and I lived a Jewish life in the town with my grandfather. I was his inseparable companion on the street and in the synagogue, where he kept me protected under his legs that rhythmically followed the cadence of the prayers. Grandfather was my first hero, my first ideal. He was a strong and honest man, and people respected and loved him in that small Jewish community, which was his world.

Our house in Poland was large. The living room was the soul of the house.

That was where the workshop was. My grandfather and my uncles labored around a large and narrow table, making shoes for the Christian peasants in the area. During the week we ate in the kitchen where there were two large wooden barrels, one full of pickles and the other with herring. But on Fridays, in the afternoon, they took away all the shoetrees, the soles, the half finished shoes, and they thoroughly cleaned the room. They set up a large table with an impressive white tablecloth, big plates and antique silverware. Everyone took a bath and put on clean clothes and began the ritual of the Jewish Sabbath.

Between tangos and pasodobles, Berol the dance king

When I returned to the Island in 1935, I was five years old. I didn't speak Spanish, only Yiddish. They took me from a traditional Jewish home in Poland to a not so traditional one in Cuba. Although at home they spoke in Yiddish about Israel, Moses, Solomon, and Herzl, and they celebrated the Jewish holidays and didn't eat pork, my parents were not religious. Mama was a wonderful cook. She made soup with *kneidlach*, with noodles, the stuffed chicken necks. Our rice was potatoes. Peddlers came from Havana and brought *jering, jrein*, and black bread.

There was a small synagogue in Santa Clara. It wasn't like the one in Poland to which you entered by ascending a big stairway. It was on some upper floor in a building on Independencía Street. We were about fifty Jewish families; the majority, like my father, came from eastern and central Europe. There were also turcos who came before we did. I remember Feldman, who had a store called CAÑÓN ALEMÁN (GERMAN CANNON), Blacher, who was a business partner of Papa's, Gabroviecki, Esquenazi, the owner of CASA MOISÉS, and the Schub family, who were good friends of mine...

My father was not only a man dedicated to business, very hardworking and exacting, but he also enjoyed life. He played the mandolin and sang, and when they gave parties in the synagogue, he was the dance king. He danced the tango and the pasodoble. He went around the city on a motorcycle when that wasn't very common, and he was a womanizer —that's the only way in which I am not like him.

From a Jewish boy to a Cuban boy

I studied at the neighborhood public school. My teacher was named Inés: a dark, dark black woman, who was the prettiest thing you can imagine. When my mother took me to school, Inés had difficulty pronouncing my strange Polish surname. She was my teacher in fourth and fifth grade. I was a beautiful little blond, and Inés adopted me and was my godmother. She had an incredible knowledge of Cuban history and taught me to understand all the periods of our history: the Indians, Columbus, slavery, the wars of independence. She spoke to me about the races that made up Cuba, and she made me totally anti-racist. She is the one who converted Martí, Maceo and Gómez into my new heroes, justice into the meaning of my life and Cuba into my country.

Thus, I evolved very early from being a Jewish boy to being a Cuban boy. My first problem, my first contradiction, came when I began to prepare for my *Bar Mitzvah*, which I didn't want to do. The teacher was an old Viennese cantor who had lost his voice and was in charge of the synagogue in Santa Clara. He was a good and intelligent man, more cultured than those Russian and Polish Jews that had practically come straight from the *ghetto* to get the boat to come to America. By thirteen, I had read all the history and science books that Inés had loaned me, and as my knowledge grew, my questions about religion increased. I expressed my first doubts about the logic of religion to the teacher. He used arguments against me that were much more elaborate than those of my father or his friends, who simply took refuge in some citation from the Bible. I asked him what it meant to be a Jew, and I said to him that if it was a nation, then my nation was Cuba, I was Cuban. If it was a religion, I didn't believe in religions; I only believed in reason. In the end, so as not to hurt my parents, I made my *Bar Mitzvah*, but I didn't give in later when the second contradiction presented itself, and I decided to marry Marta.

Marta's family did not oppose our relationship. In Cuba, in mixed marriages, the opposition usually came from the Jewish side. One of the things that has maintained the Hebrew people and has permitted them to survive, despite being dispersed throughout the world, has been not to inter-marry. I took Marta home a few times so my parents could get to know her and to create a favorable environment. They liked her a lot, but they hoped I would marry a Jewish girl like everyone in their family had. When I finally told them I was going to marry Marta —after she gave up her religion—my mother said it was impossible, that she preferred to die first, that I couldn't renounce a tradition of more than five thousand years, that our family had always been Jewish. They both started to cry. It was the first time in my life that I saw my father cry. However, with time and grandchildren, they got used to it.

136

Latin American student fraternity at the University of Miami.
1949.

From Miami to the July 26th

My father, who had begun with a small factory where he made shoes he named Alfa, formed partnerships and set up other factories in nearby towns like Camajuaní, Remedios, Manicaragua, and Placetas. Later on, he opened a wholesale business where he sold materials for making shoes. In partnership with my uncle León Osacki, of Holguín, and his brother-in-law Moisés Kubiliun, he bought the tannery of Santa Clara. He made a considerable fortune and decided I should go to the United States to study. I went in 1948, at sixteen. I returned at twenty three in 1955. I studied for five years at the University of Miami and worked for two as an architect, designing houses, a hotel on Miami Beach and a commercial center in the city.

When I left, it was the time of Chibás and Prío. Although I supported Chibás and went to hear him, I wasn't an activist. Nor was I a Marxist. I knew who Marx was, but I didn't have a clear idea of what he really thought. At the University, we formed a Fraternity with certain conspiratorial aspects, which, behind the facade of an entity dedicated to social activities, brought together students from Latin America. Our symbol was Bolivar and our objective and secret slogan was to unite all the peoples of the continent into one great nation or federation of States.

Very quickly, I became president of the Foreign Student Association. Later, I was elected to one of the three highest leadership posts of the entire University.

One of the other leaders was a brilliant American girl, a leftist. We became very good friends, and she gave me a book on the history of philosophy as told through the lives of the twenty most important philosophers of humanity. When I read it, I understood Marx's ideas for the first time. I liked them a lot, but I thought the world he proposed was utopian. Although just and correct, it was a utopia. Later she gave me *Capital*, of which I could understand only about ten percent. Finally, I read the book that.converted me into a revolutionary: *Three who made a Revolution*. It was the history of the Russian Revolution based on the biographies of Trotsky, Lenin and Stalin, told in a way that was so human that it made that epic saga seem normal and logical. I was no longer the same. Something changed in me.

Batista seized power in a coup d'etat on March 10, 1952. That year, as always, I traveled to Cuba in June, July and August and went to Santa Clara. I was a very good friend of Marta's brother, Guillermito,[1] who was studying medicine at the University of Havana. He already was a member of the MNR,[2] and I told him my desire to join the struggle. We came to Havana and went with Faustino Pérez and Armando Hart to see García Bárcena, who named me delegate of the organization in Miami. My job was to mobilize student opinion and that of the Cuban colony there, and to obtain resources for the armed struggle. My friend David did not support me; he said Jews shouldn't get mixed up in the internal politics of any country. As an example, he pointed out what had happened in Russia, Germany and France; he argued that our true homeland was Israel and that here, after Fidel attacked the Moncada, anyone could be killed. I answered: "Since there are many Jews who think like you do, I feel even more committed."

Afterwards, the MNR fell apart. When I went back to Cuba in 1955, the July 26th Movement, the Directorio and the OA[3] were organizing. One of my friends from the MNR suggested I go see the people of the Communist Party. We went, but since they were opposed to armed struggle and we believed it was the

---

[1] Guillermo Rodríguez, member of the July 26th Movement. After 1959, he was a General in the FAR, occupying different posts.

[2] M.N.R.: "Nationalist Revolutionary Movement," led by Rafael García Bárcena, former student leader against the Machado dictatorship, who opposed the coup d'etat of Batista.

[3] O.A.: "Authentic Organization," one of the movements that fought against the Batista dictatorship.

only possible way to defeat Batista, we decided to join the July 26th Movement. I began working in the section of finances and information dissemination. Later, they named me head of Civil Resistance, an organization parallel to the July 26th, that brought together all the professionals, women and businessmen who, although not full activists in the 26th, raised funds, offered their homes for meetings, distributed leaflets and hid comrades who were being pursued. At that time, I worked at Shell. I took my *nom de guerre* out of the telephone book, looking for one that, like Shell, began with "S". That's how I became "Angel Sierra".

In 1957, Shell sent me to be the chief technician in the provinces of Matanzas, Las Villas and Camagüey. Batista had a close relationship with the president of the company, which turned out to be beneficial because it became a kind of safe haven that facilitated our movement. In January 1958, they designated me head of the July 26th Movement in Las Villas, a position I held until the end of the insurrection.

When Fidel came from Oriente in the caravan going to Havana, he stayed in the house of Marta's parents. We talked, and I told him that, since I had now fulfilled my duty, I would soon renew my work as an engineer to which he responded: "You think you have finished, but you don't realize that now is when the real revolution begins." Three days later, on January 9, they sent for me to go to the Presidential Palace and informed me that I had just been named Minister of Communications. I didn't even know where the Ministry of Communications was, or what it did. I thought, what in hell am I going to do now?

Ché's *polaquito*, the youngest minister

From that moment, I started a new stage of my life. The Ministry established Prensa Latina and Radio Habana Cuba, so that the Revolution would have an independent media and voice because at that time all of our communications went through the United States. We also created the program "The Revolution explains its work," which consisted of a weekly dialogue, in popular and common language, between an invited minister, the host of the program and the public. At the beginning, when I was looking for space for it, Goar Mestre, the owner of CMQ, the main TV station of the country, refused, saying that Cubans don't like political programs. When we occupied fourth place among programs of the widest audience, Mestre called me to say that the ministers

As Minister of Communications at the TV Program "The Revolution Explains its Work." Havana, 1959.

would not last long and that, when they took me off the air, I should go work for him as a host on Channel 6. But instead of doing that, in the mid 1960s, I went to work with Ché as a vice minister of Industries.

I have thousands of memories of Ché. Of the struggle in Las Villas, of the jokes we told in the early morning hours waiting to leave for voluntary work, of the chess games that he played with his bodyguards, singing softly and very out of tune the old tangos of his childhood, of the day my mother died when he spent the entire night talking to me until dawn. Later, he visited me when I was vice minister of the Central Planning Board, and we would lie on a rug on the floor, making plans for the world.

I remember the time I asked him to please talk to my father, who admired him so much. I explained to him that when all the Jews of Santa Clara left, my father had remained on account of me, without my having asked him to, because he understood that, if I was one of the revolutionary leaders, his duty was to support me with his presence. He had always been a man of action, and now he felt like his life was empty, without direction. Ché received him and asked him to talk about his experience in shoe making. My father suggested what could be done to increase shoe production. After listening to him, Ché

140

asked him to become the national supervisor of that industry —he helped my father find new meaning in his life.

When I learned that Ché was preparing to leave, I sent him a letter with Pachungo, signed "El Polaquito" (the "Little Pole"), which is what he always called me. I asked him to allow me to accompany him. He responded that he agreed, but that I should wait until they had already consolidated a territory because he wanted me as an administrator not as a guerrilla fighter. The news of his death destroyed us, but we got back up because the principal lesson Ché left us by his example is that he was an attainable paradigm and that struggle must continue until final victory.

Return to the land: a Jewish farmer

I told Fidel that I didn't want to continue working at the Ministry and that I liked the countryside, nature, and agriculture. He responded: "What a good idea; you begin tomorrow." He named me director of the main cattle development project of the Island. With Marta and our four children, I went to live in a small house, surrounded by fields, cows and horses. I had never before ridden a horse or herded cows. It wasn't easy, but on one trip to Turiguanó I found a book entitled *Learn to ride a horse in fifteen lessons*, by Count Renato Prodi, who had been the equestrian champion of Italy fifteen times. I read it in the car on the way home. I asked Manolo, the administrator —who always pointed out that I had never learned to ride— to saddle up the horse. We went for a ride, and he exclaimed in astonishment: "Chief, where did you learn to ride?" He was even more surprised when I told him: "In my car."

Since 1971, I have been working as Vice Minister of the Fishing Industry, in charge of production. I am also president of the Council of Collaborators of the José Martí Program and the Martí Club "Faustino Pérez." I have dedicated myself to spread the political thinking of Martí and Maceo, and I write when I can. I have already published two books. Surprisingly, there are people who visit Cuba who have read them and express an interest in meeting me. Others send emails or phone me. The books even served to put me in touch with the children of two of my father's brothers who survived the war. A few months ago, I received a call from an unknown cousin. He had bought the book in Australia and learned of my existence. There is no greater pleasure than —and Martí was also so right about this— to have a child, plant a tree and write a book. I have done all three things.

Now, I spend Sundays planting here in the yard of the house. Planting, I forget all of my problems. I go out at nine in the morning and leave at dusk. Here there are one hundred twenty banana trees, plus tomatoes and cucumbers that I planted.

If there is consciousness, there is hope.

When they invited me to Israel to see the possibilities of development in aquiculture, I marveled at the ultra modern and very productive techniques they had applied in the desert. I spent about fifteen days touring the country. At night we stayed in the Kibbutz. There, upon finding out that I was a Jewish Cuban revolutionary, they asked me a million questions. Naturally, they sympathized with the Revolution. There I saw up close something that Ché told me about when I began to work with him and he found out I was Jewish: "Have you heard of the kibbutz? I want you to know that it is the only place where true communism exists. We are centuries behind in comparison to them."

It was an experience. I went to the Museum of the Diaspora, to the Wall. I especially asked them to take me to the cemetery because I wanted to see the grave of Golda Meier, whom I admired a lot. I don't practice Judaism, but I don't hide my origins either. Judaism is a religion and a nation. There are two things I liked about the religion when I studied philosophy, searching for truth: That there is one God and God is a being like us, not a stone, not the rain, nor the sun; and the Ten Commandments, because it is the first time in the history of mankind that a religion instilled ethics in a very concrete way. In truth, I always wanted my children to know the history of the Jewish people, which is beautiful and often sad. They should know that they are descendants of Jews on their father's side.

All of my father's and mother's family were exterminated by the Nazis in the Holocaust, except one of my mother's brothers, Leon, who already lived in Cuba, and one of my father's brothers who joined the Red Army and escaped. When he returned to Poland, he found they had killed them all: the women, the elders, and the children.

When the Germans came, my grandfather —this I recount in my book— hid in the house of one of the peasants for whom he made shoes. Since in the first days nothing happened, he decided to go back to town. Then the Germans concentrated the entire Jewish population, and grandfather, with his granddaughter in his arms, hid under the wooden bridge that led to the house,

142

without knowing why or what for. Three days later he was found because of the cries of the girl, half dead with hunger and cold. They took away his clothes and made him walk naked through the town. Outside the town, at the side of the river, he dug his own grave. I was ten years old when I heard the story from my mother's lips, between sobs. I went to the bathroom and closed the door. "I imagined my grandfather as I remembered him, dignified, erect, serene, marching naked through the streets. I imagined his white body, now helpless in its nakedness, and I cried the bitterest tears I have ever cried."[4]

It is not possible for the world —and the Jews as part of it— to continue to live like that, between wars and assassinations. Rabin knew. He wanted and could have achieved peace, but they killed him. The Arab groups that bomb the kibbutz and blow up buses, and the fundamentalist Jews, who assassinated him and shoot at the faithful as they pray, with their fanaticism condemn millions of human beings. This "you kill me, I kill you" cannot go on. There are some opposed to it. My first cousin, who lives in Israel, supports the Cuban Revolution. His wife travels the world speaking about uniting Jews and Arabs. When I was in Israel, I participated as an invited guest in a meeting of one of the Jewish-Arab groups that fought to unite both peoples. This is important. If there is consciousness, there is hope.

---

[4] Enrique Oltuski, Pescando Recuerdos, Havana, 2004, p. 67.

With his mother in Poland.
1933.

His Bar Mitzvah in Santa Clara.
1943.

With Fidel Castro and Osvaldo Dorticós, president of
Cuba, at the carnival in Havana,1959.
Oltuski is at the far right.

Oltuski in his garden.
Havana, 2005.
(Photo by Maritza Corrales)

145

PART TWO
The Jews of the Central Highway

(Photo by Maritza Corrales)

David Tacher Romano

And you are Jewish....that still exists?

My family is *turca* on both sides. They came to Cuba at the end of the 1920s and dispersed throughout the Island as peddlers and shoemakers. First, they settled in Havana, later in Camagüey and, finally, in Santa Clara. My father, Isidoro Tacher Balestra, was brought as a child from Silivri, during the First World War. My mother, Virginia Romano Assa, was born in Cuba, but my maternal grandparents came from Istanbul.

I was born and raised, until I was nine, in the old part of Havana, very close to the Chevet Ahim Synagogue. We were a family of modest means and practically lived from day to day. I studied for two years at the *Albert Einstein* school in Miramar, from 1957-1958. David Pérez was the director.

Papa began as a peddler and later had a small workshop on Santa Clara Street, around the corner from the Synagogue. It was a jewelry shop where they made rings from old gold. He didn't have the heart for business. He sold on credit, but if people couldn't pay, he didn't collect. I only saw my father happy and free of economic problems after the Revolution when he went to work for the State.

149

On the weekends, for Sabbath, we went to the home of my paternal grandparents. We used to eat *borekas*, *fila*, rose marzipan, baklava, *dolma*, trushi (raw cabbage in salty water). Jewish life was very different than the one here, in the province. I remember that on Pesach, we sang the *Song of the Little Goat*: twelve Tribes of Israel, eleven Stars in Joseph's dream, the Commandments are ten...

Even though we were living in the interior, I made my Bar Mitzvah in Havana at Chevet Ahim. The people of the province who had young daughters moved to Havana so they could get them married and avoid marriages with gentiles, which at that time was very painful. Even a marriage between Sephardic and Ashkenazi Jews wasn't seen as a good thing.

My family was very respectful of traditions. They raised and educated their children with Jewish values and great love for the country that had embraced them. One of my uncles, Elías Tacher, fought in the war for Israel in 1948. My maternal grandfather, Víctor Romano, was the treasurer of the last board of directors of the community of Santa Clara and of the Synagogue on Independencia Street. They handed over the Synagogue, but asked that the cemetery remain. But it wasn't that way. They nationalized it and it slowly deteriorated. Papa became frightened and asked to be buried in Havana.

In 1959, Papa, who was a member of the July 26th Movement, was sent to Caibarién to run the match factory. Already, in those years, our parents didn't teach us. We were two different generations. For that reason, I never related to the Jewish families in Caibarién. Besides, I studied in Havana. There I met my wife, a Uruguayan Catholic who didn't want to convert, and we went to live in Santiago de Cuba where I studied economics. When Papa got sick, I returned to Santa Clara.

In Santa Clara, we were very few Jews, and we all needed each other. First, we began to connect up with other communities on the Island. We read a book called *The Jewish Book of Why*. We read it because we didn't know what to do. When we spoke to someone here in Santa Clara, he asked us in surprise: You are Jewish...that still exists?

We called our Community *Or Jadash* (New Light), because it was reborn on Rosh Hashanah in the year 5756.[1] We are all Sephardic Jews, but we pray with Ashkenazi *siddurims*. We are so few that we cannot establish those differences.

---

[1] 5756: the year in the Jewish calendar that is equivalent to 1995.

Before having a synagogue, we decided to restore the cemetery, which was in a state of total disrepair. A community that doesn't respect its dead doesn't respect itself.

When an exhibit about Anne Frank came to our community, we wanted to make a monument to the Holocaust. The desire became a dream that this city should have a remembrance of what fascism had been so all could see it and remember it.

As long as that hope survives, so will the Jews

For almost two years, North American friends of the *Cuba International Community Builders Project*, run by Miriam Saul, tried to acquire an object connected to the Shoah that would help us with this dream. One day, a woman arrived with a package: a stone from Chlodno Street in the Warsaw Ghetto, which had been donated by the Holocaust Museum in Washington. When she showed us the stone, we were all overcome by a very strong emotion. There was a deep silence; everyone was lost in his own thoughts. The dream had become a reality. Here we are, despite everything, ready to continue living with the principles and values that have been passed on from generation to generation, convinced that, at the end of the day, a brighter world will arise and a future generation will be able to experience that glorious time. As long as that hope survives, so will the Jews.

Our community has been gradually integrating into the life of the city and into all spheres of its social life. They called us from the Cultural House to come to a meeting of the ethnic minorities in Santa Clara, and there we were able to thank the people of the city who welcomed our parents and grandparents so openly, permitting them to settle in the area. Very modestly, we sponsored some prizes in an event of the Cine-Clubs. We displayed our traditional and religious objects in an exhibit of eastern cultures at the Museum, and we taught the museum guides so that they could explain our culture to visitors.

A silent meeting

One day, the Association for the Deaf asked us for some "noise makers" —the kind we use on Purim— to help some deaf and blind children by penetrating their world of silence through vibrations. Of course, we gave them to them as well as a *Megillat Esther*, so that they would know the story of the noise makers and what they meant to us. One day, they invited us to one of their Assemblies, and there I learned that our Purim noise makers had served not only to drown out the name of *Haman*,[2] but also to help others improve their lives. Together, we sang the National Anthem, we with our voices and they with their hands. There were no differences between us; we were living a unique moment joined by the hand of Silence.

What Torquemada didn't understand

In order to commemorate the Shoah, we held a regional Ecumenical Meeting between Christians and Jews, with the Bishop of Santa Clara and Dr. Miller, president of the community. We gave matzoh to the churches, and they set their tables with our matzoh. I think all religions are about love and shouldn't instill hatred of others. We loaned books to the Christians, and they told us: "But this is the same thing we do."

One last anecdote. Since we didn't have a place to study for our conversions, we gave classes in the Cathedral. A very fine detail: When the bishop entered where we were meeting, he was very thoughtful and put his crucifix in his pocket. I would like to peek through a hole and see our grandparents in heaven —what would they think of the fact that yesterday we were persecuted, but today we are united here as true brothers. I am thankful for the present understanding. Who would have said to Torquemada that a Jew and a Christian were going to join together to do something like this.

---

[2] On Purim, during the reading of the Meguillat Esther, every time the name of Haman or Aman —the prime minister of King Asuero of Persia, who attempted to kill all Jews in the realm— is mentioned those present make noise by shaking rattles or pounding the floor with their feet, so that, symbolically, his name is erased.

Youth of the Santa Clara Jewish Community
at an exhibit about Anne Frank.
2002.

Jewish cemetery of Santa Clara after its restoration.
2000.

Monument to the Holocaust in Santa Clara's Jewish cemetery.
2003.

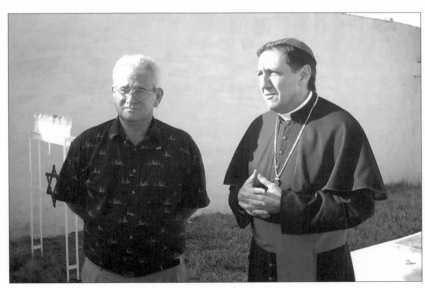

With the Bishop of Santa Clara at the dedication of the monument to the Holocaust.
2003.

(Photo by Tatiana Santos)

Moisés Naé

Chevet Ahim and its cemetery: among the first on the Island

My parents were *turcos*, descendants of Spaniards. My paternal grandparents, Moisés Naé and Rica Mizrahi, lived in *Iderné*,[1] and my maternal grandparents, Josef Assa and Bella Benador, in Smirna where Grandfather was a Rabbi. They lived there until they moved to *Iderné* where my parents met. In 1923, my mother's family came to Banes, a small town in Oriente province. Papa arrived on the steamship "Orinoco" in 1924 and went first to Sagua la Grande, in the central part of the country. Later, he went to Santiago de Cuba, the capital of Oriente where someone told him that there was a family in Banes with my mother's surname, and he went to look for her.

He started out as a peddler in Antilla, Mayarí, peddling throughout the northern region. Then, in 1927, he opened a store that he called EL ZEPPELÍN, because at the time those air balloons were the rage. Later on, when I was an adult, papa transferred the store to me, and we changed the name to CASA DE

---

[1] Edirne in the diction of the interviewee

LOS RETAZOS (REMNANT HOUSE). I was in it until 1961, when it was nationalized. I had worked in all the stores of Banes, always as a salesman, which is what I liked. I stayed here. I never wanted to leave.

At the beginning, the Jewish businesses in Banes didn't open on Saturdays. At least Papa and my uncles never worked on the Sabbath. Nor did they allow anyone to light the fire. They paid a boy to do it. When the economic situation of the country became very difficult, we were forced to open the store on the Sabbath, but they always closed on Rosh Hashanah and Kippur.

There were more *turcos* than *polacos* in Banes. None of the *turcos* came from Arab countries. Nevertheless, when the Society held its first meeting on July 29, 1926, it took place in the house of the *polaco* Pesah Heller. We belonged to Chevet Ahim, the association of the Sephardic Jews in Havana, and for that reason we named the Society La Unión Israelita Chevet Ahim. All the founders, except Heller and Dubinski, were *turcos*, and at the first board meeting, only Dubinski was elected a member. The president was Moisés Pardo, and my uncle Isidoro Assa, the General Secretary. Afterwards, they set it up in the Kal, and later in my Grandfather's house. There was a department where they had the *Sefer Torah*, the *Teba*, everything. When Grandfather died, the only *Jazanim* left were Alberto and Isidoro Assa. They were the ones who read the Torah.

We celebrated the eight days of Pesach. The first and second nights we did in my grandfather's house. He invited many of the merchants who usually came to town to sell. The matzoh was sent from Havana by express.

On Purim, Papa ordered caramel and mint sweets that were shaped like pretzels and made by a Jamaican woman. For the *birí*,[2] sometimes they brought Rabbi Nissim Maya or my grandfather did it. I made my Bar Mitzvah in Santiago. Since we didn't have Jewish schools, we studied in the regular schools here. I went to Los Amigos, which was Quaker, but Papa always read the Bible to me at home. When the Society in Banes closed, we joined the one in Santiago de Cuba and later the one in Havana.

Mama loved to cook. Papa slaughtered the chickens because there wasn't a *shochet*, but everything was kosher. She made *takayú* (a pastry of eggplant), *borrequitas* of cheese, *dolmaika* stuffed with tomatoes and peppers, pickles made with sugar and lemon, *trushi* (raw cabbage in salty water), *baklava*...

---

[2] *Brit Milá*, as it is pronounced by the *turcos*.

The need to have a cemetery arose very quickly on October 1 of that same year, 1926. Its construction was finished in 1927. Primitivo Silva[3] generously donated a parcel of two thousand square yards. Jews from nearby areas were buried here. After the Revolution, as the land area was very large and the number of persons buried very few, they asked us to consider giving up a part for a Monument to the Martyrs. We agreed to give them half, with the promise that they would restore the rest, but they didn't. One day a man from Santiago de Cuba came and closed it.

I moved my grandparents and my aunt to Havana. Only the son of the Epelbaum family remains here. When Mama died, the cemetery didn't exist anymore. Some friends gave me their pantheon. Her remains were there for twenty years until I took them to Miami where my father, who had died while visiting family, was buried. So, now, finally, they are together again.

---

[3] Primitivo Silva, a wealthy Catholic neighbor in Banes.

Acta

En el pueblo de Banes, siendo las ocho de la noche del día 29 de Julio de Mil Novecientos veinte y seis, previa citación en la Casa del Sr Pesah Heller, situada en la Calle D número cinco, los Señores Moisés Pardo, Rafael Matatia, Alberto Adato, Roberto Albala, Alberto Eskinazi, Alberto Vae, Lauro Pardo, Marco Cohen, Henrique Abut, José Chalom, Jacobo Pardo, Jacobo Matatia, Salomon Benbaras, Isidoro Asa, Samuel Maya, Dionisio Abut, Mayr Dubinski y Pesah Heller, al objeto de tratar sobre la constitución de una Sociedad Benéfica Mutua y Hebrea, de la cual forman parte todos los Hebreos residentes en esta localidad, idea iniciada por los Señores Moisés Pardo, Henrique Abut, Mayr Dubinski y Rafael Matatia.

Abierta el acta por la Comisión iniciadora se concedió la palabra al Señor Moisés Pardo, quien explicó a los concurrentes el objeto de aquella junta que no era otra si no el de constituir una asociación Benéfica Mutua, entre todos los elementos Hebreos de la comarca, la cual brindara a sus componentes ayuda protección y robustez bajo los principios de Unión y fraternidad que deben reunir en toda Sociedad y a fin de poder ejercer todos los ritos y costumbres

Document recording the founding of the Unión Israelita
Chevet Ahim of Banes.
July 29th, 1926.

With his father in the store "The Zeppelin," Banes, Cuba.
1940s.

Bond sold to raise funds for the construction of the Jewish cemetery in Banes.
1927.

(Photo by Maritza Corrales)

Raquel Romano Mechulam

Those people came and took everything without paying

My parents were from Galata, a neighborhood in Constantinople. Papa came to Cuba from Turkey in 1925, when he was twenty years old. His mother sent him because my grandfather had died in one of those internal wars they had over there, and she didn't want her son also to be killed. Papa was the oldest and already of age for military service. So, he embarked for Cuba because his future brother-in-law was living in Camagüey.[1] He and Mama were already engaged. She followed him in 1926, and they married here. They had four children: my sister, who was a laboratory technician and died very young; myself, born in 1930; and two brothers, one who is a doctor living in Havana, and the other who was a merchant and a teacher. All are buried here, in our cemetery.

Papa began working with my uncle and was a peddler for many years. They went out with a bundle on their shoulders and walked the street. Now, I don't

---

[1] Camagüey: capital of the province of the same name. One of the first towns founded during the Spanish Conquest in this part of the Island.

know how they did it with this heat. They sold on credit in the city and nearby towns. First, he peddled fabric, then jewelry. Later, he went back to fabric for a short time until he opened a tiny variety store in the Santa Rosa Market in 1958. He usually bought merchandise from my uncle, or he brought it from Havana. He sold everything: soaps, perfume. My brother, the doctor, was then in high school and used to help him so he could leave for lunch.

It was a very difficult life. During Batista's regime, the police took things. There were days when Papa hadn't sold even thirty pesos, and those guys would come in with their hard faces and take things without paying. After 1959, merchandise became scarce for the peddlers as well as for the stores, and Papa had to close the store in 1962.

República and San José: the streets preferred by the Jews

The stores were primarily located on República Street. For example, CASA JAIME was on República and Santa Rita. I don't remember the owner's name —it was a strange Polish surname. Today, the store is a *shopping*,[2] but you can still read the original sign engraved in the floor. There were others on Estrada Palma. My uncle owned the FARMACIA MECHULAM on Avellaneda.

San José was the street preferred by the Jews. I still live there. Some Ashkenazi and Sephardic Jews also lived on Santa Rosa and Palma —all in this area. At the beginning, they lived wherever they could, but when they found a house closer, they moved. I was born on San Esteban, one of my brothers on San Martín and the other on Pobres. When my parents improved their situation, we moved to San José.

I have my religion, and you must respect it

In 1960, I started to work in the traffic section of the Telephone Company. After six years, I was promoted to head of shift, and I was there until 1993 when I retired. I was the girlfriend of one of the engineers in the company, but his mother, who was from Camagüey and very Catholic, demanded that I convert. I said that I was Jewish, that I had my religion and if I respected hers, she had to respect mine. In the end, we broke off the relationship.

For Sabbath, mama lit toothpicks with cotton wicks soaked in oil. It wasn't like now that they light candles. Every Friday, she lit the oil lamp. On Yom

---

[2] *Shopping*: Cuban name for the stores that operate in freely convertible currency.

Maimonides Library
of the Jewish Community.
Camagüey, 2003.
(Photo by Maritza Corrales)

Kippur they dressed up; they got very elegant for the Holidays. Mama sang Turkish songs, and sometimes when she could get music from there on the radio, she would dance.

The Ashkenazi Jews had their community on San Esteban. Ours was on Pobres Street, but we had a common cemetery. There was no bakery or kosher butcher shop here like there was in Havana where we went to buy salami, black olives, matzoh. There were some very delicious things. At home, we ate chicken, turkey and fish, but nothing with lard or pork. Everything was cooked in oil. Mama made sweets, turnovers and stuffed eggplant with cheese and potatoes, sponge cakes. But over the years, the traditional cooking was lost.

After the triumph of the Revolution, the important people of the community emigrated. The elderly who stayed have died and we, the youngest, did not have a very active life in the synagogue. So, the memory began slipping away; it was being lost. But there was always something, that little thread that never broke, like the arrival of the products for Pesach. At that moment we always reaffirmed that we were Jews, and that we belonged to the Jewish people.

Our community still conserved the books of the Minutes of the Society *Tiferet Israel,* which was founded in 1927. Albojaire gave them to his daughter to keep and asked her to treat them with the utmost care. In 1994, we began to regroup ourselves in Albojaire's home, in the Levy's house and later here. We are now 30 families. We have a youth group of *rikudim,* a small school and a modest library so that all may learn about our history.

Former building used by Tiferet Israel
Synagogue in the 1930s.

Dedication of the Camagüey Synagogue.
1998.

164

(Photo by Tatiana Santos)

Julio Rodríguez Ely

"Julito the *polaco*"

My family's story is the same as that of all Jewish immigrants. My maternal grandfather came from Turkey, Kirklisse or Kirkisiá, as they called it, with my grandmother and my mother's older sister, Sarah. When they landed, they settled in Camagüey where my grandfather, Rafael Ely Levy, was one of the founders of the Jewish community, the one who bought the cemetery in the 1920s. They lived on Pobres Street, close to the synagogue. Grandfather was a businessman. Uncle Salvador, who was born in Camagüey, worked in some stores.

My uncle Isaac is the youngest and was born in Havana. First, he worked in some stores owned by Jews on Muralla Street. Afterwards, he had a jewelry store across from the tobacco factory on Egido Street, called EL ORIENTE, in partnership with a Spaniard. Later, he opened another jewelry store on Muralla. "Iche," which is how the *polacos* called someone named Isaac, was a *turco*, but he married Clarita who was a *polaca*. My other aunt was married to a non-Jewish Cuban, a ball player named Adriano Aguilar or "Machito" as he was known in the world of Jai Alai.

My paternal grandfather, Julio Rodríguez Bembasat, was in the military in Turkey where, as you know, they no sooner ended one war when they started another. It seems that Grandfather got tired of it, deserted and came to America. That was before 1915, more or less. He left my father, who was still a child, in Turkey with my grandmother. He came to Caibarién,[1] where a first cousin was living. During that time, there was an epidemic in Turkey and my grandmother, the wife of my grandfather the soldier, died. Papa stayed under the care of my great grandmother. As it was common for cousins to marry each other to perpetuate the family fortune and the race, they brought over a cousin from Turkey, Violeta Rodríguez Behar, to marry my grandfather. As a consequence of this custom, we have some in our family that are named Levy Levy Levy.[2]

Grandfather sent for papa, who was then eleven. He arrived in Cuba, entering by way of Tiscornia. He brought heavy winter clothes, which were useless here, and uncle Vitalio threw them into the sea. He found his father, who had remarried, in Caibarién together with his three new brothers. The first business that Grandfather set up was a partnership with a cousin. They named it La Cuba Libre (The Free Cuba). It was on Máximo Gómez Street, one of the commercial streets in Caibarién along with Céspedes Street. When the partnership broke up, he set up La Bandera Cubana (The Cuban Flag), a clothing and fabric store on Máximo Gómez between Jiménez and Falguero Streets.

Papa didn't want to be a businessman. He wanted to be a musician, but Grandfather wouldn't let him because he said that musicians were lazy bums. He never wanted to give him the twenty cents that the book cost so he could study. So, Papa forced me to become a musician, and what I wanted to be was a baseball player. That's life. Of music, what I liked most was the piano, but in small towns there were a lot of prejudices, and they didn't believe that men should be pianists. So Papa decided I should learn to play saxophone. He bought a piano for my sister. She didn't like it, although she had talent. Later, the piano got eaten by termites, and I transformed it into a piece of furniture with the star of David and a menorah. That's life.

---

[1] Caibarién: port on the sea north of Camajuaní, in the present province of Villa Clara.
[2] In Cuba, as in Spain, people have two surnames: their father's and mother's first surnames. After marriage, it is customary for the wife to keep her surnames. Since children assume the first surnames of both of their parents, the surnames might be the same if their parents are related.

José Gorión, a Jew who "invented his life story"

In the 1930s, Papa went to Havana to look for work, but at that time, they didn't hire foreigners. Since the old man didn't have an accent, he changed his name and called himself José Gorión and said that he was from Santa Cruz del Sur and that all his personal papers had been lost in a storm that leveled the town. That's how he invented the story of his life in Havana and got a job as a laborer wielding a pick and shovel on a construction crew that was building the National Amphitheater.

But, you know, the Jews have a charm. It's true that they can make money out of a little spot of earth, with sacrifice, naturally. The other workers got up at five in the morning and Papa at three. He made coffee and sold it to the others. It was hard work. He had circulatory problems from so much walking in the fields with a package of clothes over his shoulder and a small suitcase in the other hand or with a little cart of clothes. If they didn't have money to pay him, they gave him chickens or eggs. After things got better, he got a motorcycle and later a car.

Finally, my father not only took over my grandfather's store, but he also started a business selling mattresses, jewelry and bicycles on credit. He bought gold in the countryside. He remained a peddler until, in the 1960s, they prohibited sales on credit. When they nationalized the store, there were a lot of people who owed him money.

My uncle, who had studied Commercial Sciences, worked for the government and was a founder of Plantas Mecánicas, a factory in Santa Clara. However, Papa, being the eldest, had to work and wasn't able to study past sixth grade.

The communities of Caibarién and Remedios

In the decade of the 1930s, there was a community made up of Jews from Remedios and Caibarién. By its name, *Bikur Holim* (Aid to the Sick), we knew that they were carrying out beautiful communitarian work. I remember the metal boxes I used to see in Jewish homes that had an inscription and a map of the Holy Land, which were for collecting money to help needy persons. My grandfather told me that part of the money was sent to Palestine, before and after the founding of the State of Israel.

There were two stores in addition to ours and LA CUBA LIBRE, which Moisés Rodríguez had kept on Máximo Gómez Street: CASA JACOBO (owned by Jacobo Hasday), and CASA ISIDORO (owned by Isidoro Rodríguez Hasday, another of

Bikur Holim of Caibarién and Remedios.
1931.

Papa's cousins). Yoya and Israel Chiprut and the Levy family also lived here. Now the only ones that remain are the Rodríguez (us) and the Levy family.

Since there was no Hebrew school here, we studied in the best schools available. My cousins in Havana were able to study in Jewish schools. I went to school at the Progresiva de Cárdenas, which was Presbyterian, because the other private school in Caibarién was the one run by Marista priests, which had nothing to do with our tradition whatsoever.

My family wasn't orthodox, but we didn't eat pork. They cooked the typical dishes: *borekas*, *yaprake* (cabbage with ground meat), *agristada* (brain soup with lemon), and breaded sliced tongue. Every year, Papa brought Jewish food from Havana. Maybe we weren't more religious because the synagogues were so far away. On Yom Kippur we went to the one in Santa Clara and for Pesach to the one on Inquisidor Street, the Chevet Ahim, in Old Havana. Mama's family was more religious. They also lived in Havana and had more possibilities there. I remember that Grandfather took us to the kal for the *Hashkavah*. It's like the *yizkor* of the Ashkenazi, but it's not the same because the name of the dead person is not said.

There were some things they didn't accept. The day my aunt Berta married a Cuban Catholic, my grandfather tore up his clothes. He used a Turkish expression, *almina*, and tore up his clothes with his hands. My aunt was the first to break the tradition, but she was very happy in her marriage. They even named my cousin Barbara, for Saint Barbara.

In the town, they call us the *polacos*. I am "Julito, the *polaco*." My wife, who converted a short time ago, is called "The professor, the *polaca*" even though the community here was and is entirely Sephardic. However, at school in Cárdenas, they did call me "*the turco*." But that's not so strange; they call the Jewish cemetery in Santa Clara "the cemetery of the Syrians."

The cemeteries of the "sirios" in Camajuaní and Santa Clara

When my little sister died, the cemetery of Santa Clara was already in total disrepair. There wasn't any fence, and people took materials from the graves to build. Grandfather Julio's grave was the only one left standing. In 1977, my father died and since he was a mason, he was buried in a plot belonging to the San Juan Lodge. So, we decided to build a pantheon in the Catholic cemetery in Caibarién. We thought, even though it was Christian, it would be cared for better. We also buried León Dueñas there; he had served as our Rabbi and had also been a soldier in the Turkish army after which he studied at the Sorbonne. We buried the Levy family, my uncle and my mother there as well.

With empty hands and a hopeful heart

The Jews, our parents, didn't have a high educational level. They came to Cuba with only the clothes on their backs, and everything they did, they did with a sense of sacrifice and love of family. They arrived with their hands empty but their hearts full of love and hope. They instilled in us a love for work, family values, and very beautiful sentiments of patriotism and gratitude to the country that took them in and which they made their own. For example, I went to study in Cárdenas, and even though Papa could pay the whole tuition, he wanted me to get a partial scholarship. That meant that every afternoon I had to sweep around the front of the building where I studied in order to, symbolically, pay the difference.

Here, in Caibarién, after school and my classes at the music academy, I went to work in the store. It didn't matter that I was the owner's son. He would just as easily send me to collect bills on bicycle as make me clean the windows, and

Julio playing the sax in Caibarién´s park.
2004.
(Photo by June Safran)

he paid me, so that I would learn the value of money. I remember that Papa always said to me: "Julito, don't spend it all, save."

After the Revolution, even though they took their stores, Papa and Uncle Isidoro decided not to leave Cuba. They were of a certain age and didn't want to emigrate again. A funny thing happened when they nationalized the store. The person in charge told Uncle Isidoro that his store was going to be transferred to the hands of the people, and he responded: "That seems like a good idea to me, let's go distribute it." And he began to throw the merchandise outside. The police came and arrested him because he was throwing all the clothes onto the street.

Thanks to papa's insistence I have two skills: I am a musician and a teacher. As a musician I have played with jazz groups and in the Municipal Band of Caibarién. As a teacher, I began in 1966 in a secondary school. After I got my degree, I was one of the founders of the schools in the countryside. I have been a department head, school principal and regional director of teaching methodology. I spent thirty-three years at the Ministry of Education. And now, the only thing I do is play the saxophone.

170

Brit ceremony in Chevet Ahim.
Havana, 1951.

Customers in front of his father's store "The Cuban Flag."
Caibarién, 1956.

171

With his father.
Caibarién, 1952.

Julio and Sarah Berta in front of the family pantheon
in the Catholic cemetery in Caibarién.
2004.

(Photo by Maritza Corrales)

172

A Jewish furniture born from the piano.
Caibarién, 2004.
(Photo by June Safran)

Observing the Sabbath with members of the Jewish community.
Caibarién, 2004.
(Photo by June Safran)

173

Orestes Larios Zaak

We lived on Pobres[1] Street and we were really very poor

My two maternal grandparents were Jewish. Grandfather, Saúl Zaak, was from a small town in Lithuania, on the Polish border. Although he was Lithuanian, he always considered himself Polish. My grandmother, Doba Potazsnik, was from Vilna, the "Jerusalem of Europe" that the Nazis practically wiped out during the war. My grandmother's entire family died in the Holocaust. My grandfather came to Cuba in 1923 and, with a lot of hard work and the help of some Jewish friends who had immigrated earlier and had a piece of land in Florida, in the province of Camagüey,[2] he was able to bring grandmother from Poland the following year. They were married in Havana and settled in Camagüey. They were a little like gypsies.

Grandfather was a blacksmith and he had a smith shop on Verges Street. Perhaps I got the artist in me from him. He made some pieces in stainless steel

---

[1] The Spanish word "pobres" means poor in English.
[2] Florida: a village in the old province of Camagüey. Today, it belongs to the province of Ciego de Ávila.

and some beautiful spurs for horses. He could forge a plow as well as a tiny pair of earrings, which he bartered to a friend in Florida. My uncles followed the tradition and also became blacksmiths.

At the beginning, my grandmother and aunt were peddlers, street venders. They went up and down the streets selling little things. Later, grandmother had a mobile shop with threads and needles that she would set it up in the doorway of the house, a kind of display case on metal wheels. Even during the most difficult times after the Revolution, they continued to peddle. They stood on lines (colas)[3] to acquire products; they bought small things like combs, buttons, and razor blades and then would sell what they bought for five cents more.

We lived on Pobres Street, at the intersection with San José. The name of the street suited us because we were really very poor. My grandmother had her little stand there. Everyone called it "Dora's store," which was the name most similar to Doba. A majority of the Jews lived in this neighborhood, and, over time, a good portion of the small stores on República Street came to belong to Jews. The people in Camagüey, just like those in Havana, called them *polacos* or *turcos*.

There were two synagogues in the neighborhood on the same street: one Sephardic and the other Ashkenazi. There is only one Ashkenazi family left in Camagüey, mine, because my brother and my nieces emigrated to Israel. There is also another Polish family in Nuevitas. The majority of the communities in the interior were *turcos*. There are two families here that are Turkish from their maternal side, the Romano's and the Levy's. The others descend from more distant relatives.

Mama married my father who was Spanish, but she made a Jewish life because my grandmother insisted. I remember that when I was a child, they took me to synagogue. After 1959, when the majority of the Jews had left, religious life, in general, declined in the country, and it became more and more difficult for Mama to maintain the tradition.

In Camagüey I began to know my Judaism

I was born in 1953; so, I was six years old when the Revolution began. From the time I was a child, I was always attracted to art. I was one of the first

---

[3] Because of the scarcity of products it was necessary to stand on line ("hacer cola") in front of stores in order to buy things.

students enrolled[4] in the Provincial Art School of Camagüey and the National Art School in Havana. In addition, I also graduated in Art Education from the José Martí Superior Institute of Pedagogy.

When I finished my studies, I did my social service in Havana at the Experimental Studio of the FAR,[5] where I carried out a project consisting of painting the military in their daily life, in combat, with my own style of socialist realism, more photographic and hyper-realist. However, when I was in the war in Africa between 1977 and 1978, first in Eritrea and later in the Ogaden desert, I didn't paint anything, although I still remember it.

I don't paint Jewish subjects. I participated in the first exhibit of Cuban and Cuban-American Jews in the United States with works depicting the preservation of the environment and ecology, which was the work I was doing at the time. In 2000, I won first prize from the World Food Program of the FAO (Food and Agricultural Organization of the United Nations), with a painting dealing with sustainable development and environmental protection. That year, I was the first Latin American to design the logo of HSL, an important communications company of Genoa.

As you see, I was born in Camagüey, I studied in Havana, and I became fully involved in the activities of the Revolution. I was in the war in Africa, and I have traveled and resided in Europe. I am very restless. Although I inherited something of the gypsy from my grandparents, I always return to Cuba, to Camagüey. This is my spiritual refuge, where I began to know my Judaism.

---

[4] The interviewee uses the word "becado," the literal meaning of which is " having received a scholarship," but in post-Revolutionary Cuba, it refers to students who live at the school while studying. Since education is free for all Cubans, from primary through post graduate, including living expenses, students who graduate from university level schools are obligated to give two years of social service in their field of study.
[5] FAR: Ministry of the Revolutionary Armed Forces.

Identification card that
entitled poor people
to receive medical services.
1949.

With his grandfather in Camagüey.
1970s.

Still life painting by Orestes.
(Photo by Michel Coviellas)

(Photo by Maritza Corrales)

Isidoro Barlía Loyarte

A love immortalized in stones

Papa, Sanjún (Salomón) Barlía Bensusen, was born in Rodemstam, Turkey, in 1914. He was ten years old when he arrived in Cuba in 1924 with my grandparents Isidoro and Violeta (Nissan and Zimbul) and his three brothers. The family settled in Camagüey, but life turned out to be very difficult there, and they came to Sancti-Spíritus.[1] They looked for the settlements of Spaniards from the Canary Islands in Cabaiguán, an area very rich in tobacco and sugar cane. Here, they opened a clothing and accessory store on Independencia Street, in front of the statue of Judas.

One of the brothers became a salesman and was always wandering from one country to another, until he went to Puerto Rico in the 1950s. Another opened a store in the 1940s, also on Independencia Street, and a cousin opened a business called EL SELLITO COMERCIAL. They initiated an original system of

---

[1] Sancti-Spiritus: a town in south-central Cuba, founded by the Spanish conquerors in 1514. Today, it is the capital of the province with the same name.

sales promotion, up to then unknown in Cuba: for each purchase, they gave you a series of stamps and a book. When you filled the book, you had the right to a product free of charge, depending on the type of book.

Papa first married Elisa Behar Tacher, a woman from Turkey he had met in Camagüey. She died in childbirth in 1946, and that inspired one of those love stories that are found in cemeteries. Papa built the most attractive grave in the Sephardic Cemetery in Havana, with its little angels (now disappeared), truncated column and crown (also lost), and a poem that he wrote for her. A little before Elisa died, he built this house, which he named VILLA ELISA. It's not just any house, but a Jewish home, which you can tell by all its six pointed stars.

After my mother, Zoila Oyarte López, converted, they were married. I was born in 1952. We didn't have a synagogue here. Oddly, the community of Sancti-Spíritus (some fifteen families) was always linked to the communities of Caibarién, Camajuaní and Camagüey, but not to Santa Clara. Maybe this was because of family ties or because there were many Ashkenazi in that community. I don't know. Even our Jews asked to be buried in the Camagüey cemetery or in the one in Camajuaní. So much so, that it wasn't until I was an adult that I found out that there is a cemetery in Santa Clara. Usually, we went to Camagüey or to Havana for the High Holidays, and to Caibarién just to visit. There was a dance hall in the community of Havana which I went to in the 1970s on Prado Street, next to the Arab Union.

At home, we observed the Sabbath, and we celebrated Pesach. I was circumcised on the eighth day by a mohel they brought from Havana. Papa didn't permit anyone to buy pork or shrimp. He fasted on *Tishah B'Av* and Kippur. But our Judaism centered on Yom Kippur, which was the most sacred day. I remember that once I was playing sports, and I forgot. My father was furious. Papa was very dogmatic; he never explained anything.

Community life as such, didn't exist. I don't think that they knew much about the precepts of Judaism. I don't remember a single activity for *Shavuot* or *Sukkot*. There was no Jewish school. Those that could, sent their children to the best private schools in the city, which were those of the Presbyterians or the priests. I studied at the Presbyterian School, but all of my cousins went to La Salle.

The families in Sancti-Spíritus were divided by rank. Those who were well off went to Camagüey and Havana for the holidays and weddings, and they followed some traditions, even though their children were being educated

The outside gate at Villa Elisa.
Sancti Spíritus, 2003.
(Photo by Maritza Corrales)

in Catholic schools. The poorest slowly moved away from Jewish life. In the provinces, there was a time when Judaism was practiced very independently, within the family. In Havana, life was different.

After 1959, only two Hebrew families remained in Sancti-Spíritus: ours and that of Samuel and Victoria Saltiel. Naturally, Jewish life practically disappeared. My courtship and marriage to Daisy, who is not Jewish, created problems with my father. He had chosen a bride for me in Havana, a niece of León Baruch. Papa had made mother convert before he married her, but in 1975, it wasn't so easy to convert. Daisy had to go to Havana many times to meet with Abraham Berezniak[2] who made her fast, gave her books on religion and got her interested in knowing about Judaism.

When Papa died in 1978, the only link we had left were the monthly dues that we paid to Adath Israel, and the products we bought for Pesach. It's been a long time since Abraham came to see if there were babies to be circumcised. There was one, but his mother didn't want to do it. We returned to the Patronato when the Jewish community re-emerged, and everyone in the provinces was

---

[2] Abraham Berezniak, in charge of the orthodox synagogue Adath Israel of Havana. His interview appears in Part Three.

taken care of by them, instead of by Adath Israel. In 1996, Feldhandler, who was from the community of Cienfuegos, came to see us. He brought the first books and invited us to a Purim celebration. In 1997, Robin Senderowitz of the *Joint* gave us the idea to form our own community, *Javaiá* that began to function in 1996. My daughter Ana went door to door, knocking on those of everyone who was of Jewish origin. She got together a group of children from eight to ten years old, who are today's youngsters. Now, we are twelve families, with forty seven members. The majority have not yet converted.

The Jews didn't have time to get the bread

We have a little school, the *Maguen David*, which functions on Sunday mornings, with seven children between three and nine years of age. We tell them about the different holidays. One day, it was Pesach, and someone mentioned the word *pizza*, and Claudia, my granddaughter, jumped up and said that on Pesach we don't eat pizza and we don't eat bread. There was an Israeli with us who asked her "why?" And Claudia answered: "Because the Jews left Egypt very fast, and they didn't have time to go get the bread."[3]

We have now begun a course for young adults, which eighteen people attend. Each semester we give a new course. The young people have a space, they study and they dance. With the help of the *Cuba-America Jewish Mission* of San Francisco, directed by June Safran, we formed a dance group of Rikudim. We all work for the advancement of the community. I am the president, but I continue working as a mathematics teacher at the Facultad Obrera Campesina.[4] My four children, my wife and the youth are the driving force of Jewish life, to keep its presence forever. This house, with its stars of David, is everyone's home, the meeting place, the Synagogue of Sancti-Spíritus.

---

[3] In Cuba today, bakeries give out bread daily on the ration system although one can buy it as well. It is a daily routine to go to the bakery every day "to go get the bread."

[4] Worker Peasant Faculty: A high school level faculty created for the training of workers and peasants who worked during the day.

His father Salomon, in front of the monument to Elisa. Sephardic Jewish cemetery of Guanabacoa. 1947-48.

At his son's Bar Mitzvah, Beth Shalom Synagogue. Havana, 2004.

(Photo by Tatiana Santos)

183

(Photo by June Safran)

Nissim Franco

"Misimico": the last of the *turcos*

I got the nickname, "Misimico," because I was very naughty and always ran in the streets with my friends. My mother would shout to me: Nissim, Nissi! She spoke a bit differently, and the neighbors understood her to say "misi." So, since I was very small, they started to call me "Misi," "Misimico," and it stuck.

In 1960, Papa was not well, and I didn't want to leave him. When they nationalized the shoe store, a friend found me a job in the sugar refinery, in the mills. I worked for four years shoveling and another four on the conveyor belt feeding sugar into the mill. I will tell you an anecdote. One day the pressure started to go down and down. The comrades shouted that I should leave because it was dangerous. But I kept feeding in sugar until the pressure went back up again. The Party congratulated me and awarded me a medal for being the "best worker of the conveyor and rake." Now I no longer work, and I receive a small pension from Social Security and what the B'nei B'rith and the community send me from Havana: a little money and the things for Pesach.

My parents came from Constantinople, very young: my father was sixteen, and my mother a little younger. They met and married there. Papa was born in 1901. He left Turkey for fear of the war. He landed in Cuba in 1918 and settled in Camajuaní[1] because he had relatives here who had immigrated earlier and had told him about the place.

At the beginning, he sold clothes in Yaguajay and Meneses. He was a peddler, with his "sack on his back." Later, Isidoro and Israel Franco, who worked in shoes, encouraged him to go into shoemaking. Papa put it this way: "I am going to set up a shoemaking shop and see what happens." But, really, he didn't make any money until I began to cut for him. I had been working with Isidoro and Israel who paid me two *kilos* a day and one *peseta* a week.[2] The cutter that Papa had did things aimlessly. Not me, I was a pattern maker and the preparer. I made innovations in the clasps and forty other things. With what Papa earned, he bought four houses and paid for my brother's studies so he could become an accountant. The store was called LA CAMPESINA, and it still exists today on Boulevard Street.

Papa died in 1966. He is buried in the Hebrew cemetery of Guanabacoa, head to head with Jacobo Susi, the *Jajam* of our Kal.

The Benei Israel cemetery: Hilda Franco and Marcos Barrocas

The story of my sister is a very sad story. Mama said to me: "Look after the baby in the crib because I am washing clothes." But when I went to see her, she was already dead. She was only seven or eight months old. That was 1932.

Some guys tricked Marcos into going out to the sugar plantation to buy old gold, and they knifed him in the back. They killed him to get his money and jewels. However, we never had problems because we were *turcos* or *sirios*, as they called us. We formed part of the village.

The Jewish community of Camajuaní was fully integrated into the social life and customs of the Cuban people. Already, in 1929, it had formed a kite team with the Chinese and had built a float entitled *"The Queen of Turkey"* that represented one of the rival neighborhoods. The float went out escorted by the rural army guard because they said the jewels the woman wore were all genuine. I was only three at the time, but I always remember them talking about it. I am

---

[1] Camajuaní: a town in the north of the central province of Las Villas.
[2] Kilo: a popular word for one cent. Peseta: twenty cents.

seventy-six years old now and have excellent memory. I remember even the charts of mammals that they showed us in eighth grade.

Here we had a Society, *Benei Israel*, and a Kal. Papa took us to the Kal. When I was small, the Kal was on Fomento Street. Afterwards, they moved it to the end of the town. Papa was always a member of the Directors of Benei Israel, as treasurer, general secretary and president until he died. From the 1950s on, I also participated, first as an alternate director and later as vice president and president. During Pesach we all got together and ate *fango*, ground raisins, a paste Mama made that we ate with meat. My family observed the Sabbath. On Friday, my mother cleaned the whole house.

All our countrymen were in business selling clothes and shoes, mostly in stores although a few were peddlers. There was LA BANDERA CUBANA, owned by Alfredo Franco, Policart's cafeteria, Jaime Maya's tobacco shop, and EL CAÑÓN ALEMÁN that was owned by the *polaco*, Sansanowitz. There were many Jewish families: Franco, Dueñas, Maya, Behar, Policart, Sansanowitz, Pinto, Motola, Susi, Lew, Barrocas... many. But none remain. Only me.

"The Queen of Turkey" float, Camajuaní parrandas.
1929

(Courtesy of René Batista)

Jewish cemetery of Camajuaní.
2004.

(Photo by Maritza Corrales)

(Photo by Tatiana Santos)

Donna Albalah Levy

From Istanbul to Santiago de Cuba: the last immigrant

I was born in Istanbul in 1937, in a Sephardic Jewish family that had been established for centuries in Turkey. I was raised in a neighborhood where even the butcher was Jewish. Behind the house was a factory where they made matzoh for the whole city. In most of the countries in which they settle Jews live in a particular area: the rich among the rich, the middle class among the middle class, and the poor among the poor. There were various neighborhoods in Istanbul: Pera, Galata.

We first lived in Pera, and later, in 1950, we moved to the outskirts. We were a well-to-do family, all living in Turkey, except an uncle who had gone to Palestine in the 1930s. After the founding of the State of Israel in 1948, a good part of my family moved there even though life in Israel was not the best for immigrants. Mainly, people went because of economic difficulties, or because their children had gone as youngsters, guided by Zionist ideals.

Our house was next to the Kal. In Turkey, it wasn't like it is here. Jewish life wasn't centered in the synagogue. Only my father went to the synagogue. On

189

Fridays, everything in the neighborhood closed at four in the afternoon, and peddlers used to go out on the street to sell flowers. I have a very beautiful memory from my childhood: Mama cleaning the house, cooking the meals, and Papa coming through the door on Friday night with a bouquet of flowers in his hand, to await the Sabbath. This was the customary ritual every week.

The school was a block and a half from home. I studied there the first six years because the Hebrew school was only a primary school. Later, I went to a French school run by nuns, Notre Dame de Sion, where there were children of different creeds: Jews, Orthodox Greeks, Catholics, and Muslims. They taught the Catechism, but, naturally, we Jews didn't participate. The fashion of the time among the upper class was to send their boys to attend the English school and the girls to the French school. Since I liked to sew and paint a lot, I enrolled also to study dressmaking, embroidery, painting and textile design twice a week. I drew stylized tiles; I painted mosques and palaces like the one in Labensk, a very famous place.

Later, we moved to another section in which we lived together with Turks, English, and Germans, and we went to a club where I began to relate to non-Jews. But at home we maintained the tradition as always. On the Sabbath, Kippur, and Pesach, the whole family got together —my parents and my uncles. I remember that on Kippur they stayed overnight, but they didn't sleep in beds. Preparations for Pesach took a month— to take down the curtains, remove the rugs, and eliminate the stove. That house shined. It was a holiday of a lot of work, but very joyful.

We were observant like the majority of families in Turkey at that time; there were practically no orthodox. The ones that I knew mainly kept Kippur and Pesach. On the Sabbath, the Muslim doorman of the building was the one who turned on the lights, and I went around with my money in a handkerchief because it was forbidden to touch it. Although we didn't mix cheese with meat, we had only one set of dishes. We didn't cook, but we did go out in the car for a ride. It was this attachment to customs and traditions that kept us from disappearing as a people in the thousands of years of the Diaspora.

After Sefarad, Turkey

In Turkey, there wasn't anti-Semitism, but there was a difference. Our parents kept us separate for fear we would fall in love and marry outside our religion. Although we talked to the gentiles, all our friends were Jewish. Turkey didn't

Donna, her mother, grandmother and aunt in Turkey. 1937.

participate in the Second World War, which is why its Jewish population did not suffer Nazi extermination. However, ninety-nine percent of its inhabitants are Muslims. So, every time there was a political problem, that there was a student protest, they always blamed the non-Muslims: the Greeks because of Cyprus and, in one way or another, the Jews were also involved.

For example, they passed a law that imposed very high taxes on members of the other religious denominations. If you couldn't pay, you lost everything and were sent to forced labor in Anatolia. My identity card specifies that I am Jewish. The first thing the Turks say to me when they hear my last name is, "you aren't Turkish," even though we Jews have been living there for five centuries. It's incredible that after five hundred years they still do not consider us legitimate Turks.

Nevertheless, the place where the Jews lived the best after leaving *Sefarad* in 1492, was Turkey. At that time, the Sultan allowed them to settle southwest of Istanbul. They could always practice their religion, and the government didn't persecute them, despite the taxes.

Return to Cuba

In 1954, my younger brother, Israel, got sick with rheumatic fever. At that time, they started to sell cortisone in the black market. Although the treatment helped him, the doctors suggested that he move to a warm country, until he was bigger. For us, there were only two warm countries: Israel and Cuba.

In the 1920s, my father, Mordejai Albalah Adato, had lived in Cuba when he was very young —sixteen or seventeen years old. After the war, many like him were orphaned in their native city of Edirne. He was the oldest of four brothers. There was terrible misery that made them emigrate. At that time, Cuba had a booming economy, and those who were already on the Island wrote to their families about it. That's how my father came.

First he went to Havana, where he worked carrying sacks on the docks. Later, he went to Santa Clara with an uncle who was living there; then, to Santiago de Cuba and from there to Banes because the friends with whom he traveled on the ship had settled there. In Santiago and in Banes, he began to peddle like all the others because he had no capital. They didn't like working for anyone and didn't have professional skills suitable for other employment. Besides, business among the Jews is something very natural.

They slept in boarding houses, three in a room, working non-stop in order to send money to Turkey to support their families. When he had enough money, he sent for his younger brother and set him up in peddling. After ten years in Cuba, in 1933, he began to yearn to see his family, and he returned to Turkey. At this time, Cuba was in a critical economic, social and political situation because of Machado.

My uncles had already moved to Istanbul where he met my mother, Luna Levy Baruj, an orphan, fourteen years old, and a very beautiful girl. They were married, and they prospered in a food supply business. Nothing to do with fabrics. The whole family worked in food supplies, even those who died during the First World War had a cheese factory in Edirne. Papa made a lot of money during the Second World War with his food warehouses. By 1950, we had moved to the other neighborhood that I told you about. We had the store below —a residential food delivery service that Mama set up— and the house above. Mama was very special in everything, including business.

When my brother got sick, Papa didn't want to come to Cuba because he knew what life here was like and was afraid that Mama wouldn't adapt. She led a very active social life that he thought she wouldn't be able to recreate in

Cuba. But my mother, who had longed to go to *America* since she was a child, rejected the idea of Israel and opted for Cuba where her brother was. Within three months, they sold everything, including her store and Papa's warehouse. The fact is that they thought they would only live on the Island some five or six years, but they didn't want to risk leaving capital behind in case something happened. I came under protest. I was seventeen years old and in love for the first time. I cried a lot.

I thought that Cubans were different

We left Istanbul for Athens and Paris. We stayed two days in each of those cities to visit relatives. From Paris we took the KLM flight to New York, where bad weather detained us for more than twelve hours, and from there, finally, to Havana and then on to Santiago de Cuba.[1] The first trauma of my arrival in Cuba occurred when I got on that little airplane and landed at a provisional airport in Santiago, which was just a wooden building with a porch that looked like one of those houses in the western movies. I saw my aunt in sandals and a colorful dress without sleeves. We came from Paris and New York on big, comfortable trans-Atlantic airplanes, smartly dressed in suits and jackets.

I didn't want to be in a strange country that separated me from everything I loved, my best friend, my cousin whom I adored, and my boyfriend. I was dead tired after six days traveling and had never seen a man this color. The only image I had of a black man that I remembered was that of the *Mau Mau* in American movies, who ate people. Where have they brought me? I asked myself.

The days passed. All my father's old friends who lived in Santiago, in San Pedro, Trinidad and Corona, where the Jews were mainly concentrated, invited us out. I wasn't like the people here; I was an introvert, and the Cubans were very extrovert. At seventeen, I still went around in ankle socks, without makeup. Here all the girls wore makeup, went around with their shoulders and legs exposed, they laughed with the boys and went out alone. To make matters worse, every time I tried to talk, I did it in Ladino, and, naturally, they laughed at me because I seemed funny to them.

I admit that the first time I saw the Carnival, I thought the people were some kind of savages, those dances, that smell of sweat. Without doubt, I

---

[1] Santiago de Cuba: the second city of importance on the Island; one of the villages of the most eastern part, founded by the Spanish at the beginning of the Conquest.

thought the Cubans were different. But then, the second year, I was *congueando*[2] with the savages. And I became more *conguera* than all of them. What I liked most was to dance.

Jewish life was also different

Here, they were much less observant than in Turkey. Until I arrived in Cuba, I had never seen a live pig, nor one sold in a butcher shop. In Istanbul, there were only a few places that offered ham for non-Jews, like something very refined. The *Haggadah* of Pesach wasn't like the one there. The synagogue was a house to which only some older persons, the old ones, went. The *jajam* was a peddler who had become a Rabbi along the way, not like in Turkey where we had an Orthodox Rabbi who inspired a lot of respect.

The community reached its high point with our arrival because Mama began to organize parties with Turkish dances and songs. She cooked borekas and sold them to make money. The youth didn't have the same upbringing, but there weren't mixed marriages. The only one I remember was Castiel who married a non-Jew, but even though they frowned on her, she participated in all the activities. The others who had married outside the religion had already moved away from the community, and I didn't meet them.

In Santiago, we didn't have a kosher butcher or Jewish schools, only a Kal. Papa, who was a peddler, brought meat from Palma and San Luís, because it was of better quality, and we all ate it. My group was all Jewish. The first year I spent embroidering, painting and cooking, because I liked it. I wanted to study architecture, but in Santiago there wasn't a school for that, and my father said that no daughter of his was going to go to Havana to live in a boarding house. Later, we moved permanently to Havana, and then my Jewish life developed here in the Sephardic temple.

---

[2] Conga, *congueando*: a verb form that comes from the word *conga*, a Cuban dance rhythm, very popular in the carnivals.

Donna with her brother and mother
in front of their store in Turkey.
1950.

A wedding at the Synagogue of Santiago de Cuba.
1954.

(Courtesy of Rafael Pilossof)

195

Facade of the synagogue.
Santiago de Cuba, 2003.
(Photo by Maritza Corrales)

At the Kotel (Wailling Wall).
Jerusalem, 1997.

PART THREE
Those who stayed to rebuild

Abraham Marcus Matterin (1916-1983)

Collaborative member of the Sociedad Colombista Panamericana of the Institución Hispano-Cubana de Cultura, secretary of publications of the Asociación Nacional de Escritores, Poetas y Amigos del Arte and the Círculo de Periodistas y Escritores Hebreos de Cuba. His articles appeared in the newspaper *El Mundo* of Cuba and in the press in Argentina, Mexico, Venezuela and the United States. Founder and director of the magazines *Hebraica* (1947-1949), *Israelia* (1950-1952) and of the newspaper *Reflejos Israelitas* (1953-1954). Author of *Los hebreos y la bandera cubana* (1950), *Martí y las discriminaciones raciales* (1953); translated into Yiddish the poem Martí, by Eliécer Aronowsky. A director of IWO; president of the Queen Esther Competition (1949-1954); founder and president of the Unión Juvenil Hebrea de Cuba (1939-1942); secretary of culture of the B'nei B'rith (1948) and secretary general (1951); founder and first vice president of the Agrupación Cultural Hebrea Cubana (1952-1954); secretary general of the Sociedad de Amigos de la Universidad Hebrea de Jerusalem (1950); president of public relations of the Comunidad Hebrea de Cuba since 1950; director of the Library of the Patronato since 1954 and vicepresident of the Patronato, from 1970 until his death in 1983. Decorated with the Order of the Centennial of the Cuban Flag (1950) and Gentleman of the National Order Carlos Manuel de Céspedes (1958).

A Cuban Jew

In the early 1960s, I met Abraham in the office of Luis Gómez Wanguemert, director of the newspaper *El Mundo*. I enjoyed talking with him. I was attracted by the pride with which he spoke of his people and of my Island. His love and loyalty to Judaism and his ever present recognition of Cuba was inspiring. Because of him, I began to go to the library of the Patronato and to eat in its restaurant. As a child, I had participated in the Hebrew traditions and customs. However, it was because of his influence that I became interested, as an adolescent, in that secular and fascinating history. I never formally interviewed him because I had not yet begun to write about the Hebrew presence in Cuba. Thus, I include things he said to me during our conversations, remembrances that other friends have passed on to me and details of some interviews conducted abroad.

The grandson of *Jone der Shuster*

Matterin was born on April 1, 1916, in Kaunas, the capital of Lithuania, which at that time formed part of the tsarist empire. He was the grandson of Jonas Marcus (*Jone der Shuster*), "a man so dedicated to his people that he took food to Jewish prisoners in jail every Sabbath" and "he helped the sick as well as the Hebrew brides who didn't have a dowry."[1] His grandfather was such an important philanthropist and social activist in Kaunas that, when he died, all activity stopped and twenty thousand Jews attended his funeral.[2]

Matterin's grandparents were very religious, very orthodox. His father "told him that they lived in the United States after the First World War, but they didn't want to stay and returned to Lithuania because he said that the Jews there were not true Jews because they worked on Saturdays and smoked." He only remembered two things about his town: "an enormous tree that was in front of his house and one of the visits on which he accompanied his grandfather to the jails."[3]

Like so many other Jews, his father, León Marcus, decided to emigrate. After a brief stay in the United States, he arrived in Havana on February 2, 1924 on the ship "Edda." His wife and his three sons came with him, among them Abraham who was almost eight years old. First, they lived in Old Havana, in

---

[1] Unattributed interview conducted in the United States. Archives of Marcus Matterin in the Museum of the City, Havana, Cuba. [hereinafter: Unattributed interview]
[2] *Israelia*, No. VI, Year II, August 1951, p. 8, Havana, Cuba.
[3] Unattributed interview.

a small hotel across from the telephone company. Later, they moved close to Damas Street. They had a very hard life, and when his father became sick with typhus, they were left without money. León became a shoemaker. His mother cooked for guests who rented rooms in her house, and she sewed underwear for men under subcontract until three in the morning.

He went to a public school in the neighborhood and later to the Centro Israelita. His drawing teacher, Schwartz, recommended him for a scholarship to San Alejandro. He had only studied two months when he began to work as a shoe maker. Although it was his dream, he could not finish his studies, and he had to learn to read and develop on his own.

His father instilled in him the beautiful Jewish traditions of love, justice and peace, as well as affection for Cuba. León Marcus died relatively young, but in his short life he was very active socially. He was president of the Comité Hebreo Anti-Nazi during the Second World War, of the Asociación de Fabricantes de Calzado de La Habana and a leader of the Sociedad de Hebreos Oriundos de Lituania.

"The most integrated Jew in Cuba"

Cuba penetrated Matterin's soul. He was both proud to be Jewish and proud to be Cuban. He alternated his daily work with that which gave him more pleasure: public speaking, relating to people, disseminating Jewish culture, being a bridge between this immigrant minority and the society that had so generously taken him in. At one of those lectures, Don Fernando Ortiz[4] introduced him as "the most integrated Jew in Cuba."

He made friends with important Cuban intellectuals, artists and journalists, whether they were Communist or of the center, including Fernando Ortiz, Juan Marinello, Nicolás Guillén, Labrador Ruiz, Lezama Lima, both Salvadores (Bueno and García Agüero), Calixto Masó, Roig de Leuchsenring, Juan David, Arroyito, Father Gaztelu, Cintio Vitier, Juan Emilio Friguls, Pablo Armando Fernández, Wanguemert, José Luciano Franco, Samuel Feijoó, and José Antonio Portuondo. They always responded to his requests: they were lecturers at the institutions in which he carried out his untiring promotional

---

[4] Fernando Ortiz, the most representative and encyclopedic figure of Cuban culture of the first half of the Twentieth Century. His scientific work covers anthropology, ethnography, sociology, linguistics, history, folklore, and archeology. He is called the "Third Discoverer of Cuba," after Columbus and the Baron Alexander Von Humboldt.

Membership card No.001 as president of the Unión Juvenil Hebrea.
Havana, 1940.

work; they gave him space in newspapers; and they used their own pen to write about the history, triumphs and contributions of this Hebrew minority to the Cuban economy, society and culture. I think this was his main gift: an intelligent and pertinent promoter. He organized and participated in activities involving international cultural figures who visited the country, such as Pablo Neruda, Gabriela Mistral, and Ernest Hemingway.

His links to leftist groups date far back. On June 13, 1940, he registered as member No. 1 in the Unión Juvenil Hebrea del Centro Israelita, the secretary general of which was Arón Radlow, one of Cuba's most important Jewish Communist leaders.

"Working like an ant, in solitude, and not always understood"

Fernando Campoamor described him well in his article "Pecho Adentro" published in 1959: "Abraham Marcus Matterin did not lose time working for the Hebrew colony; he worked each day like an ant, at times completely alone and not always understood. He dedicated his life to the book that is the everlasting symbol of Judaism, because the book never let go of the hand of

202

the Diaspora nor deserted its struggle in exile. [...] This good man has done more than anyone else to fill the emptiness and silence of others, generously and with modesty. What he has done for the Hebrew cause in human terms, without noting it in accounting books, leaves a balance of respect for his unfaltering work."[5]

As examples, we have the special magazine he promoted in the newspaper *El Mundo* to celebrate the New Year 5720 (1959), the cover of which he, himself, designed; the volume dedicated to *The Jewish Mother in Literature and Art* (1959); the special issue of *Hasefer* (The Book) of August, 1958; the pamphlets on *The Cuban Flag* and *Martí and Racial Discrimination*, of 1953, for which he also did the cover; the magazines that he founded —*Hebraica, Reflejos Israelitas, and Israelia*; the innumerable lectures given and organized on his preferred subjects— Martí, Einstein, Bergson, Maimonides, and Herzl; the concerts of classical, folklore and synagogal music; and the participation of Jews in chess.

Faithful to the tradition of the book, he set up a printing press in his home from which he conducted the major part of his work of disseminating information to the community. Among the most important activities were those commemorating the Centennial Anniversary of the birth of José Martí, in which the Cuban Hebrews, led by Marco Pitchón, that original and tireless Sephardic Jew, and Matterin, organized the most impressive series of homages that any minority had ever dedicated to the National Hero.

"A small country of great men"

"My Judaism, which is not religious but one of tradition, makes me genuinely proud to be Jewish, of the history of our people, of the contribution of its ideology to the life and ethic of society, and of the great figures of its history. But at the same time, I am proud to be Cuban, of its historic leaders like José Martí, Maceo, and Máximo Gómez, as well as of the great Cuban intellectuals and artists. I once gave a lecture entitled 'The Small Country of Great Men.' Although Cuba is a small country, its scientific, cultural and historical achievements far surpass that of small countries. To live in a country for fifty-six years makes one proud of that.

There is an anecdote I will never forget that has to do with Erich María Remarque. When fascism began to strangle Germany, he went to live in

---

[5] Fernando Campoamor, "Pecho Adentro," *El Mundo*, Havana, October 4, 1959.

His favorite place: The Patronato library.
Havana, 1970s.

Switzerland. He was interviewed there, and the only question that remains engraved in my mind was: Mr. Remarque, did you feel very lonely living so many years in Germany? The answer was an immediate no. The journalist asked why, and Remarque answered: 'Because I am a German Jew.' And I am a Cuban Jew. Do you understand? It is a duality in which one does not exclude the other. Of course, the history of Cuba does not have the centuries of recorded history that Israel has, but it is a passionate history. Among the Cuban people, the Jews and Cubans complement each other. That is my sincere opinion, without false patriotism, without chauvinism…with nothing of that. I can say that I am a Cuban Jew."[6]

"In those hours when work is put to rest, a beehive remains illuminated…the library where Abraham constructs his vigil, honoring tradition."[7] There, in his library, that Cuban Ashkenazi Jew remained working continuously. Together, he and the persistent Sephardic Jew, Marco Pitchón, formed the perfect binomial square that built so many bridges between our two cultures.

---

[6] Unattributed interview.
[7] Fernando Campoamor, op.cit.

With the Chilean poet Pablo Neruda.
Havana, 1942.

Making a donation at the State of Israel Public School.
Havana, 1970.

205

Ida Portnoy (1906-1992)[1]

Cofounder of the Asociación Femenina Hebrea de Cuba (1926), for many years its treasurer and vice president; founder and president of the Asociación de Damas del Patronato de la Casa and Templo de la Comunidad Hebrea (1952-1961); vice president del Patronato (1966 - 1992).

Not very religious, but she observed the traditions

From the time I can remember, Ida was involved in the activities of the Patronato. She was its vice president. I saw her grow old and continue to attend services even in her wheel chair, pushed by her faithful Eladio. She was there until the end, tied to the life of her community with a sense of being rooted to the Jewish people and strength that neither old age nor illness could defeat. Her bright blue eyes never reflected the passing of years.

She was born in 1906, in Nicolaev, Ukraine, of a Polish mother and Russian father who immigrated to Mexico so that their sons could avoid having to go to

---

[1] In addition to the memories I have of Ida, I have included testimonies of Dalia Gómez, secretary of the Patronato, Adela Dworin, vice president of the Patronato, and Eladio Moreno, a young Catholic, who took care of her and was her support until the end.

Her family in Nikolaev.
Rusia, 1910.

war. Like all Jews who were forced to emigrate, they suffered great hardships. She told stories about how, in the Ukraine, her mother used to make soup from onion skins only for the children, and how she used to burn the house furniture in order to cook and keep it warm.

She came to Cuba on July 10, 1925 from Mexico where her father's potato business had failed. She always said: "We had nothing else, but we always had potatoes."

In the Ukraine, she finished second grade. She did not study in Cuba. She knew Spanish, a little German, Yiddish and Russian, although she always preferred to speak Russian. She spoke to her parents in Russian on the days of *yizkor*, in front of the peculiar lamp that lit up the Star of David. She said that they understood each other better in that language. And it was in Russian that she spoke her last words on February 10, 1992.

She was proud to be Russian and that her family were not Poles from the *shtetl*. She also had a brother who was a doctor, something unusual in the Jewish community in that period. She adored her parents. Their graves in the cemetery are very lovely, and she even left a space so that she could be buried next to them.

Soon after landing on the Island, she married Aarón Pelinowsky, also Russian, who was a fabric merchant and had a store on Muralla Street. From then on, she began to devote her life to the community, and participated in the founding of the Asociación Femenina Hebrea of Cuba and was president and treasurer for many years of its Women's Committee.

Her long and fruitful dedication to this work stopped only with her death.

When she first arrived in Cuba, she attended Adath Israel Synagogue, which was then located on Jesús María Street in Old Havana. Even after her parents moved to Vedado, they continued going to that synagogue until she became a founding member of the Patronato and its synagogue was built. I would not say that Ida was a very religious person, but she did observe the traditions. Eladio recalls that she lit candles on Fridays, commemorated the anniversaries of the dead, cooked blintzes, gefilte fish, and ate matzoh during Passover.

The Marilyn Monroe of the community and a *goy*

Ida divorced Aarón and remarried. At that time, it was scandalous for a Jewish woman and leader of the community to marry a Catholic. Her parents, especially her mother and uncle, with whom she had always lived, were very religious. However, in the end, her uncle was the only member of the family who opposed her marriage to the famous doctor Otón Madariaga because he was Catholic and *goy*. Later, Madariaga became a patron of the Patronato, one of three Cubans who appear in the list of its Second Founders, those who gave money to save the mortgage.

Ida was a little like the Marilyn Monroe —the glamour girl— of the community, says Adela Dworin, not just because she was pretty, but also because she led a very active social life in both the Jewish world and in Cuban society. At that time, there were no Jewish women who had a chauffer; I think she was the only one. She always remained concerned about looking her best and wore clothes by the most famous designers, and she traveled a lot. She was both envied and a role model. All the women of the community wanted to imitate her. She was cheerful and pretty. She loved to dance and go to parties. When she became ill with cancer, the radiation treatments caused her to lose her hair, her beautiful hair. But even so, Ida put on her makeup and went out in her high heels, continuing to dress up and participate in all the activities of the community like when she was young, like the first day.

The glamour girl of the Community.
Havana, 1930.

As President of the Women's Committee of the Patronato.
Havana, 1958.

(All photos courtesy of Eladio Moreno)

(Courtesy Susan Barstein)

Luis Chanivecky Rawet (1927-2000)

A musical family

I was born in Havana in 1927. My father, Chaskell, was from Kiev, Ukraine, but he spent most of his youth in Budapest studying the violin. My grandparents had taken him out of Russia because he had deserted from the army. While he was in Hungary, he married, and my sister Rosita was born. Papa became a widower and came to Cuba in 1923. He wanted to join his brothers who were in Canada, but, like so many Jews who arrived here with the hope of going to the United States, he didn't get a visa. He worked in Cuba and in the end decided to stay. That is the story of the origin of the community on the Island.

My mother, Feigele Rawet, was from Warsaw, the Polish capital. She met my father in her brother's store where she was a salesgirl. He loved the aroma of her cooking; he fell in love, and they married in 1924. First, they settled in Old Havana, close to the docks, in the area where mainly the Sephardic Jews were concentrated. After, they moved to Regla where my father set up a workshop and I studied at the San Juan School, a private Catholic school.

My father was a very good violinist, and he taught Rosita. But he couldn't

213

earn a living from music in Cuba and had to work at other things. He set up a store, later a workshop, and, when that didn't go well, he closed it, and we worked together as itinerant wholesalers. Papa also played the mandolin. My musical career began when I found his mandolin behind the wardrobe by accident.

Only when I was at the point of retiring did I begin to seriously publish my own music: scores for theater, boleros, and children's music for cartoons on television. Later, I composed music for the production of the play "Anne Frank," which was performed in a program in the United States on Jews in Cuba. My songs have done well. Some of my compositions became hits sung by Los Zafiros:[1] "La luna en tu mirada," "Locura azul," and "Bossa cubana." There are many records and cassette recordings of them, and they have even been performed in documentaries and in a movie.

In Cuba they treated us as equals

My family adapted very well to life in Cuba; they became rooted. They spoke perfect Spanish. They didn't miss the place they came from where they had suffered discrimination and persecution. Here, we were treated as equals. There were never bad feelings against the Jews. Many did not even know what a Jew was; they had no consciousness of that. How could there be anti-Semitism if they didn't know what it was?

Jewish life was carried on freely. On the religious holidays, Rosh Hashanah and Yom Kippur, my parents took us to the Centro Israelita. They spoke perfect Yiddish. In addition, Papa spoke Hungarian, Russian, and Polish. Mama cooked very well. She made Polish style borscht, cold with an egg, and Russian style, with meat, potatoes and vegetables. She made meat with prunes and potatoes. But there was no special religious life. I am circumcised, and I made my Bar Mitzvah —the traditional things.

The path to a national home

I became affiliated with the Betar and Irgún. I went to the club on Bernaza Street, and I was there when Beguin visited us. I was a traveling salesman and worked from one end of the Island to the other, which permitted me to be in contact with the communities in the interior. Those were times of a lot of pain

---

[1] Los Zafiros: a famous Cuban vocal group, whose style was similar to The Platters.

In the synagogue, as Ba'al Tefillah.
Havana, 2000.
(Photo by Peggy Myers)

and confusion. The majority believed that we should have a national home so that the victims who survived the Shoah would have a place in Zion where they could begin a new life, but we disagreed on the road to follow. Everyone had lost relatives in the Holocaust, killed by the Nazis. In both my father's and mother's families we had news of only one survivor. It was something horrible to see how entire families were wiped out.

The *ba'al tefillah* and the *gabai* of the synagogue

Blumenkrantz was old and looking for someone to take his place in the synagogue. At the beginning, it was very difficult for me, but now, every time a service ends, I feel a very special inner peace that fills me spiritually.

Chanivecky could be found in the Patronato at all hours. He was always ready to help the youngest with a friendly word, and incapable of being two-faced. I like the way someone of the community described him: "Above all, Luis was a good man. He was good because he didn't know how else to be."

215

His parents upon their arrival to Cuba.
Havana, 1924.

His wedding at the Patronato.
Havana, 1956.

(Photo by Tatiana Santos)

Jose Miller Fredman

A Jew secretly baptized on paper

My parents arrived in 1924. Mama came from Pinsk, Poland, and papa from Quedania, Lithuania. Both of them came to Cuba in order to get to the United States. My father emigrated when he was twenty two years old for the same reasons as many Jews: to flee compulsory military service, which for them was terrible. I know that Papa was the youngest of four siblings, although he didn't talk much about his family. Mama had been left an orphan when she was five.

As far as I know, through letters and photographs, the family lived in a suburban area, semi-rural, with their animals, geese and chicken. Everyone in the family, with the exception of one who lives in Israel and my grandfather, was exterminated in the Holocaust. According to what my mother told me, my grandfather died during a pogrom from the blows they gave him.

When my parents arrived in Cuba, they earned a living as itinerant venders in Havana. Later, they moved to Yaguajay, a town in the northern part of Las Villas province, where one of my mother's sisters lived. There, they opened a variety store that they called LA ECONOMÍA.

217

I was born in Yaguajay, in August of 1925, almost at the same time as the Cuban Communist Party. My parents had rented a room in the home of a very Catholic family, where a very strange thing happened. When I enrolled in the University, they asked me for my birth certificate, and when I applied for a copy, it turned out that I had two birth registrations. In one, my father, instead of being Yona, was listed as Juan and as a business owner, and Mama wasn't Yashke, but rather Josefa, and did typical women's work. The other registration was normal and had only one error: my surname is actually Ferdman (man-horse), but they had inverted a letter, and I was registered as Fredman. It was only as a result of this incident that I became aware that they had baptized me in secret, at least on paper, and had re-registered my birth.

At the time, there were six Jewish families living in Yaguajay: the Gribov's, the Krost's, the Sussi's, the Barroca's, one of my father's sisters, and us. The Sussi's went to Tunisia, and when the returned to Cuba, the father became the *Hazzan* of Chevet Ahim and performed my brother's *Brit*, a big event because they had never seen one in our town. The Crasin and Feldman families lived in the town of Meneses. There were three families in Iguará: the Zimmerman's, the Usher's, and the Dworin's. All had stores in good locations: La Catalana, El Paraíso, the Bazar Hamburgo and Villa de París. They were well placed in two neighborhoods of the town: in Sansarí (the Hawk) and in the Loma (the Cock), where the well-to-do lived. The area of the hardware stores was between the bridge and the neighborhood of Sansarí. Above it, were the fabric stores; it was the best location because normally no one bought in the first store he found.

The merchandise arrived through Iguará, which was the best road out of Yaguajay to civilization. There were wholesalers in Santa Clara who sold to us, above all those in leather and shoes: Enrique Oltuski's father and the father of Abel Holtz. Traveling salesmen also came, like in Arthur Miller's novel. My father knew some of them from his first years in Havana, and they even stayed overnight in our house instead of a hotel in order to save money, Jews as well as Spaniards. After 1945, when I came to Havana, I bought for them. Also, around the time of Pesach, Papa came to Havana to get the matzoh and took advantage of his time to purchase other goods as well.

My mother and father were not very religious; they weren't orthodox, but they were kosher. At home, we ate the meat from the butcher shop in Havana; my father used to buy live chickens from the farmers and slaughtered them himself. My mother kept track of all the Holidays, with or without a calendar. She made traditional desserts: cookies (*kijalaj*) covered with powdered sugar for which she cut the dough with an upside down glass, and blintzes. She also made *gejakte leber*, chopped chicken liver with egg and onion.

A Cuban couple with a lot of children lived across the street from our house. They cooked very well. We didn't eat fillet mignon, but there they ate nothing but fillet. They would kill a pig and store the meat in pork lard. I ate everything. I enjoyed spending Christmas Eve in the homes of all my friends in town. For me, it was a punishment to have to eat the gefilte fish and matzoth ball soup in my aunt's house. I couldn't stand the sticky gelatin.

The Cubans were always open, friendly and welcoming. This country does not have a history of religious conflict. There had never been anti-Semitism in Cuba. Sometimes they called me "*polaco*," but that was not important. I never felt discrimination or disrespect. Not at the University, either. While I was living in the countryside, I had no idea what a Muslim was, nor much idea what an Arab was. People were identified as *sirios*, *moros* or *libaneses*. There was never a single incident among the different groups, nor with the Cuban people. Everyone I knew —Elías, Miguel the Moro, Yunes— was Christian. I always went around with the Fernández kids, who were very Catholic. Although I knew I wasn't the same as they, that they understood each other better, I never had any difficulty being part of their club.

Andrés Dworin was the only mason, but there were many in the United Hebrew Congregation in Havana, the institution of the American Jews on 21st Street and G, which hosted all the sessions of the B'nei B'rith. No doubt the masons ideas were behind the creation of that fraternal organization.

A Jew attracted to politics

My father, my uncle Benjamin, and the people I knew did not get involved politically. I was the only one who got involved. I belonged to the Liberal Youth, was secretary of the Anti-Fascist Front and, later, a supporter of the Socialist Youth. The office of the Communists was in a place that Papa had rented to the Popular Socialist Party next door to my home. Carlos Rafael Rodríguez, Fabio Grobart, Gaspar Jorge García Galló, Raul Ferrer and many more went there. They were friends of mine. Maybe Papa didn't like it, but he never mentioned it to me. I was attracted to politics. My connection to the Communists was through a lawyer they had sent to town, and I spent a lot of time talking to him in the house. The lawyer was José Felipe Carneado.[1]

In Yaguajay, there was a relatively big group of Communists. The political activity in support of the Spanish Republic was very strong, mainly among the workers at the sugar mills. The town had three mills and most people depended on them for work, but they only worked ninety days a year. In one of them, the Narcisa, 97.5% of the workers were Communists. It was difficult to live there, to see the frequent and numerous evictions of the peasants, to see entire families homeless, sleeping in the doorway of my house, the abuses of the rural guards. You couldn't be a young person and witness that with indifference.

I'll tell you a story. In Yaguajay there was an army officer by the name of Corporal Perdomo, who, they said, had killed a boy in the area. Later, Batista made him a colonel. When we were living in Havana, my sister was studying law, and one of her classmates noticed my books. Soon after, the Military Intelligence Service came, seized the books and arrested my father. When we arrived at the police station, they were already taking his fingerprints and photograph. Suddenly, an officer comes in, and I tell him that I think I know him. It was Corporal Perdomo. Fifteen minutes later, my father was released. That's the way Cuba was.

Cubans and Jews at the same time

My link to B'nei B'rith was through Marco Pitchón. I began to participate in the youth group, *Hillel*, in 1946, and I ended up being secretary of the B'nei in 1950. I took on other responsibilities as I matured. We were young, and we had intellectual and political concerns. We all felt we were Cubans, and, at the same time, we felt we were Jews. We didn't want it to be seen as ambivalence, but rather as a manifestation of our dual identity and understood by all those around us who weren't Jews.

At that time, the State of Israel had recently come into existence, and some people were influenced by what they read in *El Diario de la Marina*, which didn't hide its reactionary leanings and was very critical of the creation of Israel. We wanted to promote understanding between Cuba and Israel. For that reason, many participated in the founding of the Agrupación Cultural Hebrea-Cubana. Dialogue was strengthened with other organizations, above all with the B'nei.

---

[1] José Felipe Carneado, leader of the old Communist Party. After the Revolution, he was head of the Office of Religious Affairs of the Central Committee of the Party.

In a meeting of the Agrupación Cultural Hebreo-Cubana.
Havana, 1950s.

Fathers Biaín and Aldeaseca, as well as many professors, like J. B. Kourí and
Virgilio Beato Núñez, were invited to the activities. I think it was one of the
best periods of community work in Cuba.

In the early years, Gromyko was one of the defenders of the State of Israel.
The defeat in the 1948 war convinced the Arabs that the decadent monarchies
had to be replaced with younger and more popular governments. Thus, the
movement emerged that brought Naguib and later Nasser to power. It also
resulted in Soviet support for Arab nationalism.

We were leftists, but not Communists. LA VICTORIA, on Obispo Street, was
Marcus Matterin's favorite book shop and mine as well. A circle of intellectuals
used to meet there, including Lezama Lima, Isidro Méndez and others. There
was also another book store LA ECONÓMICA that was owned by the Party. It was
better to relate to the people that you met there than with any others. The only
thing the Communists had was their ideals: they wanted to help the poorest,
the most humble. They were heroes, and. I don't regret having known these
people. I do regret, however, not discovering earlier the evil of Joseph Stalin.
I began to distance myself from my Communist friends during the trial of the
ten doctors, after the death of Andrei Zhdanov.

The most difficult was the decision to leave

I think the most difficult moment for the Jews in Cuba was the moment when they decided to leave. Almost all were merchants —small, medium, rich. My sister, who was a lawyer, decided not to stay because all her clients had left. I didn't have a reason to leave. Papa didn't want to emigrate, his business hadn't been nationalized, and he was making good money. He didn't decide to leave until it was nationalized in 1968, but at that time my son was of age for military service, I was married to Dalia, and our youngest child had been born. Really, I have never regretted staying because the final outcome is what counts, and it hasn't been bad for me.

I had friends in the Ministry of Public Health from the days of the Socialist Youth, who acted as advisors. Three or four months after the triumph of the Revolution, they offered me a post as a dentist in the army, in the Tactical Forces. I was there until 1961 when I went to work at the Military Hospital.

The return of the prodigal son

As soon as I left the Revolutionary Armed Forces in 1968, I returned to the Patronato. I no longer felt comfortable in the military because of the war of 1967 in Israel. I had an opportunity to change jobs, and I took it. They placed me for a year in the Orthopedic Hospital in Camagüey, and afterwards, I went to work at the National Hospital from which I also attended patients at the William Soler Hospital. I entered the Patronato when it could no longer be considered a community. Before that, I had not been a member of either the United Hebrew Congregation or the Patronato, for the same reason that many who are here today weren't members. It can't be said that the Patronato was in its time, at the beginning, really a popular institution among the Jews. It was elitist, more elitist than the Centro Israelita. My uncles were old members. Nevertheless, I got married at the United Hebrew since I had a connection with them through the B'nei B'rith because many of its members also belonged to the B'nei.

My work in the community has had two phases: the first, when I returned and became involved in community activity; and the second, when I became president of the Patronato. During the first, I began to direct the B'nei B'rith, which had been left without a president and owed its existence to the efforts of Isidoro Stettner who kept it active during the 1970s. They were eager for new people, and I organized a few activities that were very well received. I was forty five, and I was much younger than those who were the leaders. Although not everyone had left in the 1960s, everyday more people abandoned the country, and nothing could prevent the decline of community life.

We miss our Jewish home

Ten percent of the Cuban population, one million people, emigrated. Among that million and something were thirteen thousand Jews, but those thirteen thousand Jews represented not ten percent, but ninety percent of the community. And they were the most involved, the most observant of its members. So, our community not only declined numerically, but also —and this is even more important— its identity diminished and was being lost in Cuba. The elders continued to age, and the young grew up without a Jewish education. They did not have their Brit or Bar Mitzvah. But a sufficient number stayed so that Jewish life didn't die altogether. We remembered our Jewish home, and we missed it. We wanted our children to know about it and tried to reconstruct a little of that life.

By 1968, community life was already very reduced and getting worse each day. The leaders of the community had considered it very important that there be an Israeli representation in Cuba and that Cuba maintain relations, as it had in the 1960s and, even more significantly, after the Six Day War in 1967. For that reason, the breaking of relations with Israel in 1973 left the leadership of the Patronato somewhat limited. Until then, they had used the Legation of Israel to communicate the things they wanted to say to the Government and the department of the Communist Party concerned with ecumenical relations.

After the Yom Kippur War, Israeli politics took a turn. The Labor Party lost control of the Government for the first time and a center-left coalition yielded to Menahem Beguin. Carter assumed the presidency of the United States and Sadat took power in Egypt. That, undoubtedly, caused and brought about a situation favorable to the peace process between Egypt and Israel, with the return of the Sinai.

It is a contradiction. At the moment that there is a great change between the most important Arab country and Israel, the Arab reaction is to call a boycott, a policy related to the price of oil as a result of the 1973 war, and they threaten nations that maintain relations with Israel. That scenario —Sadat in Jerusalem, a US president supporting the peace process and Beguin, who despite his past also wants peace— was not the best time to mount the anti-Zionist, anti-Israel policy, which arose in this period.

What is certain is that the dissemination of anti-Zionist propaganda, which had not previously been heard in Cuba, impeded the activity of the leaders and considerably diminished the possibilities for a resurgence of Jewish community life, which was already very reduced and insignificant. Some of the leaders became old and died. Others, of greater importance because of their national stature and knowledge of the international Jewry, such as Baldas,[2] thought that little was left for them to do for the community and its Zionist projection.

In 1978, they closed the Unión Sionista. Baldas thought that his being a Zionist militant was harming the community and that he was no longer accepted as before. He really did a lot for the Patronato. He applied for the exit papers of those who wanted to leave, obtained the import of eggs and tires from Israel and made the links with agricultural technicians in the citrus projects. But he did something that I consider a mistake: he used the Legation of Israel in Cuba as the intermediary instead of establishing direct contact with the department of Mier Febles, which dealt with the community at the Communist Party of Cuba at that time.

Baldas asked me to stay. We had worked together and, although we didn't always agree, we maintained a good relationship. Also because I knew José Felipe Carneado. Baldas had a hand in my taking leadership of the Patronato, even though there were other qualified people. Maybe because of the way I related to others outside the community, or for the work I did in the country, he thought that I was well thought of by others. In his opinion, my success did not reflect marginalization as a Jew, but rather, being a Jew, I was doing quite well in this society.

Avoiding confrontation

A new period began in Cuba in 1978-1979. The Interests Section of the United States was established, political prisoners were freed and, although this is not directly related to the community, the liberalization favored the few Jews who had been penalized for illegal money changing.

One of my goals as president of the Patronato was never to let it get into a situation of confrontation. We kept active and waited for the appropriate moment to reconstruct it, which happened after the historic meeting with

---

[2] Moisés Baldas, president of the Jewish Community of Cuba, from the great exodus of the 1960s to 1981, the year in which he immigrated to Israel.

With Fidel Castro during the visit of Rabbi Lau, Great Rabbi of Israel.
Havana, 1993.

Fidel in 1990. We then asked for support from the Joint, and we sought out those who had Jewish ancestors to come and form a new community with very different characteristics.

That moment also coincided with an ideological opening in Cuba, after *perestroika*, and the collapse of the Soviet Union and also with a change in attitude that had been growing in Israel that resulted in Rabin's election in 1992 and opened the way for the Oslo accords. This political move put the State of Israel and the world Jewish movement on a different footing.

Remember, world public opinion at that time was very different compared to that of today in relation to the Israeli-Palestinian conflict, independently of which side is right. Israeli politicians should understand that we cannot turn our backs on world public opinion and that, if we are in a situation that is not evident to the rest of the world, we must defend our policy in a way that non-Jews can also understand. I don't think that Israel manages the art of communication and political discourse very well.

Israel does not have any kind of policy to help the communities of the

Diaspora. They want the Diaspora to end and everyone to go to Israel. The Israeli concept is that it is the State where all Jews should live. The policy is motivated by demographic phenomena more than anything else, which is contradictory. They cannot accept that the Palestinians establish the law of return. More than half a million Arabs live in Israel, who are Israeli because they live there. It is like a *sudeten*,[3] but it has been respected. We Jews understand it, but the rest of the world doesn't. Nevertheless, the majority of Jews, inside and outside of Israel, agree that there should not be Jewish settlements in Palestinian territory.

Disagreements have to be accepted

I believe, but I don't want you to think I am being immodest. Maybe yes, maybe no. One can't say that someone else wouldn't have done the same. I believe it lead to positive results. As a leader of the Jewish community, you have to work in collaboration and perfect understanding with the Office of Religious Affairs. One is trusted because one understands the process and why the government makes certain decisions. On occasions, only a thin line divides conduct that is justified and acceptable and that which is not justifiable or correct. We have always paid attention to that.

Everyone has to accept disagreement, but when you disagree, you have to be careful not to cross the line. To be in disagreement is not the same as being an adversary. My objective has been to prevent our becoming an element of friction and to maintain a good equilibrium. I have tried to be on the side of reason, justice and what is decent, without ever being influenced by any type of partisan politics. Let others judge if that is easy to achieve.

---

[3] *Sudeten*: Sudetenland in German, a region of the former Czechoslovakia occupied by a significant German minority that was annexed to the Third Reich in 1938.

With his parents.
Yaguajay, 1929.

Representing the Agrupación Cultural Hebreo-Cubana in an
assembly of different institutions of the Community.
Havana, 1950s.

227

Conmemorating the Anniversary of Jose Martí, Fragua Martiana.
Havana, 1955.

With Daniel Barenboim.
Havana, late 1990s.

228

(Photo by Maritza Corrales)

Alberto Mechulam Cohen

My grandparents were true Jews:
they didn't understand anything else

My name is Alberto Mechulam Cohen. "Mechulam" in Hebrew means well paid. I fulfill my name: I pay well, but I don't know if people pay me well. My maternal grandmother was Bulgarian, from Sofia. They had shops, but the war created a very difficult economic situation, and they had problems. So, they emigrated with my mother in 1924. Grandfather came with his two children. The daughter was very little, and she became a Cuban citizen.

My father was born in Istanbul. He worked there in a caviar factory that exported to Russia. He landed in Cuba in 1923. All his siblings died in the Holocaust, in Petain's France, and my other grandparents in Turkey. They couldn't come because he didn't have the money to bring them over.

My mother married and had a son, who now lives in the United States and is a widower. Later, she met my father, and they were married in 1933. My sister was born first, and I was born in 1936.

229

We lived in Luyanó, a neighborhood of the capital. We were extremely poor, and for many years we all slept in one room until we went to Güines, a town in the former province of Havana. There, Papa worked together with José Ojalvo as an itinerant fabric vender. On Sundays, I also went out to the countryside to sell with Salomón Schved. Although we continued to live on very little, I could study. When I was in the sixth grade, I prepared to enter high school to get my degree.

In Güines, there were sixteen Jewish families, including the Lieberman's, Barrocas's, Pinto's, Cohen's, Franco's, Elnecave's, Gut's, Schved's, Gurinsky's, Weiss's, who taught me some Yiddish, the Ojalvo's, and us. Almost all of them had stores. Elnecave owned the Ten Cent; Schved, a stand in the Market; and Gut had a mattress store. After 1961, they all left Cuba, except Weiss, who was very Zionist. He died in San José de las Lajas. Although we were very integrated into Cuban society, we felt very committed to Judaism. As young people, we organized our own activities, and on the Holidays we all went to Havana, to Chevet Ahim or the Patronato.

I founded the first Jewish organization in Güines. We even edited a small newspaper, with a monogram that Marcos Barrocas designed, that we distributed monthly. We held our meetings at the Ten Cent in town, which was the home of the Elnecave family. The Club, which was called Weissman, didn't last long. We held sessions to learn about Jewish history, and, in order to strengthen our roots, we read news about Israel and the Jewish world in newspapers that were sent to me from Havana.

My family was very religious, orthodox. They were also very Zionist. Grandfather had an important position in the synagogue: he was Cohen and Levy.[1] They were true Jews; they didn't understand anything else. They spoke Hebrew, and grandfather wrote Ladino with Hebrew letters. He was always very concerned with tradition. They had one table for meat and another for cheese. Grandfather used to buy grapes and made wine himself that he drank on Saturday. He prepared it by hand. Grandmother made *borekas, trushí, yaprake, bulemas, tishpishtí,* and *almodrote*. Because she was Bulgarian, she made a lot of yoghurt and rose marzipan. They lived on the corner of Chevet Ahim, the

---

[1] "Cohen," from the Hebrew, meaning priest. In the Tabernacle and in the first and second Temple, the Cohen carried out functions that required special sanctity. Today, they are the first called to read the Torah in the synagogue. The "Levy" are the second called to read and are in charge of pouring water into the hands of the Cohen before they bless the people.

Sephardic synagogue in Old Havana, on the third floor, close to the ocean, because if they had to flee it was easier to pack their bags quickly and escape. They observed the Sabbath and cleaned on Friday night. They ate what there was and often didn't eat anything. We were so poor, so poor that I could not make my Bar Mitzvah.

In 1952, I came to Havana to study. Since I had no money, my plan was to go to the United States. But my brother worked for a very rich Jew in Havana, Isidoro Abravanel Varón, and he suggested that I work there during vacations to make some money for my studies. My brother introduced me and explained my situation. Abravanel asked me how much the tuition cost, which was seventy pesos, and he took them out of his wallet and gave them to me. I worked in his factory until 1960, more or less, and every month he gave me a little money. After they nationalized the factory, I began to work in the Aid House of Mantilla, in Los Pinos,[2] in the Maternity Home and some clinics, to support my studies.

Amnón Mechulam, the last president of Macabi

In 1953, I joined the Hanoar Hatzioni, which was at that time on Prado. My name in the organization was Amnón Mechulam. I was the *Madrij, Mazkir*. Later, I became a member of the *ken* Volpi of the Unión Sionista, which was across from the Capitol building. I was there until I graduated as the *Rosh Ken* (Head of the Group), in 1960.

We made a lot of excursions. We had camp sites, like the *scouts*. We also prepared ourselves to make *aliya* to Israel, but not like the Hashomer, who were more disciplined, dedicated, and leftist. Those in the Hashomer, already knew by age sixteen that they would make *aliya*. The Hanoar were more bourgeois, they did it if they wanted to. Some —Nathan Berezdivin, Dov Kramer, Soshana Perelis— who were from Betar, the other Zionist organization that was more to the right, went to the *kibbutzim*. Later, in 1961, I began in the Macabi, where I was vice president and ended up being the last of its presidents. Our organization was no longer as it was before, when we had sports teams, but we met and had outings and a lot of dance parties. We had such a good time that those of the Patronato, almost all of whom were Ashkenazi, were amazed when they visited us.

---

[2] Mantilla and Los Pinos are boroughs of the City of Havana.

Purim Festival.
Havana, 1962.

A *turco* and a *polaquita*: love at first site

I met my wife, who is a *polaquita*, at one of the Youth activities for Purim at
the Patronato. It was love at first site. I was president of the Macabi and I saw
her by chance, from afar, when I was talking from the dais. Then, when the
other boys wanted to go talk to her, I told them I had priority because being
president had to have some perks. I even told them to lock in the bathroom
the guy who offered to accompany her home. Everything was very fast, very
fast. We met in March, we were sweethearts in April, and we married in June
in the Patronato because I was going to the provinces to complete my rural
medical service. We took a honeymoon, and when we returned, we had to
sign some papers that had been missing. My in-laws were more liberal, but my
mother wanted a *turquita* for me. She said that the *polacos* caused a lot of friction
because they were a little patronizing, but my parents were flexible and didn't
take it badly. We had two children: Moisés, who studied with the Lubavitch, is
very orthodox and works in Argentina with a Rabbi; and Esther, who lives in
the United States.

In 1963, they assigned me to Nícaro, to finish my degree. There, I met Roberto Namer. We went to his house for Sabbath, and he read. In the 1970s, I moved to Manzanillo where there were a number of Jewish families living, among them the Motola. I invited them to our house and gave them newspapers that were sent to me from Havana. It was a way of circulating Judaism from one place on the Island to another.

This is a Jewish church?

Later, I was transferred to Havana. Jewish life had declined a lot because of the exodus of the community. In the four synagogues there almost wasn't a *minyan* left. Practically an entire generation was lost, a generation that could not transmit the values of Judaism to their children or their grandchildren. In 1984 or 1985 the *sheliaj* of the Rebe Luvabitch, Rabbi Appel from Brazil, came to organize a school. At the beginning it was a lot of work. We spoke with the Patronato and they gave us a small space, and the Lubavitch got us a car to pick up the children. We succeeded in getting twelve children to attend the little school.

When Moisés Asis left, I was alone until the *Joint* came in 1993 and began to prepare teachers. Then we had more resources, and people began to return to the synagogue. Many who had closed the door in my face when I went to find children, because they were afraid to send their children to a Jewish school, are now attending themselves. The most important thing is that the children are bringing their parents who were assimilated, and they are bringing their parents who had also been distant. Today, we have students who are over eighty years old. We have involved all who have a Jewish soul, and they are coming. There are some funny stories. One day, one of those fathers showed up and asked me if this was the "Jewish church;" that's how estranged they were.

Xiomara Rozenczwaig was the first teacher of Yiddish for a year and a half. We think that Yiddish is very important because it is what united the Jews in Europe. My father-in-law was a fanatic about Yiddish. We mainly teach classes on Jewish history and Hebrew at the Sunday school, but we also have a lot of workshop activities, a theatre group, a dance group, and a very good library with material on Judaism.

Now, with the support of the Joint, we have ninety-five students and a faculty of fifteen teachers. We have various levels: first, children up to four years old; then up to ten; up to thirteen; and up to twenty years old. The school for adults is located at the Centro Sefardí and has an enrollment of thirty. In these last four years, about one hundred thirty students who have passed through our classrooms have made their *aliya* to Israel.

We give each child a Hebrew name and teach them to put on the *kipa*. The girls learn to light the candles. Many, the majority, arrive not knowing anything at all. When they began, they didn't even know the meaning of the word Shoah. We have now made a small Holocaust museum so that young people know and never forget what must never be forgotten.

Mechulam's grandparents.
Turkey, 1923.

Teaching Hebrew at the Sunday school when it was first started.
Havana, 1985.

(Photo by Tatiana Santos)

Rebeca Peison Weiner

Instead of the *Gospels*, the Old *Testament*

My parents came from Poland in 1935, fleeing from the war that was already approaching. Mama was from Bialystok; Papa from a village where he worked in a saw mill. Everyone in my mother's family died in the Holocaust. Only she, a brother who already was in Cuba, and a sister, who had emigrated to Argentina, survived. Mama came when she was very young, only twenty years old. She traveled alone from Europe. On my father's side, my grandparents escaped to Russia where they later died, and the rest of the siblings were able to enter the United States.

Papa came to Cuba because two of his brothers were already living in Rodas, a town in the south-central part of the Island. My parents were married in 1939. My brother, Jacob, was born first, and four years later I was born here, in Havana, but we moved to Rodas where my father opened a shoe factory with his brothers. Later, we went to live in Cienfuegos where papa set up a big store for shoes, clothing and dry goods, LA CASA GIL, at No. 80 D'Clouet Street.

We attended an American school called Eliza Bowman. In Cienfuegos, there were a lot of Catholic schools, but my parents chose an evangelist school, in order to avoid putting us in one of those. Mama and other Jewish mothers reached an agreement with the director that when they gave classes in the catechism and taught the Gospels, they would take all the Jews to the library and teach them the Old Testament.

At that time, in Cienfuegos, there were some eight Jewish families: the Mandel's, Lichtenstein's, Rousso's, Adato's, Kraveca's, Behar's, Levy's, and ours. We met in a house on Castillo Street that served as the synagogue where my father, Chilke Peison Kuzmireck, led the services. It had a Bima, *Torah* and everything. If I remember well, it was established at the end of the 1940s. But we went to Santa Clara on Rosh Hashanah and Yom Kippur, where they had a larger community and synagogue.

Although my father opened the store on Saturday, my family was very religious. Mama cooked on Friday mornings, and in the afternoon it was eaten cold, hard boiled eggs, salad. She lit the candles. There was always gefilte fish, which was handmade and not from cans like we eat today, the *kijalaj*, the *halle*, and the *lekaj*, which was a cake made with dark honey. Supplies were brought from Old Havana, from the Pesate grocery store, which was the most famous. My uncles made up the list and sent the products to Cienfuegos. My parents always spoke Yiddish between themselves and with us also, but we answered in Spanish because we wanted to be Cubans.

We moved back to Havana in 1962. Since papa was a shoe cutter, he found work at the Amadeo factory, one of the best in the country. He worked there until he suffered a heart attack and retired.

He always attended Adath Israel synagogue. After his heart attack, he began to help Geiholtz and was the president of the orthodox synagogue for many years. He stayed until the end, as long as he could. When Mama became ill with cancer, he went everyday. Even after she died, he continued going, but it wasn't the same and he began to fade. He was seventy-three. Abraham Berezniak replaced him.

Rebecca's mother with friends in Poland.
1933.

Cienfuegos Jewish Community.
1948.

(Photo by Tatiana Santos)

Adela Dworin

In what kind of country have we landed?

My father came to Cuba in 1924. He arrived with nothing. A friend picked him up at the dock, loaned him thirty dollars to disembark and invited him for coffee near the docks where he asked for two glasses of cold water. Papa told me that he thought, in addition to how good it was, that it was free, and that it would be a happy day when he also could say in Spanish: "Give me two glasses of cold water." They took him to a rooming house in Old Havana where nine or ten boys and girls slept together in the same room. My father was very correct, very noble. There was one girl who asked him to sleep in the bed next to hers, and Papa always did.

His father died when he was eight. He had a younger brother, Moishe, and his mother was widowed very young. He was brought up with his uncles and cousins. When he was eighteen, the economic situation was very bad, and he had to enter military service in Pinsk, the Polish town where he was born. The family decided that he should emigrate to America and later get them out. It was 1924 and very difficult to get a visa to the United States. Papa could only get a visa for Cuba, and he came here with the idea of staying a short time and then continuing on, like the rest, to the United States. Of course, he had to work. One of his countrymen introduced him to the suppliers so that they would give him some merchandise, and he could begin to peddle.

Mama emigrated in 1930, also from Pinsk, because her older brother lived in Cuba. She came with my grandmother, who was also a widow, and with a younger brother who was fourteen. They arrived on December 31, and, since it was a holiday, they were sent to Tiscornia. For my grandmother, who was very religious, that time was like Yom Kippur for her: "I won't eat this because I don't know what it is; I won't eat that either because I don't know how they cooked it..." She repeated the anecdote about how they served white rice and black beans, something unusual in Europe. Expressing both astonishment and some repugnance, she asked: "In what kind of country have we landed, where they don't even have white beans, and they eat black ones, and only God knows if they are dirty?" As years passed, Grandma learned to cook black beans. They were delicious, and she loved them.

They were in Tiscornia for two or three days. When they got out, my uncle took them to the home of a Jewish family that had many children and rented rooms. They lived there several years. Mama had to work in a sweat shop that belonged to another countryman, who, of course, verbally abused her. Her fingers were full of needle pricks because she didn't know how to sew and was slow. The owner used to say to her: "*Nu, griner* —so, green (that's what they called the immigrants)— when are you going to finish making the hems?" They worked from eight in the morning until twelve at night during the period of the sugar harvest, which was before the May 20 celebration when everyone dressed in Drill 100[1] and white. They gave them one hour off to go home, bathe and eat something. She told me that she cried many tears, but when there wasn't so much work, and she could leave earlier, she got dressed and went with friends to walk on the Prado, to the Parque de la Fraternidad. She loved to go out, to dance, and to enjoy life.

A *shadjnte* for the *pinsker* of Havana
In Pinsk, my paternal grandmother found out that there was a family that was emigrating to Cuba and went to see them to send letters and some gifts for

---

[1] "Drill 100:" special fabric used for tropical suits.

my father. Without meaning to, she became a *shadjnte*. In Havana, my mother and my grandmother had already asked the Bakalchuk about the *Pinsker* family. They invited my father to tea, and that's how they met.

Papa had a girlfriend in the United States, a second cousin, who was doing the paper work to get him there, and he told my mother that he was only in Cuba temporarily. My mother told me that from the moment she saw him, she said: "This is a good match; you can see from his face that he is a good man, handsome, honest and very sweet. I can't let him escape."

So, they began going out together. They sat on the wall of the Malecón, on the Prado. Papa told her about the small store he had in Alquízar, and Mama answered that she had not left Pinsk to go live in a small town. She proposed that he sell the store and settle in Havana, and they were married in a civil ceremony because she wanted to make sure that, if the visa came, he wouldn't go to the United States. Papa delayed eight months in selling the store. When he returned, they were married in the synagogue in 1931 or 1932. I asked her where they spent their honeymoon, and she said that there wasn't any honeymoon in those times, they were poor and after the wedding, they went back to the house where they were living. Papa moved with Mama, Grandma and my uncle to the Brum family's house. My sister was born there.

Mama stopped working, and, with the money from the sale of the small shop, my father bought a store at 224 Bernaza in partnership with Motel Hertz. They called it HERTZ Y DWORIN. Hertz manufactured pants and Papa, shirts. So, by getting together, they dressed a whole person. The business prospered, and they moved to 19 Curazao, where I was born. Then, father decided to go into business independently and opened another store at 25 Cristo. He made shirts and children's clothes. Mama helped him with the showcase, and my sister assisted in the office.

In the store there was a workshop with an electric cutter where Papa and the cutters worked, but the sewers were subcontracted. Once the clothes were cut, they were delivered to the workshops for finishing. Later, they put them in boxes. My father preferred to sell wholesale, although he also made some retail sales in the showroom. He supplied the smallest shops, the stands. At the end of the 1950s, when his production was of better quality, he signed a contract with EL ENCANTO and other large stores, but, above all, he supplied stores in the countryside, Jewish as well as Arab.

Extra, extra! The nationalization!
Extra, extra, they took away the stores!

The day of Saint Barbara, December 4, 1962, the Revolution began the great nationalization of stores that had employees. At that time, there were still sellers of newspapers who shouted the news on the streets, and at five in the morning, I heard: "Extra, extra…the nationalization! Extra, extra, they took away the stores!" I turned on the radio, and I understood that my father came within the law. I knocked on his room and woke him up. I remember that I said to him: "Don't worry; we are going to be ok. I am going to call so that you continue working in the store." Papa went to Cristo Street and found that the interveners were already there. They only paid him for the merchandise, not the store. The inventory amounted to ten thousand pesos, and they paid him over ten years.

Papa saw that I was so positive that I think I transmitted some of my optimism to him. He was a little over fifty years old. He went to the Ministry of Domestic Commerce to get a job. They asked him where he wanted to work, and he said near where we lived. They assigned him to the boutique at the Hotel Capri, EL PATIO, which had belonged to one of my father's cousins; it was one of the stores of the Habif. He worked there until he died in 1971.

Something questionable in the refrigerator

I grew up in a very orthodox home, because my grandmother Miriam was. My parents were more liberal, but Grandmother held the reins in the house. I remember her devotedly praying early in the morning with her old *Siddur* with torn pages that she had brought from Pinsk. Grandma did not allow anyone in the kitchen, even mama couldn't enter. There were two sinks: one for dairy and the other for meats. When we rented our present house in Vedado, fifty years ago, the first thing she did was to go to the kitchen to see if it had two sinks. If not, we couldn't move in.

At the beginning, we had only one refrigerator, but with a separate shelf for dairy. To have even one refrigerator at that time was a luxury. One day, the family below, who weren't Jewish, made a flan and asked to keep it in our house. My mother, out of guilt, said ok. When Grandmother saw the neighbor coming with that in her hands to put it in her kosher refrigerator, she roundly objected saying: "No, they can't keep it here. And if it has pork?" She didn't talk to mama for two days for having put "something of questionable origin" in her refrigerator.

We bought meat at the Resnick butcher shop, which is the only one that still exists today. The employee, a non Jewish Cuban who had learned Yiddish, delivered the meat to the house. Grandmother put it in water and then salted it, just as I do now. She had a lot of influence over me. I was instilled with such fanaticism; I was like her clone.

Saturday was the most tedious day of all because I couldn't do anything. I didn't talk on the telephone, and I didn't ride. Grandmother went to synagogue, to Adath Israel or to Knesset Israel, but I stayed home and couldn't go shopping or to the movies, or play or put on makeup or turn on the radio. So, I spent the day reading. I only attended synagogue for a Bar Mitzvah, a wedding and the High Holidays.

At home, we cooked on Friday before Sabbath. We made *schont*, although not too much because it was very heavy, with a base of lima beans, very greasy breast meat and a lot of potatoes. Grandmother prepared a typical dish which is stuffed chicken necks. I remember the aroma. She put it in the oven, which was permitted because you couldn't see the flame, and left it there until the next day. The smell permeated the whole house and, I think, the entire neighborhood. That is one of the smells of my childhood and part of my youth.

She also made gefilte fish. On Friday morning, she bought the fish. She cut the fish with carrots and onions with a small machete. She made it as it really is supposed to be, not the balls. She was an artist. She peeled it, taking off the skin very carefully, filled it and then put the skin back on and put it in the oven. When she set the table on Friday night, it was a work of art. The fish, with its eye and everything, seemed like it was still whole.

You are drinking Christ's blood

Everything was very animated and cheerful for Pesach. We had to clean the house to eliminate the *hametz*. Grandmother didn't even permit coffee that week. They completely changed the dishes. We had two sets for the year and a different one for Pesach, plus a double set of pots and pans. There was a frying pan that was used to make blintzes, which have a cheese base, to which she attached a small string to differentiate it from the one used for meat.

It was very exciting because during eight days we ate on new plates, with new flatware. Grandmother made wine from raisins. She prepared it months ahead of time in large pickle jars. She put in a filter that she opened from time to time to see how it was fermenting. We didn't eat rice or beans. The cakes weren't very tasty because they were made with matzoth meal, but there were many other delicious things. I liked the egg with onion a lot and the *jrein*, which made everyone cry. Grandmother bought the radish, grated it and prepared it herself. The family got together and some friends, some ten or fifteen people. Since I was the youngest, I asked the four questions in Hebrew, Yiddish and Spanish.[2]

Another typical dish was borscht. A non-Jewish maid worked in the house. Normally, we gave her vacation during Pesach because many times it coincided with Holy Week. One year she didn't want to take vacation, and when she saw the red soup, she said to me: "Honey, don't eat that soup, because you are Jews and you are drinking Christ's blood." Although I told her that the color was from the beets, it must have had an affect on my subconscious because afterwards I couldn't stand borscht. I can't bear the color or the flavor.

Grandmother gave Papa a cushion so that he could eat reclining. We ate chicken soup, matzoth ball soup, *kneidlach*, wine (that night, they let us). The dessert always came from abroad. Later, the Jewish bakers learned to make it and called it "coquitos." Another thing I remember is going to Pesate's store on Acosta Street to buy the Passover products. I liked it because it was always very decorated.

Besides being a good cook, grandmother was a baker. She made bread, apple strudel and kijalaj to lick ones fingers. We liked to drink tea. We would put out the samovar and take six or seven glasses. Russian style, we put sugar cubes or *vareniye* on a small plate and poured the tea on top.

A Jewish boy on the wrong path

Grandmother was a real character. I am going to tell you a story that defines her head to toe. She always lived with us, except for a brief time when she went to Chicago with two younger aunts. I was ten or twelve at the time. Although she had gone to stay permanently with an immigrant visa, she could only stand it for fifteen months.

She only spoke Yiddish and so spent a lot of time alone, but since the two aunts were as observant as she was, she felt like a fish in water. In Chicago, in winter, you had to put on the heat, and so on Fridays they hired a *shabbes goy*. One Friday, the boy didn't come, and they spent a terrible night. The following

---

[2] At the Passover Seder, children participate by asking four questions. They were designed to convey moral teaching and also to include the participation of children in the ritual.

Friday, when he appeared, they reproached him: "What happened that you left us freezing and with nothing to eat?" To which the boy responded: "I couldn't come because it was my Bar Mitzvah." Horrors! The aunts and my grandmother had sinned doubly. And right there and then, they fired him. They had put a good Jewish boy on the wrong path.

Grandmother gave it all up. Although they told her that she could not return to the United States, she said that it didn't matter. She wanted to return to Cuba and her granddaughters.

The antithesis of Yentl

I think that, in many ways, Grandmother was an exception. The women of her time were not instructed in the Jewish religion. But she had many brothers and she was brought up with them and had the same religious education. When she went to the synagogue in Havana, the men asked her: "Miriam, what comes next?" She answered them: "It's unbelievable that you don't know." She read in Hebrew perfectly. I wrote the dictates and she reviewed them. She spoke Russian, Yiddish, German, Hebrew, and, I think, Polish also. On Pesach, she sat at the head of the table at the Seder. She had as much say in the house as my father, and my father was her son in law, not her son.

I studied in a religious school, and I still fast on Kippur. For me it was because of the fear of God and continuing tradition. Mama followed tradition, although maybe less strictly with respect to the kashrut. When Grandma died at ninety-six, my mother entered the kitchen for the first time at the age of eighty something. During all the time that mama was cooking, I'm not sure if I ever ate something that wasn't kosher.

The Jewish schools: Sephardic and Ashkenazi

The customs, the language and the food of the two groups were different. There were no Sephardic Jews in either of my two schools because the classes were in Yiddish, and that was the language in which we talked among ourselves. They went to Theodore Herzl. We were also separated in the clubs. If you look at the list of founders of the Patronato, you won't find even two. There were some in Pérez's preparatory school and at the Havana High School. They called us the *polacos*. They didn't discriminate against us, nor did we against them, but we had our own group.

First, I studied at the Tarbut, which was on the upper floor at Acosta and

The little "sailors" of the Tarbut School.
Havana, 1941.

Habana Streets. The director was Ida Cohen. It was a private kindergarten for members of the community, some fifteen or twenty children of both sexes. There, I met some of my life-long friends: Fanny, Eva Rubin, Elenita Gurwitz, Elenita Kubiliun, and David Rot. I think that David Pérez was one of the teachers at the school.

Later, I went to primary school at the Instituto Yavne, on Damas Street, between Acosta and Luz. The director was José Abrami, my *lehrerke* (my Yiddish teacher) was Malka Shojet, and two marvelous mulattas, Estela and Antonia Madruga, taught me Spanish. When I was in fifth grade, I was very good in Yiddish and Hebrew, but very slow in Spanish, history, geography, and mathematics, and the teacher, Dr. María Despaigne, said to me: "I think you are intelligent, but you are lazy and don't study. I am only going to let you pass the grade because I don't want to separate you from your little friends." It was the biggest embarrassment of my life, but it was effective. I studied and did fifth and sixth grades with excellent marks.

At school, we were all very afraid of Abrami. We didn't know anything about his private life. He wasn't married and didn't have any children. We celebrated

248

his birthday, and they prepared us to sing and to recite poems, and, after, he gave a thank you speech. Every year, he always told us that he was "foitytree" years, and we all laughed.

In the morning we studied Yiddish and a little Hebrew, in order to read the *Humash*. They put more emphasis on Yiddish. At that time, Hebrew was still the religious language, the State of Israel didn't exist, and it was considered blasphemy to use Hebrew for everyday things. For Jewish history, we used the book by Simón Dubnov. The rest of the curriculum followed the normal plan of studies of the country.

Although it was a private school, they didn't charge some of the students. The uniform of Tarbut was beautiful, copied from the European style, maybe Russian: A blue *jumper* with little straps, a blouse with ruffled sleeves with lace and elastic, and an apron. The formal uniform was all white silk, with a scarf with the letters CT, and a white and blue beret like the one sailors wear. The one at Yavne was all white, with pleats in the front, a black belt and a monogram in light blue with the flag of Israel, with the letters IY. The daily uniform was made of cotton, and the one for civic activities was silk.

Every Friday, we said the pledge to the flag just like in the Cuban schools. We had a dais with the two flags, we sang both anthems, the National and the Hatikva, and we recited poetry. We preferred to go to the Jewish school because we had double vacations: on the Cuban patriotic holidays (May 20, October 10, and December 7) plus the weeks of Pesach, Purim, Rosh Hashanah and Yom Kippur, although that also meant that they pushed us more in our studies so we could finish.

A Jewish *rebel without a cause*

The course did not end in June, but in December, in order to coincide with Chanukah. It was a lovely holiday. We always celebrated it in the Artística Gallega, which had a theater. Starting in October, the dance teacher, Porras, began to prepare us and demanded perfection. I assure you that we could compete with La Colmenita.[3] I have photos of the different dances. Sometimes, I would dress up as a gypsy or a Chinese girl. A blond Chinese! The doll costume was fantastic. I was six or seven. The stage set consisted of some boxes, and we, dressed as dolls, came out of the boxes. Another was the Fire Dance, the one

---

[3] La Colmenita: a contemporary Cuban children's theater group that has performed internationally.

by de Falla that Blanca danced. For the other three numbers, we were in the chorus. Blanca was the most daring and irreverent. I remember that when we had the Humash classes, it seemed to us like God was inside the book, and we kissed it. One day, when she saw us squares, she took it away from us, threw it on the ground and said: "See, nothing happened to us."

We sang Jewish and traditional Cuban songs. The parties at Yavne were unforgettable, except the one for sixth grade because by then the school had lost many students to the Centro Israelita on Egido and Dragones. We stayed until the end because of our parents' loyalty to Abrami. It was sad at the end of the course, because they were closing the school.

From there, I went to the preparatory school of David Pérez on Sol Street. Non-Jews also studied there, not only in the preparatory, but also in the commerce school as well. Some of my classmates, whose fathers had achieved a good economic position and didn't want them go to a public school, enrolled in Baldor and in the Ruston Academy. We, the inseparable, went to the Havana High School. There, I met Pereli, Alberto Toruncha, Jaime Wiener, Israel Percal, Charles Gojer, Sarita Aronowski, and Dora Matz. Many Jews studied at the high school because we still lived in Old Havana.

You have planted a tree in the name of your granddaughter.

My earliest memory is the blue collection box of Keren Kayemet Leisrael with a map of what Israel would be later. There was almost a competition between my friends' boxes and mine. We put in part of our snack money, and we were proud when the delegate came by with his key and opened them to see who had made the largest contribution —not because it meant who was the richest or gave more, but because we were thinking about the future of Israel. On our birthdays, Grandmother always gave each of us a diploma that said: "You have planted a tree in Israel in the name of your granddaughter."

I remember one day that papa was very distressed. I was about ten years old. It was the day they brought to Cuba from a concentration camp some bars of soap made of human fat, and they buried them in the Cemetery of Guanabacoa. They took all the children from school. Mama and Grandmother didn't want me to go, because papa had lost his entire family in the Holocaust. And I cried and said: "I want to go. Maybe in one of those bars of soap is a little fat from my grandma" —of the grandmother I never knew, my father's mother.

250

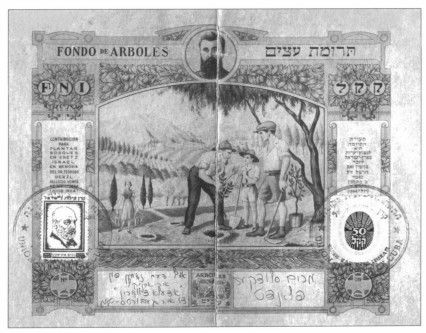

Bond of the Keren Kayemet Leisrael to raise money for the Herzl forest.
1940s.

My parents went to the Centro Israelita a lot; they were very active. Every once in a while a lecturer came to do *fund raising* and talked about what the State of Israel was going to be like. I was a little girl in 1947, but I will never forget the great joy we felt when Israel was established and the equally great sorrow that Cuba was the only Latin American country to vote against the partition. We had a very moving activity at school, which combined the happiness of seeing the flag waving and the pain of hearing of the first losses.

Machado and Batista: two different reactions

The Kultur Farain existed and was a force as long as there were poor Jews. In the 1940s, many became capitalists and wanted to erase their past. When they moved to Vedado and Miramar, they forgot their Communism. The poorest remained Communist, those that in some way hadn't prospered so much. Sometimes, I passed by the Folkcenter or the Sholem Aleijim, and the majority of those who were there were very, very poor.

251

When I was in my third year in high school, the incidents against Batista began and, naturally, our parents were worried. They still had a ghetto mentality. They were super grateful to the country and to the Cubans because they had received and treated them well. They never felt anti-Semitism, but ghetto mentality is difficult to change. We dealt with the gentiles, we loved them, they were our friends, but we never invited them to our home. There was always the fear that we would fall in love with a non-Jew. They still had the idea, even at that time, that we were aliens in Cuba, and that was decisive.

As soon as trouble began, they immediately wanted to switch us to private schools, and we protested. Where would we find better teachers than the ones we had at the high school. We all sympathized with the revolutionaries, we all suffered from Batista's take over, but we were afraid of rejection, that they might say we weren't Cubans.

There never was any Jew left abandoned

My father always was involved with charitable organizations, above all with the Tuberculosis and Mentally Ill Protective Committee, of which he was a founder. On Sundays, a group of the directors went to visit those who had tuberculosis in La Esperanza Hospital, and the mental patients at Mazorra. Mama and grandma got up very early to prepare a typical Jewish meal (*kutlet*, gefilte fish) for them. I was small and didn't understand why the only day that papa had to be home, I couldn't go to the movies or the circus with him and had to go without his company because he was having lunch with them, at those places, and didn't come back until after five in the afternoon. One day, papa came home with his arm bandaged, and I got very scared. One of the patients had taken a bottle and wounded him. I was traumatized. I was always afraid when he went to Mazorra and pleaded with him not to go.

Later, when I was already working at the Patronato, I had to go to Mazorra on several occasions because there were two patients who only spoke Yiddish, and it was very difficult for them to communicate with the doctors. Now, we don't have anyone there, but we have groups of people who visit any member of the community that needs it.

I think it would be fitting if one day some recognition is given to our elders for the work they did; they not only visited the sick, but they had a small clinic in their social club, the antecedent of the family doctor.[4] Since they arrived in Cuba "with only the shirts on their backs," they created organizations to assist others. There has never been a Jewish beggar here or anyone left abandoned without help. These organizations even paid for care in private clinics (Our Lady of Carmen) so that three hundred needy Jews didn't have to go to a public aid home or a public hospital.

Change in the Jewish identity process

I already spoke about the time my father lost his business, in 1963, and went to work at the *boutique* at the Hotel Capri. At that time, the only tourists that came to Cuba were the Russians. Papa loved human relations and, when they told him they were interested in visiting a Cuban home, he immediately invited them. But I thought: Why do they want to come here? Our home is not a typical Cuban home; we don't eat pork or fried pork rinds; we don't speak Spanish to each other. After two or three glasses of tea, the reason became evident. Many began to cry and admitted to us that they had Jewish blood, but they couldn't say it openly.

That shocked me. In Cuba —before and with socialism— we never had to deny our Jewish ancestry. We have practiced our religion openly without having to hide, and we never suffered pogroms or anti-Semitism. My nieces and nephews, who were born after the Revolution, know all the Holidays, go to synagogue and are proud to be Jews.

---

[4] Since the 1980s, Cuba has had a program of placing doctors —"family doctors"— in every neighborhood to provide primary care to about 200-400 people. All medical services in Cuba are free of charge.

The Dworin-Slucker family.
Havana, 1943.

Board of the Tuberculosis and Mentally Ill Protective Committee.
Havana, 1945.

With schoolmates in her dance costume.
Havana, 1945.

With US filmmaker
Steven Spielberg
at the Jewish cemetery.
Havana, 2003.

(Photo by Tatiana Santos)

Isaac Rousso Lilo

What it is to be "extremely poor"

My father was born in the Dardanelles, in Turkey. When he was thirteen, there was a quarrel in the family. His father had died, and his mother had married an uncle. So, he became a stowaway and landed in India. From there, tumbling around the planet, he arrived in Mexico where he lived for a time, until he came to Cuba. That would be around 1913 or 1914. I remember the date, because he was one of the founders of the Unión Hebrea Chevet Ahim, which was organized in 1914.

Mama was from Ankara. She was fourteen when her entire family decided to immigrate to Cuba. They first lived in Sagua la Grande, in Las Villas province, and later they settled in Havana where she met my father. They married and had three children. I am the youngest.

For a time, papa had a good position. He began, like everyone, as a peddler. Later, he opened a small business, but when the economic crisis came, it went under and never came back. But, in truth, I once heard that he had lost everything gambling. He was always in sales, until he got run over by a car and was left lame. He never worked again. Mama sewed underwear with a Singer sewing machine for a countryman on Bernaza Street.

I was raised in a very poor family. I was enrolled at Theodore Herzl School as a scholarship student, which, at that time, meant that you were extremely poor. We lived in a tenement house on Cuba Street, across from the Merced Church. When all three of us were working and we earned more money, we moved to Ayestarán. My sister was the cashier in a shoe store called MIAMI, owned by the Olenberg's. Salomón worked in Brinberg's leather warehouse on Amargura Street, and I worked for B'nei B'rith with Marco Pitchón.

1959 and 1994: a closed cycle

Between 1952 and 1956, I got my first job at the B'nei B'rith Lodge, which operated out of the home of its president, Marco Pitchón, on Aranguren Street. He was a commission agent for foreign firms. I was his secretary in his personal business for half of the day, and the rest I worked for the Lodge. Alberto Toruncha, my schoolmate from primary school, recommended me when they needed to add personnel. After me, his sister entered along with another boy, who emigrated to the United States after the triumph of the Revolution.

Toruncha, who was also very poor, started studying medicine, and I covered for him when he escaped to study. From the time he was twelve years old, he knew that the only way to pursue a career was to win the Bachiller and Morales prize in high school, which meant getting the best grades in all his courses. It was very difficult to win because there were four high schools, and the one in Havana, where we studied, was the hardest.

Pitchón had begun historical research on the role of the Jews in the War for Independence. I was the one who went everyday to the National Library and the National Archives to look for documentation. I was paid by Pitchón to read the *Gaceta de La Habana*, from 1850 to 1895. I also wrote all the letters to international personalities and leaders for the Martí book, asking them their opinions of our National Hero, and it irritated me to have to write to that group of degenerates, like Somoza and Trujillo. I was already in high school, the environment was heating up, and I began to think differently.

The cycle begun in 1959 came to a close in 1994, and I returned. I can talk about that time, but not the time before or after Pitchón. That's why I want to produce a small publication so that people will know. I became interested in the Lodge again because it was a lay organization. I am not a believer. I am not for the "religionization" of anything, but for the inter-relation and coexistence with other groups. I think that the B'nei, in addition to being a philanthropic organization, was always a cultural center within the community, and that it should open itself to the society in which we live and leave the spore.

Zionism or Revolution

In 1956 and 1957, I was president of the Macabi youth organization, which was next to where the Provincial Court is today, on Prado. We were about forty members. We took excursions and held dances. Although there had been a strong sports league, by my time it no longer existed. The baseball team was very good; they played in the stadium in Regla.

At that time, I was already a member of a cell in the July 26th Movement, and I know that I was president because I sent myself a letter warning me not to hold parties because that was not appropriate under the circumstances.

I got involved in Macabi simply because it was an organization of young Sephardic Jews. Likewise, when an activist came from Mexico specifically to create Hanoar Hatzioni, Alberto and I joined. The main idea was to train in Israel. I remember that Isaac Barrocas went and came back as a trainer. I wasn't in it very long. Alberto stayed a little longer. When the Revolution triumphed, I was nominally the president and we continued meeting on Prado, but by the end of 1960, I was working as an accountant at the Ministry of Embezzled Assets,[1] and I stopped going.

In December, I was mobilized to train in the School for Militia Officers. I returned to Havana at the time of the US presidential elections, and I remained mobilized until Kennedy took office. Then, they sent us to "clean the Escambray,"[2] and within a week of my return, we went to the Bay of Pigs. When it all ended, we stayed at Campo Florido.

Once on leave, I went to a meeting of the Macabi in the Centro Sefardí, dressed in uniform. It was an odd situation. There was one group of people who already had a visa to leave the country, another in the process of getting visas, and another who were beginning to make their applications. There I was in the midst of all of them dressed in my infantry uniform and another fellow, whose name I don't remember, was in his artillery uniform. Naturally,

---

[1] A Ministry set up to pursue assets that had been embezzled during the Batista dictatorship.
[2] "Clean the Escambray": a military operation that defeated the counter revolutionaries gathered in the Escambray Mountains, in the center of the Island.

they looked at us and asked what we were doing there. We didn't have the same goals: They were leaving, and we were defending the Revolution.

So, I decided to leave. I remember that when I crossed the threshold, I promised I would never return, and I didn't return until my mother died in 1972.

I have to be buried in the Jewish cemetery

Mama was very sick and when she emerged from a coma for a moment, she said to me: "Isaac, I have to be buried in the Jewish cemetery." I went to Chevet Ahim and spoke to Jacobo, the brother of the teacher Pérez, to arrange everything. She died on the last day of Sukkot, which also fell on a Friday. It was Sabbath and Simchat Torah, and she couldn't be buried. The cemetery was full of my comrades and those of Salomón, non-Jews. We spent hours —six, seven o'clock at night, and it still wasn't dark. They didn't understand anything, and everyone asked why she wasn't being buried. It seemed like a story by Tomás Gutiérrez Alea[3] and Poe. Finally, the sun went down, and we could bury her.

Because we were so poor,
we didn't observe anything very strictly

Mama was very religious, but she never went to the synagogue. I think she was ashamed of her poverty. She always fasted on Kippur, even when she was diabetic, and she didn't eat pork. But on Pesach, when we didn't have enough money to buy the matzoh or the oil, we ate bread, and she cooked with pork lard. That was the only sin she committed. Because we were so poor, we couldn't observe anything very strictly.

I remember that she cooked many dishes. Her famous *borekas*, some pickled salad of cabbage, tomato and onion which was exquisite, and the *garato*, a raw fish like seviche. She cooked very well, because my grandfather had owned a grocery store in Turkey. They didn't sell the merchandise there as they do here; they sold what they, themselves, prepared.

By 1957-1958, I had a girlfriend who was the daughter of Mexicans, half Indian. When Mama saw her, she was categorically opposed. She said she was black. Later, my sister married a gentile, and I think that opened the way. In addition, since my wife was from Sagua, the first town in Cuba in which she had lived and had fond memories, she finally accepted it.

---

[3] One of Cuba's most notable filmmakers who made a comedy in the 1970s called "Death of a Bureaucrat."

I was the rich one in the family

I went through primary school at the Theodore Herzl, the school of the Sephardic Jews, which was on Inquisidor Street, where Clara Cheni and Pérez were teachers. I began in 1943 and finished in 1948. From there, I went on to the preparatory school that Pérez had upstairs at 57 Sol. I was the rich one in the family because I could get my high school degree. My brother didn't. He had to go out and sell knives and combs, riding on street cars, while I attended high school and studied business, accounting, stenography and typing.

When I finished high school, the University was closed. In 1959, I began to study Business Sciences, and when, in 1962, they opened the Faculty of Economics, I switched into it. Later, I worked as an internationalist in Laos. Currently, I became the chief of accounting at FINTUR, the financial company of the Ministry of Tourism. I became a member of the Communist Party of Cuba and am secretary of my cell in the Association of Combatants of the Cuban Revolution.

The blows that I didn't get from Carratalá, my mother gave me

There weren't many of us Jews involved in the movements against Batista. I remember that after the uprising in Cienfuegos, I brought to one of the meetings of the Macabi a pamphlet I had mimeographed at work to hand out, and no one wanted anything to do with it.

Papa was affiliated with the PSP, but mama wasn't because she had never given up her Turkish citizenship. However at home, we were partisans of the orthodox and *chibasistas*. On Sundays, at Chibás[4] radio hour, we were all there.

I had participated in student activities since the insurrection. I worked during the day and studied at night. One night Carratalá's[5] police went to the high school and gave everyone a thrashing. Humberto Lastra and I went to the COCO radio station to protest because they had beaten students at the Havana High School. My brother was at home, listening to the baseball game, when they interrupted the transmission to report that a commission of students had shown up to protest against Colonel Carratalá. I got home around midnight, and the blows that I didn't get from Carratalá, my mother gave me.

---

[4] Eduardo R. Chibás, founder of the Orthodox Party (1947), a split off of the Authentic Party of Grau San Martín, who was in power at that time. He was the standard bearer of a campaign to clean up the wide spread corruption. Many of the leaders of the July 26th Movement joined the youth wing of his organization.
[5] Conrado Carratalá: colonel in the Batista police force and one of Batista's most bloody henchmen.

Isaac's mother.
Havana, 1920s.

Graduation day at the Theodore Herzl School.
Havana, 1946.

New publication for the 60th Anniversary
of the Cuban branch of the B'nei B'rith.
Havana, 2003.

Aid given to the elders through the Tzedaka Fund.
Havana, 2003.

263

Rosa Behar Hazday

Doctor of Medicine and Specialist in Gastroenterology. Founder of various services of her specialty in hospitals in Havana. Head of Gastroenterology of the Calixto García Hospital (1979-1995) and member of the National Group of Gastroenterology (1979-2004). Awarded the Manuel Fajardo Medal (1979).
President of the Cuban branch of Hadassah International since its founding in 1994 and of the Women's Hebrew Association of Cuba since 1996. Received awards for her communitarian work from Hadassah International in 1999 and 2001, the B'nai B'rith Cuban Relief Project (2001-2003) and the B'nai Zion (2001).

To the Sorbonne with five dollars in his pocket

My paternal grandparents, Roberto and Hermosa Behar, arrived in Cuba with five children in 1926; they came from Kirklisse, a Turkish town. They settled in Ciego de Ávila and later in Camagüey, where my father, Moisés, was born. Grandfather first opened a fish store, later a shop, and finally he became a traveling salesman. Although my father helped him, he always wanted to study and came to Havana to go to high school.

To pay for his schooling, he worked during the day at a pharmacy and attended night classes at Havana High School. It's an interesting story. In order to save money, Papa slept in the pharmacy and studied at dawn with a little lamp. One day, the owner said: "Moisés, since you are so studious, if you finish high school, I will pay for you to go to medical school." I don't know why, but this man, who was a Spaniard, was killed, and my father had to continue working.

He had completed the first two years of medical school when the Machado dictatorship closed the University. His brothers got the money together to buy him a ticket, and, with five dollars in his pocket, he left for France to continue studying at the Sorbonne.

My father's best friend in Paris was the brother of the woman who would become my mother. Although her family was also from Kirklisse, she had been brought up in Paris. So, they met, they married, and I was born in Lille. Unfortunately, my father did not finish medical school and regretted it his entire life because he always wanted to be a doctor. From Lille, they went to live in Barcelona to find new horizons because by then they also had a daughter. He opened a little stand and began to sell anything he could find.

While they were in Barcelona, the Spanish Civil War broke out. Papa was slightly wounded and decided to go back to Paris, but, already at the end of 1938 he sensed that something bad was going to happen and told Mama that he had family in Cuba and it would be better to come here. My mother suffered a lot having to leave her family behind in such a situation. She was already thirty-three, but very much in love, and she followed him.

We came on a boat of refugees, the majority of which were Jews. First, we went to live at the Hotel Luz where they housed the Jews who entered the country, above all the Sephardic Jews. We arrived "with empty pockets," as they say. I remember that Mama wore a small purse of pink silk with golden strings around her neck, where she kept her jewelry. Each time we encountered a bad situation, she took out her little purse, and we pawned something and kept going.

The more money you had, the lower the floor
The Hotel Luz was an odd place. The last to arrive, who were the ones with the least amount of money, lived on the roof. As we improved economically, we moved down to lower floors.

In Havana, I studied at the school run by Pérez. My father was religious. He went every week to Chevet Ahim Synagogue. We celebrated Purim there, but we observed Pesach at home. All the cousins would get together and pass the matzoh with the napkin and wait for the prophet Elijah at the door. Mama cooked a Turkish Jewish meal, spinach, agristada. They purchased all the products —black bread, black olives— in the Jewish shops in Old Havana.

I lived in the Hotel from the age of three to seven until Papa began working as an insurance agent for the American National Insurance Company. In a short time, he went from the little stand in Barcelona to being president of that insurance company for the Island of Cuba. Then we moved to a building the company had on Sol and Egido Streets.

Later, my father went to work for the Laboratorios Lex, which belonged to the Sarrá family, and they sent him to Mexico as their representative. We lived there for a year and a half, and I had to adapt again to a new place. Mama was already suffering because she had lost half of her family in the war —two of her brothers and her nephews in a concentration camp and her mother who died from sorrow. She became so depressed that Papa decided to return to Cuba. We went to Ciego de Ávila and from there to Camagüey, the same road that my grandparents had taken when they arrived.

Since Mama was sick, they boarded my brother and me at Pinson School, a Methodist school where I did my primary years. Papa started to sell clothing. He began with a bicycle and ended up with a station wagon to carry the merchandise. Later, he became a specialist in precious stones, and the jewelers came to the house to buy from him.

When I finished high school, I wanted to study to be a pharmacist, but my father suggested that I study medicine. I came to Havana in 1956, a year of a great deal of revolutionary student activity, and, although I didn't belong to any of the movements, I did collaborate with the July 26th, distributing leaflets.

When the University was closed, I returned to Camagüey, but I no longer felt good in the province and wanted to return to Havana. Papa was very clear: "I will support you only if you study." I managed to convince him to let me work and study. So, I enrolled in the Gregg Academy, and I became a bilingual secretary and stenographer. In the morning, I worked for some Spaniards; in the afternoon, I was a bilingual secretary; and at night, I studied English at the Havana Business School. On Saturdays and Sundays, I went to the Casino Deportivo. I also attended lectures organized by the Patronato, and I went to their restaurant and dances, even though I wasn't a member.

We are going to continue studying

I went to Camagüey ten days before the fall of the Batista government, and I returned to Havana as soon as they opened the University. Papa insisted: "We are going to continue studying…" I didn't work anymore. He sent me money every month until the fourth year of the program when they decided to make *aliya* to Israel. They came to live their last months in Cuba in my house.

My brother had gone to the United States when he was eighteen, in one of those plans of the Joint through which they took out many Jews. Then came the Missile Crisis, and they closed the exit from the country. Papa was a French teacher at the high school in Ciego de Ávila, but he wanted to see my brother, and he was afraid of Communism. He said that he had already seen it in Spain. He got so upset that if he hadn't gone, I think he would have died.

I told him that I didn't want to go because I was at the end of my studies, and if I didn't finish, I would be like him. I had also begun a relationship with the person who would be my husband. Papa almost had a heart attack when he found out I was going out with a non-Jew, who was in the merchant marine, and, to judge by his last name, must have been German. But he finally accepted it.

In 1963, my parents went to Israel. My husband left for Europe, and I stayed with a four month old infant and in my fifth year of medical school. He cried all night, and I cried too because I wanted to study and he didn't let me, but I said that I was going to finish school, and I did. Since my husband continued sailing, I went alone with my small child to fulfill my social service in a little town in the Escambray that didn't have either an aqueduct or a telephone. I was there for two years, working in general medicine, forensics, and pediatrics. I opened the birth center and the clinic for pregnant women.

When I returned, I completed my specialty and founded the first Gastroenterology service in the city of Havana, at the Miguel Enríquez Hospital. Later, I also established one at the Calixto García Hospital. At the end of the 1970s, with grown children, I began to come more regularly to the Patronato. Before, I only attended on Rosh Hashanah and Kippur. As a doctor, I had attended the cases that Adela asked me to, but from that time on, I became involved in the activities of the community.

In 1993, I founded the pharmacy. In 1994, they elected me vice president of the Women's Association and president of Hadassah. In 1995, I became president of the Women's Association. Today, we have affiliates of Hadassah in Camagüey and Santiago, and we have some forty members. At the community

The last stop of a wandering Jew.
Her parents in Israel, 1968.

pharmacy, we classify and distribute medicines. We organize scientific lectures and give talks to educate the members of the community on personal health. We undertake a census of those who are ill in order to determine what medications are really needed.

I got where I wanted to go

Through Hadassah, I was able to see my father and my brother again after twenty-six years. My mother had died. Despite being very Cuban, Papa was happy to be in Israel. He said to me: "I got where I wanted to go."

I did too. I remember his last words before making aliya: "The Jews fight and argue, but at heart…we all get together. From now on your family is the Jewish community."

Dressed for a Purim Party.
Havana, 1941.

At the Theodore Herzl School.
Havana, 1941.

With Shimon Peres.
Israel, 2000.

At the Pharmacy.
Havana, 2005.
(Photo by Tatiana Santos)

271

Abraham Berezniak Berezniak (1946-1998)

In Cuba it is easier to assimilate than to lead a Jewish life

Papa came when he was twenty, fleeing from military service and the growing anti-Semitism in Europe. He was born in Kobrin, a small border town that was sometimes in Russia and sometimes in Poland, where mainly Jews lived, mixed with German or Russian invaders, depending on the moment. He had a small farm, but when the matter of military service began, the Jews decided that it was better to go to the United States. On the way there, they landed in Cuba. They always thought it would be transitory, but it became difficult because the admittance quotas were declining. So, people started looking for ways to adapt.

It was not an easy adaptation process because of the language and the climate, but in other ways it was easy. They came fleeing anti-Semitism and find a surprising country that doesn't know about anti-Semitism, where one can say "I am Jewish," wear the Maguen David and no one bothers you. The Cubans were always open and warm to our parents, and, for that reason, I think it was easier to assimilate than to carry on a Jewish life.

273

Some, like my father, decided to try their luck in the interior. First, he went to Camagüey and from there to Oriente, to Gibara, a town in the northern part of the province where, like almost all the Jews, he started out as a peddler, selling odds and ends. There, he met my mother, who was Cuban and not Jewish, and they were married. Since Papa was very strict, my mother had to convert to Judaism, and they were married by a Rabbi. I was born in Chaparra, on March 30, 1946, where my father had set up a store with clothing for men and women.

Grandmother Tomasa, who lived to be one hundred, was a very interesting person. Everyone loved her a lot for her generosity. She took in children and cared for them; she fed everyone who came to her. To some, she even gave them a piece of land to cultivate. During the Land Reform in 1961, her farm wasn't nationalized because it had so many people living on it to whom she had given little pieces of land that they decided to leave it as it was.

We lived in Chaparra until I was five, when Papa decided to come to the capital. We moved to Central Havana, and my father opened a store on Monte Street. I studied at the Hebrew school Tajkemoni, which was the most religious, and later at the Albert Einstein. I belonged to the choir of the Patronato where I participated in the youth activities, but mainly I went to synagogue at Adath Israel.

Papa was very demanding. He said all the daily prayers, put on the *tefillin*, celebrated the Seder, and maintained the kashrut. Mama became as observant as he was. In those difficult times, she was one of the few women who attended synagogue, together with María Diego and María Shujman, and they helped in the *Chevra Kadisha* of women.

A *shochet* with a concern for history

I worked with my father in the store and, later, in the restaurant of the Patronato. I was a good salesman because I liked it, and I had charisma. I brought people into the store; I called to them and told them we had discounted prices and good buys.

I enrolled in the Facultad Obrera and began studying Agricultural Engineering, until I was diagnosed with kidney disease in my second year and had to leave it. I always wanted to study and to have a university degree. I liked to learn. I went to see Matterin at his home and conversed a lot with him.

I became the community *shochet* because the one they had was already very old, and we had to maintain the tradition. They gave me a test to see if I could do it. They put a Humash in an outstretched hand. When they saw I could hold it up without shaking, they decided I would be the shochet. Chicken have to be slaughtered with a single cut and cattle also; there can't be several cuts because the knife can't stop, and so you have to have a steady hand and be very precise with the *challef*.

I had some stressful moments in the slaughterhouse. Once, a cow almost killed me when it fell on top of me. I wasn't used to rural things; I never worked the land, nor had I been in contact with animals.

In 1972, Lisovitch asked me to help him with the books of the *Chevra Kadisha*, but later, I had to take over everything, taking care of the dead, washing them, and helping the sick who were in the hospital. This is important work so that traditions are not lost, and also so that Jews do not feel alone because someone from the community goes to visit them and is concerned about them.

This is a community that has always been orthodox, and we make an effort to keep it that way because it is what our fathers wanted when they founded it, because we want to perpetuate our roots. Since we do not have a Rabbi, in order to maintain the community this way, I think we have to do it within the family. It's like a plant that you have to water everyday. You have to pass on to your family what you know so they will know their history. Not to turn them into fanatics, but so that they should know, and when the time comes, be able to choose the path they want.

It is no longer like it was fifteen years ago. Young people have begun to come closer and are interested in knowing about their roots. They find a Jewish environment here that welcomes them. Before, almost all the members were over sixty, but now the relief team is being formed. This is important so that Jewish life, our traditions and history never die.

YACOV BEREZNIAK: My father always took care of the elderly, of those in need, both spiritually and economically. He visited them when they were sick and also if their refrigerator broke. He rented a car and went to Mazorra to see them. Later, a Panamanian Jew gave him another car, and then he could go every Sunday.

He wanted to preserve everything so that the things of the community would not be lost. He rescued the things that belonged to the United Hebrew Congregation, and he went all the way to Santiago de Cuba and brought back the Torah and kept it until the synagogue there was reopened.

He systematically visited the provinces looking for Jews who wanted an orthodox circumcision. He spoke with the people, he asked them to organize because he was concerned about the stability of the Jews in the country. In 1991 and 1995, together with the Jewish community of Panama, they rented the CIMEQ Hospital in Havana for the circumcisions. People came from the provinces, from all parts of Cuba.

He worked so that Adath Israel would be open morning, noon and night for prayers, from Sunday to Sunday. And at that time, it wasn't easy. There weren't the resources we have now. He had to rent the hall to the orchestra of the Radio and Television Institute (ICRT) because there wasn't money to maintain it. They served tea and some crackers after services, and sometimes not even that. He updated the existing census and succeeded in getting a container of kosher products for the synagogue so that they could fulfill the religious laws and guaranty kosher food to the members all three hundred sixty five days of the year. From the time I was small, he took me to the synagogue everyday. I lived and grew up in this environment.

A religious youth by conviction

Nelsy Hernández: Abraham was very strict about the Holidays, with the formalities. He had a very strong character. Sometimes, the boy wanted to play, and he told him he should learn to pray. He was a religious person by conviction. For that reason, we —I as well as my parents who always lived with us— respected him and fulfilled all the things he asked of us. He never abandoned his ideals and got what he wanted, to keep the synagogue open and to maintain Jewish life, but with a lot of sacrifice. When we were young and I wanted to go out, he would say: "We can't because we are missing one for the ten." He was always involving me in the synagogue, always demanding of me, but also, at the same time, he allowed me to develop my career, my professional life.

When the Pope visited, at the end of January, he was already very sick and he didn't feel well, but he said to me: "I am going to go. I want to give him a small Torah, even if it is the last thing I do in life." And that's how it was; Abraham died two months later.

His father's store.
Havana, 1952.

Singing in the Patronato choir.
Havana, 1963.

His son Jacob´s Bar Mitzvah at Adath Israel.
Havana,1996.

At the cemetery as head
of the Chevra Kadisha.
Havana, 1980s.

A Jewish shochet in front of the kosher butcher shop. Havana, 1980s.

His last photograph, presenting a Torah to Pope John Paul II. Havana, 1998.

279

(Photo by Tatiana Santos)

Ida Gutsztat Gutsztat

Degree in Economic Control, University of Havana, Masters in Organizational Information Management (Cuba, Mexico, Murcia). Titled Adjunct Professor of the University of Havana. Information systems analyst (1973-1977) at the National Institute of the Tourism Industry. Professor of Information Science in the Economics Faculty of the University of Havana (1977-1979). Professor of ORT Cuba in the Patronato of the Hebrew Community (since 2002). Numerous publications and books related to philosophical aspects of systemization, analysis and design of information systems, teaching texts on Metric Methodology, Version 2 and EASYCASE, for post graduate courses, computer classes and higher education.

From Auschwitz to Havana

My family is from Poland. Papa is from Lodz, and Mama from Pioterkov. My father is a survivor of *Auschwitz*, but he never talked about his past. All I know is that on one occasion, when they were transferring them from one wagon to another, some escaped. Most of them were killed, but Papa was able to hide until the war ended. He was lucky because it was already near the end, and he didn't have to hide a long time.

When they took him prisoner, my mother fled to Siberia where she gave birth to my sister in 1942. She had a very hard time and often went hungry. She told me that, at times, she had to steal a piece of black bread so that my sister could eat. That they didn't freeze to death was a miracle because they spent two nights and three days lost in the forest.

Except for my paternal grandfather and two of my father's sisters, who had gone to the United States before 1939, the rest of the family perished in the Shoah.

A Polish product assembled in Cuba

In 1948, Grandpa asked my father to travel to the United States to see him because he didn't want to return to Poland. Mama was already pregnant with me. They didn't give him a visa because my father had been the general secretary of the Communist Party of his city after the war. Then, Grandpa suggested that they go to Cuba, which was very close, since mama was about to give birth. My sister was six years old, and I was born twenty five days after they got here in May, 1948.

When they went to register my birth, Papa said his surname was Gutsztat. Since women in Europe adopt the surname of their husbands, my mother also answered that her surname was Gutsztat when they asked her. That is the reason I have a double surname. It's better that way; I only have to spell it once. My mother's surname is really Eisenberg. Her name was Chana, Ana in Spanish, and Papa's is Guna, or Juan.

My grandfather and my father had been printers in Poland. Papa always told us how he arrived in Havana with only an American buffalo nickel in his pocket. I don't know how he was able to establish a printing press, IMPRESIONES NIGSA (New Industry of Graphics S.A.), with two non-Jewish Cuban partners and without speaking a word of Spanish.

At the beginning, we lived in a very small house in Vedado, on Calzada Street. I don't remember if we had any Jewish neighbors there. Later, we moved to Santos Suárez, and I enrolled in the Centro Israelita School where I studied up to fifth grade. All my classmates were Jewish, and we developed in a more traditional environment. In the morning, classes were in Yiddish. That was the only language that we spoke at home, until my parents learned Spanish. We went to the Patronato with Papa, but Mama didn't attend. She was very stubborn about religion, perhaps because her parents were so extremely religious. On Sabbath, he lit the candles and put on the *tallit*. As long as he was alive, we were kosher. He went and bought the products at the store on Acosta.

I remember that he liked borscht a lot, the matzoh ball soup, the gefilte fish.

My sister belonged to Hanoar Hatzioní, which was on Prado. Sometimes, I accompanied her, although I was very small. I liked to go with her, because every Saturday they had outings.

A Jewish world that disappeared twice

In Cuba, Papa didn't get involved again in anything political; not in the PCC, not in the July 26th, nothing. He worked only for subsistence. He had to feed a six year old girl, under nourished because of the war, and he didn't want her to go through the same thing. I think he carried religion within him because he survived Auschwitz and thought it was a miracle. He never talked. I remember very vividly, that after the Revolution, when they showed Russian war movies on television, Papa sat in the big chair crying. He cried in silence, and I asked him to turn off the television, that he shouldn't watch it, and he answered saying that he had to see it. Mama never watched even one. She was very extreme, very strong.

Papa didn't want to leave when Grandpa asked him to. That was a few years after he arrived in Cuba. He was then forty-five years old and had achieved a certain economic stability. He was tired, ill with asthmatic bronchitis that had gotten worse in the concentration camp. He had suffered two wars and all the persecution in Poland. It was natural that he would not want to have to start over again. Nevertheless, at the very beginning of the Revolution, he asked us if we wanted to go. My sister said no and I, who always followed her lead, also said no. Papa never touched the subject again.

I think in some ways, he was farsighted, that he became aware in time that things were going to change drastically. He was already old, his children had decided not to leave, and he assumed the position he thought most intelligent. He switched me to Edison before the Centro Israelita disappeared, and he began to limit his religious activities before the community began to decline. They did not nationalize his printing shop: rather, he sold it to the State, and they gave him a job at other government presses. He also became a Russian teacher in the language school until he retired.

He never had an objection. We became totally uninvolved. My sister, who was always very revolutionary, began to work while very young at the National Institute of Land Reform in the Ministry of Industry with Oltuski. I imitated her in everything and joined the Association of Young Rebels, then the

Communist Youth and later the Party. I got married very young, to a non-Jew. I studied economics and, for the last thirty years, I have been a professor at the University of Havana. Now, I teach at the ORT center of the Patronato.

My sister married, and her husband converted to Judaism after they got married. Later, he entered the Revolutionary Armed Forces and became a colonel. Mama worked as a translator for the Union of Communist Youth. She was fluent in Russian, Polish, Yiddish, Spanish —although she had a very strong accent— and also German, a language that she hated and couldn't bear to hear.

I am the first Cuban in the family

When Papa died, Mama did not permit us to bury him in the Jewish cemetery. She never explained why. She was very harsh, very strong. Her life was very difficult, and she was always expecting that someone was going to hurt her. Although papa had had a worse life, he wasn't like that. When she died, my sister and I decided to bury her in Guanabacoa. Later, I buried my sister there, and, now, I want to move my father there.

I would like to attend the activities of the community more frequently. That is a contradiction that I have to face. I never have enough time, I am not in the habit of doing it and don't want to turn my life around, but I think that I am the first Cuban of the family and that these are my roots, and they are very strong.

A happy life: her sister with classmates in Poland, just before the war.
1938.

With Steven Spielberg remembering her father, an Auschwitz survivor.
Havana, 2003.

(Photo by Maritza Corrales)

Karina Soriano Albo
Miriam Morales Soriano
Deborah González Morales

The return of three generations

KARINA SORIANO ALBO: My parents, Fanny Albo and Mauricio Soriano Sabán, were born in Esmirna. Papa came to Cuba in 1908 because my grandfather did not want any of his six sons to participate in the war. He said that he didn't raise his sons to be fighters. Grandfather was a very respected man, with a certain position. He made jewelry and handicrafts, but he sold his business and sent his children one by one to "the Americas," even the youngest who was twelve. They went to different places, but my father and my uncles Isaac, Samuel and Jacobo, came to Cuba.

My maternal grandmother was married in her second matrimony to the brother of my other grandmother, which is why my mother and father were raised in the same house in Turkey. It was common then to have arranged marriages. So, the family decided that they should marry, and my mother traveled to Cuba in 1914.

287

The Soriano children, with the exception of the youngest, were educated. Uncle Jacobo taught French. Papa had studied two years of medicine and had a good cultural level. He and his cousin Salvador, were the ones who brought cinema to Cuba. He was also the representative of the Pathé Freres and of Palacio sheets.

I was born in 1922, in La Víbora, a quiet section of Havana. I am the fourth of eight children. At that time, it was rare to find Jewish families in La Víbora. The majority concentrated in Old Havana. At the beginning, papa lived on Inquisidor Street, and it seems he didn't like it. He was a man with very definite ideas. He wanted his children to grow up in places that were healthy and not in the center of the city. He also used to say: "To whatever country you go, what you see is what you will do. My children are not going to be sad children. When the Wise Kings come, they are going to have Wise Kings, and when Purim comes, they will also celebrate it so that they will know that they are children of another religion, but I don't want them to suffer when they see what other children have that they don't. What they see, they have to have."

At home they spoke "turquino," which was Turkish style Spanish. Immigrants, who lived a tense life as children, do not like to lose anything, and because of that, when something broke, I remember Mama would say 'capará.'[1]

My grandfather Abraham and grandmother Estirula came to Cuba to help Mama when she got sick. They were very orthodox. Grandmother arrived with a small trunk that no one was allowed to touch because it contained her Pesach things. On Kippur, she left the house, because my mother had to feed the children, and she could not even see food. On Fridays, it was prohibited to turn on anything.

How am I going to be *turquina*; I am Cuban

MIRIAM MORALES SORIANO: Tradition was transmitted even to me, her great granddaughter. We used to call her little grandma Estirula. She was a real character. She arrived in Cuba with the lining of her coat full of money to help her children, and when my grandmother Fanny left Cuba, at seventy-two, she did the same thing. I didn't know, and if I had known, I would have fallen

---

[1] *Capará*: It is possible that this expression comes from the custom of the *caparot*, begun with the Jews in Babilonia, according to which it was possible to transfer pain, guilt, disease to another object, live or dead.

down dead at the airport. She didn't want to leave. She loved Cuba very much. She said: "I came when I was eighteen. I am now seventy. What am I? Who do I have to love? This country that gave me my sons, that gave me everything. I made my whole life in Cuba. How am I going to be *turquina*; I am Cuban. I don't want to go. Don't six million live here? I am six million and one."

The other day, Deborah brought home some Sephardic blessings, and it made me remember her. I spent every weekend in my grandparents' house, and since grandma Estirula loved wine, father used to buy a good bottle and send it to her. She used to say: "We ate, we drank and said to the good God, *bendichimos* (we bless thee)."

The first to take the "wrong step"

KARINA SORIANO ALBO: My father died very young, in 1932, at forty two. My older brother was eighteen, and I was ten. My uncles were so orthodox that Grandma decided that Uncle Isaac should move into the house and take care of the family. And that's how it was. Also the Bikur Holim helped us a lot after the death of my father. My brother had insipid diabetes, and the medicine cost a peso a day. The Bikur gave it to us and also sent the Pesach products free of charge.

My mother distanced herself a little from religion because of the whole tragedy, but my grandmother didn't, and she made her take us to Chevet Ahim. She wanted us to go there to find a Jewish husband. But this didn't even cross my mind. I didn't accept such an imposition. I went to the Club San Carlos and others in La Víbora, where I met the man who would become my husband, a Mexican Catholic. He didn't care about my religion, but my mother-in-law did. She used to say to me that the Jews killed Christ, and I said to her: "Study it, look at the documents, it wasn't like that. Look how here in Cuba there are Catholics, Christians, killing good boys for nothing." It was the period of the Batista tyranny.

As I told you, at that time, there were no Jewish families in La Víbora. I went to a public school in the neighborhood, not to a religious school. And I was the first one in my family that took "the wrong step" of marrying a non-Jew. My uncles did not accept the idea that their daughters might do the same thing, and, for that reason, they left in the 1940s.

At home, we always ate Turkish style food: *fasulias* (string beans), *bambia* (okra), *javika* (kidney beans with natural tomatoes, onions and hocks). The

COLONIA HEBREA DE CUBA

BENEFICENCIA "BIKUR HOLIM"

בקור ✡ חולים

EN CONMEMORACION DEL VIGESIMO
QUINTO ANIVERSARIO DE SU FUNDACION

ABRIL 1939   —   HABANA. CUBA

Cover of the Bikur Holim magazine. Havana, 1939.

sweets were very laborious, but exquisite. Grandma made some sweets that were so beautiful that she made a display of them: *travado*, with a base of almonds; *charope*, sugar with white cream; *piñonate* with flour that looked like a bunch of grapes. I began to eat black beans when I married the Mexican.

After marrying and when I had a better economic status, I reconnected with the Jewish world. At that time, many Jewish families were living in La Víbora. I made friends with my neighbors Sarah Pinto and Luisa Levy. We went to eat at the restaurant of the Patronato, to the Casino Deportivo. It seems that Hornedo made that Club for the Jews. We joined the WIZO[2] with Matilde Ventura, and we worked for the community.

Miriam Morales Soriano: My aunts and my mother's sisters all married Jews in the United States. They were very rich. They traveled all over the world. In the 1950s, they went to Europe and came back destroyed. The war had just ended, there was nothing, and they left all their clothes there and came back with empty suitcases. They spent the whole winter here. It was a little

---

[2] Women's International Zionist Organization.

odd: Aunt Chana and the millionaires of Miami were Communists and raised money for the Cuban Communist Party, but the first time they couldn't have fillet mignon in Cuba, they left and never came back.

Don't leave me *descuvichada*[3]

My return to the community occurred because of Grandma Estirula. She always said "they should not leave me descuvichada." When Grandma Fanny left, she made us promise to cover her mother. In 1987, my uncles came, and we agreed to make the headstone for Grandma. That is when I went to Adath Israel to make a grave for my great-grandmother, and I met Abraham Berezniak. I will always have fond memories of him. When he opened the book of burials, he was upset and asked me when was the last time I had gone to the synagogue. I explained that I was involved in the Revolution, that I was one of the people who thought that one shouldn't believe in anything, that before I used to come to the activities of the WIZO with my mother, and I wore my *chadai* until in the 1960s, in the Ministry of Industry, they told us that we couldn't wear religious symbols and I took it off. I told him that I had family buried in the cemeteries: my two great grandparents, Uncle Jacobo and Uncle Judah in the Sephardic cemetery; and my grandfather Mauricio in the one belonging to the United Hebrew Congregation. From that moment, Abraham and Rachel invited me to all the activities.

There was another incident that made our young people also begin to attend. My brother, who was a mathematical physicist and today is a professor at the University of Miami, was imprisoned for political reasons. I was worried about my nephew, I didn't want him to be out on the street, and I reasoned with him that the community had helped his parents a lot and that it was a good place for him to be. So, he began to participate in the youth activities, and I relaxed because I knew he was in a good environment. And that is how Deborita, through her cousin, became connected to the Patronato. I think she is now more orthodox than Grandma Estirula.

To find the meaning of that thing of being Jewish

DEBORAH GONZALEZ: I always knew about my origins, that my grandmother and my mother were Jewish, that I came from a Jewish home. Whether I

---

[3] Descuvichada: a grave without a headstone, in Ladino.

Deborah.
Havana, 2003.
(Photo by Tatiana Santos)

practiced or not depended on other things, not just on that knowledge, or the family in which I grew up, but also social events that happened.

I am twenty eight years old. When I was sixteen, what we call a religious opening —a resurgence— happened in the country. It was at this time that I came to the community. Not just because I am Jewish, but because of a desire to find out what it meant to be Jewish. My cousin urged me to come, but I was open to the prospect. I didn't know what I would find.

The first party to which I came alone was for some wedding. Later, without knowing how, I became involved. I arrived just at the moment that the school was being reorganized. I didn't know anything, but they needed a *morah* for the kindergarten group, for the littlest ones. It was easier, and I didn't need to have a lot of knowledge. I felt useful, I liked working with kids, and I thought that it was a way to start. I was learning and teaching at the same time, and, little by little, I learned more. We could say that the Sunday school is what has guided my life, my growth and my maturity within the community. That is how I see it.

Later, I began to assume other roles. When I learned a little more Hebrew, above all to read, I got interested in religious services. I took a course and became a *madricha* of the Youth Organization and of the adult group. In the

292

community, there was only the youth group and the Simcha that brought together the older people. However, there was an age group in the middle that wasn't organized, that didn't receive attention. Then, they formed Guesher, which includes all the members between 35 and 55 years old. People who had been totally disconnected from the community came, perhaps because their children were participating in the Sunday school.

I am also *morah* of the *Bnei Mitzvah*, of the boys who are going to make aliya to the Torah. I lead religious services at the Patronato, which is my synagogue, and I coordinate the Guesher group, which has about one hundred members. I have always been involved in education. I think if I hadn't become a doctor, I would have been a teacher because I like to teach so much.

Youth in the provincial communities

When the process of conversion began, they initiated a course in Havana for which they needed lecturers. The task was shared among the most active people, and I was selected. Later, they decided to extend the work to the provinces and they structured courses of six months to a year that met four hours a week for those who wanted to submit to a *Bet Din*, for their conversion to Judaism.

At the same time, funded by the *Joint*, a plan to support the communities in the provinces was initiated. That's how I began my work in Guantánamo. I traveled there monthly to train them, to teach them how to conduct religious services in Hebrew, because I think it is very important to know that liturgy unites us. It was very interesting. It was a very young community, with which I had to start from scratch, but I found an extraordinary human capacity in everyone and a great desire to revive the community. And I think that they have achieved it. Guantánamo now has sixty members and a place that the Joint helped us restore, which is almost a synagogue.

From there, I went on to work with Cienfuegos, and now I am in Manzanillo and Campechuela. I think it is work of great commitment, because one becomes a little like the model; they are going to imitate you, whether you like it or not. No one can imagine how much effort it requires. We are a lot of young people that have undertaken this intense community work, together with our studies, from weekend to weekend, from Friday night to Sunday night. Sometimes, when I am on duty at the hospital, I ask another doctor to cover for me, and, later, I do his shift.

A connection is also established from a professional perspective in the community as well. Through Hadassah we have organized some activities with Cuban and foreign doctors, and when we travel on outings, in addition to being the coordinator, I function as the doctor of the *machane*. The new thing I am doing, and, as always, the latest is what interests us most, is to teach the Hebrew language. I am *morah* of Hebrew in our ORT center.

Nothing in this country has made me afraid of being Jewish

All the members of my family have dedicated themselves to numbers and business. I am the first doctor. Also, I have been the first to return to active work within the community, and I drew my grandmother and my mother back in. That first generation became disconnected from the religious services and the community because of social circumstances, but I think they were the first that were waiting for someone to say "on your mark, get ready," because they wanted to return.

Of the three generations, I was the only that took a step back and married a Jew. The community has become a part of our life, without planning to be. And, naturally, it is easier if you have someone to accompany you in your community life because it demands energy, time and dedication.

I like to dance salsa, to party, and I feel I am a part of Cuban history, but above all, I am and will be Jewish. It is very organic; it has never caused me any problem of identity. There is a detail which may seem insignificant, but is transcendental: Never has anything in this country made me afraid of being Jewish. I feel enormous pleasure in recognizing who I am, and I when I say so, my comrades are fascinated. They are interested, and I have the opportunity to be the one who gives them their first glimpse of what it means to be Jewish. One explains it from the human and social point of view.

A bridge between Israel and Cuba

I defend tooth and nail the undeniable achievements of the State of Israel. I do not claim to be Zionist with the same intensity that I claim to be Jewish, but if I have no alternative, if I have to say whether I am Zionist or not, I would say yes, that I am Zionist and want to make aliya. I don't know if I would live there permanently, but I want to dedicate part of my useful life to Israel, from a professional point of view, two or three years, five or ten, I don't know. Every Jew owes it to himself and to Israel. I also feel it as an element in the formation of my Jewish identity. Zionism has many shades.

Taglit meeting.
Jerusalem, 2003.
(Courtesy Tamara Rousso)

The aliya has created a very interesting phenomenon. It is true that people go, but there is a certain link that remains. In fact, we continue to be good friends and stay in contact with those young people who went to Israel, because it is here that the little seed was born, which has grown now that there exists the program of *Taglit*. There is a retro-nourishing between those youth there and those of us who have stayed here. I feel that the Jewish community of Cuba is not weakening. On the contrary, it is getting stronger, it is growing.

The wedding of Mauricio Soriano,
the person who introduced cinema in Cuba.
Havana, 1914.

Miriam cutting sugar cane.
Havana, 1970.

296

Membership card of the Casino Deportivo,
the Jewish sports club.
Havana, 1960.

The Jewish Community of Guantánamo.
2003.

297

GLOSSARY

Almodrote: In Sephardic cooking, eggplant purée, eggs and cheese.

Aliya: "To rise." A term used to denote when a Jew rises, as in the synagogue to make a blessing before or after the reading of the Torah (Hebrew Bible), or when someone emigrates to Israel.

Ashkenazi: Name given to Jews of Central and Eastern Europe in medieval rabbinical literature.

Baclawa: A multi-layered pastry filled with pistachio nuts, very popular in the Middle East.

Ba'al Tefillah: Form of denoting the *hazzan*, the person who leads the prayers in the synagogue.

Bar Mitzvah: "Son of the law." Initiation into the religious community of a young Jew at age thirteen.

Benei Berith or B'nei B'rith: "Children of the Covenant." A brotherhood founded in 1843, in the United States, to support the moral and spiritual values of the Jewish people, to help the poor and sick and to assist those persecuted.

Benei Mitzvah: Youth who have already made their *Bar Mitzvah*.

Betar: A revisionist youth organization, affiliated with the New Zionist Organization, founded by Jabotinsky in 1923. Its name comes from a city in Palestine, the headquarters of Bar Kochba's rebellion (132-135 C.E.) which was under siege for a year and a half.

Bet Din: Tribunal of three members that decides on subjects of concern to the community. It is also convoked to oversee the process of conversion.

Bikur Holim: "Visit to the sick." In Judaism, it is a religious obligation for which societies like these are established in all Jewish communities in the world.

Bimah: In the Talmud, it is the dais where the Bible is read. It comes from the Arabic "al-minar." It is a replica of the elevation from which Ezra used to read the Torah to the people.

Blintzes: Pancakes of Hungarian origin, filled with different things, especially cream cheese. They are very popular on the holiday of Shavuot.

Borekas: Pies or turnovers filled with cheese and almonds or other nuts, typical of Sephardic cooking.

Borscht: From the Polish word *barszcz*. A soup made from red beets, very popular in Eastern Europe.

Bund, bundism: A Yiddish abbreviation of the "General Alliance of Jewish Workers of Lithuania, Poland and Russia," a Jewish socialist party founded in Vilna, in 1897. It was the first attempt to organize groups of Jewish socialist workers and artisans of Russia who only spoke Yiddish, a language that was promoted as a national language.

Bulemas: A Turkish pastry filled with spinach, cheese or sweet cabbage.

Challef: Perfectly sharpened knife used to sever the jugular vein of an animal with a single stroke.

Chanukah also Hanukah: "Festival of Lights". A celebration which lasts for eight days commemorating the victory of Judah Maccabeus over the Syrians in 164 B.C.E., which led to national independence and the purification of the Temple.

Chevra Kadisha: "Secret Society," humanitarian and social aid. An Aramaic name given to the group of persons that take on the necessary tasks after the death of a Jew: to stay at the bedside of the deceased for confession and the Shema Israel, the ritual cleaning of the body before burial, to put on the shroud and carry out the burial. There are separate groups for women and men, and they exist in all Jewish communities.

Conversos: Those who abandoned Judaism voluntarily or by force. The best known conversions were those of Spain and Portugal in the 14th and 15th centuries, after which broad sectors of the Jewish people had to live as Crypto-Jews.

Crypto-Jews: Jews who were forced to convert to Christianity or Islam, but who remained loyal to their faith, clandestinely fulling its precepts. In America, they were known as "marranos", and they were persecuted, imprisoned and executed by the Inquisition.

Diaspora: Forced expulsion of the Jewish people from their land and relocation in foreign countries, from the time of the destruction of the Second Temple.

Dolma: Stuffed vegetables, an important part of Sephardic cooking.

Elijah: One of the great biblical prophets. The name signifies "God is Yahve." During the Passover Seder, a cup of wine is filled in his honor.

Esquimo-pie: A frozen dessert, ice cream.

Fila: Very fine puff pastry, in layers, with different forms and fillings, typical of Ottoman cuisine.

Frim: In Yiddish, very religious, observant.

Gabai: In charge of the synagogue. Lay person who helps in the services during the reading of the Torah.

Gefilte fish: Fried or sautéed fish balls, typical of the Ashkenazi Jewish cuisine.

Ghetto: "Jewish Quarter." From the Italian word for foundry. Designated streets or neighborhoods in which Jews were enclosed during the Middle Ages.

Goy: Yiddish word for non-Jew, gentile.

Guesher: "Bridge," in Hebrew.

Hadassah: A zionist women's organization, founded in 1912 by Henrietta Szold to promote zionism and to improve the sanitary conditions in Eretz Israel, through campaigns against malaria, trachoma, etc.

Haggadah: Book which compiles the texts that are read at the Seder on Passover.

Halle or *Hallah*: Bread made with eggs for Sabbath.

Haman or *Aman*: Principal Minister of King Asuero and the villain of the "Book of Esther," who wanted to exterminate all the Jews of the Kingdom. He has an important role in the festival of Purim.

Hametz: For the Jewish Passover (*Pesach*) all fermented foods are eliminated from religious homes. During those days, no food prepared with yeast is consumed, and special cooking utensils are used.

Hanoar Hatzioni: A zionist youth organization that prepares young people to work in Eretz Israel, creating jalutzim (pioneers) for the reconstruction of the country. Similar to the boy scouts.

Hashomer Hatzair: "Young Guard," created to reconstruct Israel on a collective and socialist basis. Its first groups were formed in Galitzia in 1913, making it the most important Zionist youth organization.

Hatikva: Jewish national anthem since 1897, based on the poem "The Hope" by Naftali Herz Imber. Expresses the hope of the Jewish people to be established in their original homeland.

Hazzan: Singer of Hebrew liturgy, cantor.

Herzl, Theodore (1860-1904): Statesman, writer, visionary, father of political Zionism and founder of the World Zionist Organization. The manifestations of anti-Semitism in Vienna and Paris ("The Dreyfus Affair") convinced him that it was necessary to establish a state that would serve as a refuge for the Jewish people.

HIAS: Initials of *Hebrew Sheltering Immigrant Aid Society*, founded in New York, in 1909.

Hillel: Institution organized by the *B'nei B'rith* in the United States in 1921, to provide Jewish instruction to university students. In Cuba, the first Latin American affiliate was founded in 1945.

Humash: Hebrew name for the first five books of the Torah, often called the "Pentateuch."

Huppah: The marriage ritual is celebrated among Jews with a *huppa*, a type of canopy made of silk or other material, held up by four poles. The bride and groom stand under it. In accordance with the *Halacha* (Rabbinical Law), the taking of the bride to the *huppa* is the legal consummation of the wedding.

Irgún Tzvaí Leumí: "National military organization." A Nationalist patriotic movement founded in 1936, for the armed struggle in Eretz Israel against the British rule. Ideologically, it comes out of the revisionist party and the *Hagana* (Defense).

Jajam: Rabbi among Sephardic Jews.

Javaiá: "Experience" in Hebrew.

Jering: "Herring." Jewish dish typical of Eastern Europe.

Joint or *J.D.C.*: Abbreviated form of the American Jewish Joint Distribution Committee, the most important of the support institutions established abroad by North American Judaism, in1914.

Jrein: A cold and spicy relish made of horseradish typical of Ashkenazi cuisine.

Jubans: In English: a contraction of Jews-Cubans.

Kaddish: "Sanctification." Prayer recited by men in memory of the dead.

Kal: Name of the synagogue among Sephardic Jews. From the Hebrew *kahal*.

Kasher or *kosher*: "Good, appropriate for use." In rabbinical literature: the permissible and legitimate. Its most general use is related to food that is ritually pure and with the utensils that are used for its preparation.

Kashrut: A group of observances related to the *kosher*. Rules of food preparation.

Kehillah: "Community." Internal organization that characterizes the Jewish people of a specific geographic area from the time of the Second Temple (1st Century C.E.). Created for the purpose of fulfilling the religious precepts, forming social support institutions and applying the laws of the *Halacha*.

Ken: "Group," in Hebrew.

Keren Kayemet Leisrael: Its initials are KKL. Created at the 5th Zionist Congress (1901). National agrarian fund for acquiring and colonizing lands in Eretz Israel.

Kibbutz: "Collective." Colonies spread across Israel (1909-1910), founded on a cooperative and communal basis, in which private property is not permitted. Characterized by the socialization of the means of production, a shared culture, and the equal distribution of food, housing, and clothing.

Kipa: Small cap used by observant Jews to cover their heads. In Yiddish: *yarmulke*.

Klezmer: Instrumental music of the Ashkenazi Jews dating back to the Middle Ages.

Kneidlach: Popular dish of the Ashkenazi. Chicken soup with matzoh balls.

Kutlet: Hamburger.

Ladino: Language spoken by the descendants of Spanish Jews, also called *judezmo* or Judeo-Spanish. Basically a dialect dating from the end of the Middle Ages, permeated by Hebrew words and expressions, and those of the languages of the countries or regimes where Jews settled after the Expulsion from Spain: Turkey, North Africa, the Balkans, etc.

Macabi: Name of Jewish sports clubs and of their World Union.

Madrich (pl.masc. *madrichim*, fem. *madrichah*): "Youth leader," in Hebrew.

Maguen David: Six pointed star, called "Star of David." Symbol of the Jewish nation that appears on the Israeli flag.

Mameloshn: "Mother Tongue" in Yiddish.

Matzah: Unleavened cracker or bread that is eaten during the Jewish Passover (*Pesach*), as a remembrance of the exodus from Egypt.

Mazkir: "Secretary General" in Hebrew.

Mechitzah: Partition in orthodox synagogues that separates women and men in prayer.

Megillah: "Scroll," in Hebrew. Name given in antiquity to a writing consisting of a single parchment; also the name given to "The Book of Esther."

Menora: "Candelabrum." In general, signifies the sacred candelabrums of the Tabernacle. Religious symbol adopted as the emblem of the State of Israel.

Mikva or Mikveh: Pond holding approximately four hundred eighty liters of water that is not still or artificially extracted, that is used to purify the spirit and the body after menstruation as well as after forty days of pregnancy of Jewish women, or for non-Jews after the process of conversion.

Minyan: "Number." Name of the quorum of ten males over twelve years old that is necessary for Jewish religious ceremonies.

Mohel: Person who performs the circumcision.

Moreh: (fem. Morah) "Teacher," in Hebrew.

ORT: Initials of the name in Russian of the Organization for the Dissemination of Artisan Work, founded in Russia in 1880, to train Jews professionally.

Pesach: Hebrew name for Passover, a holiday that takes place at the end of March or the middle of April, lasting six days, commemorating the flight from Egypt.

Pletzlach: Onion rolls.

Purim: Holiday that commemorates the salvation of the Jews by Esther in Persia.

Rabbi: Spiritual authority in a Jewish community. In Sephardic and middle eastern communities the term used is *jajam* ("wise man").

Rikkudim: Israeli folk dances.

Rosh Hashanah: Jewish New Year.

Sefarad, sephardic: In Hebrew tradition, word used for the Iberian peninsula since the 8th Century C.E. By extension, Sephardics are Spanish Jews that were expelled from Spain in 1492.

Sefer Torah: "Book of the Torah." Rolls of the Torah that are kept in the Ark.

Sabbath: Weekly day of rest, after six days of work, on which it is forbidden to do any labor. It embodies two principles: to rest the body and soul, nourishing the spirit, and holiness. It is observed from sundown on Friday until sundown on Saturday.

Shabbes goi: A non-Jewish person that orthodox Jews employ to light fire and lights on the Sabbath.

Shadjnte: "Matchmaker" in Yiddish.

Shavuot: From the Hebrew "weeks." An agricultural festival, commemorating the moment when God gave Moses the Torah in the Sinai.

Shechita: Ritual laws of the Jews for the slaughter of cattle and foul.

Sheliaj: "Emissary, envoy." Term for representatives of the World Zionist Movement and of Israel.

Shoah: "Holocaust." The tragic culmination of European anti-Semitism, that provoked the persecution of the Jews from the time the Nazi's came into power, in 1933, and, later, the extermination of six million Jews in Europe (1941-1945), in the gas chambers and crematorium of the concentration camps, in the ghettos (neighborhoods in which Jews were confined) or mass executions in towns and villages.

Shochet: "Butcher," in charge of the sacrifice of animals in accordance with the laws of the *shechita*.

Shtetl: "Village." Jewish residential area in Eastern Europe from the 16th Century until the Second World War.

Siddur: (pl. *siddurim*) Book of prayers that contains daily orations, those of the Sabbath and of the most important holidays.

Simcha: "Joy" in Hebrew.

Simchat Torah: "Joy for the Torah." Celebrated in the synagogue at the end of the reading of the Torah, on the last day of *Sukkoth*.

Smétene: Sour cream.

Souteneur: "Procurer," from the French.

Sukkot: "Cabins," from the Hebrew. Holiday that commemorates the wandering of the Jews in the desert for forty years.

Tebah: Pulpit in a Sephardic synagogue.

Taglit: "Right to life." A program through which youth of eighteen to twenty-five visit Israel.

Tallit: Prayer shawl used by Jews for prayer and special ceremonies.

Talmud: The most important book of Judaism, together with the Bible (Old Testament). A compilation of Oral Law created by the Rabbis over centuries, from the end of the period of the destruction of the Second Temple (First Century, C.E.) until the beginning of the Middle Ages.

Tapadas: Large pastries made from same dough and filling as borekas, very popular among Jews of Turkey, Greece and the Balkans.

Tefillin: Phylacteries. Two boxes of leather that contain four parchments with passages from the Torah, with leather straps with which to fix them to the forehead and the left arm in order to always remember their content and to think of God.

Tikun Olam: "Restoration, improvement, agreement." Foundation of the Jewish ethic.

Tisha B'Av: Day of fasting, which commemorates the destruction of the two Temples of Jerusalem.

Tishpishti: Turkish tart for the Jewish Passover, made of nuts and with sugar syrup, lemon and rose water.

Torah Vadaat: Bible and wisdom.

Treif: According to Jewish dietary laws, everything that is not pure. Meat that is not kosher, mixing meat and dairy, cooking or serving food in non-kosher pots or dishes, etc. By extension, it can be used for other aspects of daily life, such as marriage to a non-Jew ("to be treif/to be kosher"), which is not accepted by Jewish law unless the person converts to Judaism before marriage.

Vareniye: "Marmalade," from Russian, transferred to Yiddish.

Yiddish: Native language of the great majority of Ashkenazi Jews of Eastern Europe, comprised of elements taken from the German of the Middle Ages, Hebrew and other Slavic and Romance languages.

Yom Kippur: "Day of Atonement", which is the culmination of the ten days of atonement beginning with *Rosh Hashanah*. It is the most sacred day of the year for the Jews, a day of fasting to expiate one's sins.

Yizkor: Prayer for the repose of the soul of the dead recited by the children or close relatives of the deceased, generally in the synagogue on the anniversary of the death.

Zionism: Movement created by Theodore Herzl in 1897. Promotes a political solution for the Jewish people, in the interest of fulfilling the millenary goal to return to Eretz Israel (Land of Israel), to create their own state and a safe haven.